Toronto Medieval Texts and Translations, 11

'PRIONS EN CHANTANT'
Devotional Songs of the Trouvères
Edited and translated by Marcia Jenneth Epstein

The rich medieval French tradition of vernacular devotional songs has not received much scrutiny. With *'Prions en chantant,'* Marcia Epstein aims to remedy that situation by offering an edition of largely anonymous trouvère devotional songs, designed for both scholars and performers, from two late-thirteenth-century manuscripts.

The majority of the music is published here for the first time. Sixty-one songs are presented, with forty-nine songs exhibited in Old French with a facing-page modern English translation followed by old musical notation and facing-page modern musical transcription. An additional twelve songs, which lack music in the original sources, are represented by the Old French text and the modern English translation only. The introduction extensively describes the social, musical, literary, and theological aspects of the trouvère songs contained in the volume. This is a valuable and welcome addition to the study of medieval music.

MARCIA J. EPSTEIN is a professor at the Faculty of General Studies, University of Calgary. She is also a performer of medieval music and a composer.

'Prions en chantant': Devotional Songs of the Trouvères

Edited and translated by
Marcia Jenneth Epstein

UNIVERSITY OF TORONTO PRESS
Toronto Buffalo London

© University of Toronto Press Incorporated 1997
Toronto Buffalo London
Printed in Canada

ISBN 0-8020-0840-2 (cloth)
ISBN 0-8020-7826-5 (paper)

∞

Printed on acid-free paper

Canadian Cataloguing in Publication Data

Epstein, Marcia Jenneth, 1951–
   Prions en chantant

   (Toronto medieval texts and translations,
   ISSN, 0821-4344 ; 11)
   Sixty-one songs in the manuscripts Paris,
   Bibliothèque nationale Fr. 24406 and
   Bibliothèque nationale N. A. Fr. 1050.
   Songs in old French, with English translation.
   Includes bibliographical references and index.
   ISBN 0-8020-0840-2 (bound)   ISBN 0-8020-7826-5 (pbk.)

   1. Trouvère songs.   2. Songs, Old French.   3. Sacred
   vocal music – France – 500–1400.   I. Bibliothèque
   nationale (France). Manuscript. Français 24406.
   II. Bibliothèque nationale (France). Manuscript.
   Nouv. acq. fr. 1050.   III. Title.   IV. Series.

   ML182.E67 1997   782.25′0944′09022   C96-932545-2

University of Toronto Press acknowledges the financial assistance to its
publishing program of the Canada Council and the Ontario Arts Council.

This book has been published with the help of a grant from the Humanities
and Social Sciences Federation of Canada, using funds provided by the
Social Sciences and Humanities Research Council of Canada.

Contents

Tables

Preface

This volume embodies a number of intentions and is directed towards a diverse audience. It is primarily an edition of two representative collections of trouvère songs with devotional texts in the Bibliothèque nationale in Paris, the trouvère manuscript X (nouvelles acquisitions françaises, 1050) and the trouvère manuscript V (fonds français 24406). The edition will, I hope, be useful to musicologists and performers, since it presents the music of many of these songs, where it exists, for the first time in published form. Its significance is enhanced by a descriptive commentary on the socio-historical context which gave rise to the phenomenon of vernacular devotional songs in late medieval Europe, thus making the songs more accessible to historians of the period. Finally, the song texts proved to be a treasure trove of clues on the attitudes of aristocrats of thirteenth-century France, for whom they were written, toward their religion. Far from consisting of a static set of doctrines, Catholicism at that time was a dynamic and changeable faith, and what the established church taught was not always what the laity chose to learn. In the songs are vivid examples of the images aristocratic laypeople had of their faith. As members of a feudal military society, they saw God the Creator as a stern overlord, Jesus Christ as a valiant commander who sacrificed himself to save his troops, Mary as a sword and shield to defend imperilled souls, and the devil as a treacherous adversary. It is hoped that the texts of their songs will bring new challenges to scholars of religious history and of lay spirituality as well as to literary historians.

In shaping this volume I have tried to follow the course of making all of its parts – history, texts, music, and interpretations – as accessible to readers of varied backgrounds as possible. A comprehensive scholarly edition was certainly considered, but it would not have reflected the needs of performers or their desire to keep the music alive. At the same time, a performing edition devoid of literary, theological, and historical contexts would have been inadequate for those whose interests lie in obtaining a greater comprehension of late medieval society and ideas. In following a middle course I have tried to strike a balance in providing background information for the general reader and technical information for the specialist. The following features are present in this volume: 1) a brief description of the manuscript sources; 2) an introductory background on the sociocultural context of the trouvère devotional songs; 3) a commentary on the form, content, and imagery of the song texts and on what they reveal about the religious beliefs of their authors and audiences; 4) a commentary on the forms and contents of the music in the songs; 5) a description of editorial methods and decisions in presenting the songs; and 6) an edition of the sixty-one songs in the two manuscript collections transcribed into modern music notation where music exists, along with supplemental translations of the texts into English and diplomatic transcriptions of the original musical notation in order to give an indication of the original intentions for phrasing.

It is therefore the purpose of this study to place the devotional songs of the trouvères in the context of their literary, musical, and sociological background, to examine them as documents attesting to the beliefs of their creators and listeners on a number of doctrinal issues, and to explore the circumstances of their creation and performance. The reader interested in the songs as devotional documents may choose to concentrate on the text commentaries and translations; the historian may peruse the background materials without concern for the music; the performer can turn directly to the edition to find recital material. It is hoped, however, that members of each group will venture beyond their usual area of expertise and investigate the phenomenon of the trouvère devotional songs as an undivided whole. To present them as anything less would be to diminish their magic.

Acknowledgments

This study has had several incarnations and a number of mentors at each stage. It has grown from the seed of my dissertation in medieval studies and musicology at the University of Toronto, where Robert Falck of the Faculty of Music first suggested the topic to me, having found – to his surprise – a musicology student passably literate in Old French. I owe that fortunate circumstance in part to the perseverance of Douglas Kelly, whose courses in Old French language and literature at the University of Wisconsin nurtured in my avid undergraduate mind an eccentric passion for the language, as did the inspiring and affectionate examples provided by Eugene and Elisabeth Vinaver. Also at Wisconsin were Larry Gushee and Milos Velimirovic, extraordinary scholars and teachers of the intricacies of music in the medieval period and of the craft of musicology.

A pilgrimage to Toronto brought me to the Centre for Medieval Studies, to its sister institution, the Pontifical Institute of Medieval Studies, and to the Faculty of Music, all of which proved to be oases on my path. Special mention is due to Andrew Hughes, Tim McGee, Tim Rice, David Klausner, George Rigg, Robert Taylor, Peter Grillo, and especially Leonard Boyle, O.P., who showed me that intellect and intuition need not be rivals. Funding from the University of Toronto enabled me to travel to Paris in order to check the original manuscripts and to breathe the essence of parchment and time that brought the project fully alive.

The next phase of my journey led to the University of Calgary, where a post-doctoral fellowship at the Calgary Institute for the Humanities enabled me to expand the dissertation into a more accessible work. Gerry Dyer at the Institute was generous with her time and energy in typing and preparing an early draft of the manuscript. Thanks to Marsha Hanen and Robert Weyant I found a continuing haven at Calgary's Faculty of General Studies, a hive of interdisciplinary activity that has honed my skills as a cultural historian. Special thanks are due as well to Christine Sutherland and the late Anthony Petti.

Richard Troeger of the University of Alberta read the next-to-last draft of the manuscript and suggested numerous improvements. Gerry Hebert assisted me in the formidable task of preparing the music transcriptions on Finale software and Brent Hay patiently untangled the technical snarls inherent in translating information from one computer system to another.

At the University of Toronto Press the late Prudence Tracy was a guiding light for the early stages of the process, as Suzanne Rancourt has been for its completion. Henri Pilon, editor *extraordinaire*, dealt with all the languages represented in this volume and saved me from a number of snares, as did Barb Porter. Brian Merrilees has provided greatly appreciated advice and assistance with the preparation of the texts.

Finally, there was the moral support team that kept me going at various stages of the project. Prominent members included Dorothy Africa, Diane Droste, Gerry and Hilary Borch, Richard Troeger and Paulette Grundeen, and Persis Ensor. Thanks also to Bernice and Herman Epstein, who have been there since the very beginning.

M.J.E.

Manuscript Sigla

All the sigla used in this edition are taken from Schwan, *Die altfranzösische Liederhandschriften* (1886) and are commonly used in text studies to represent the following manuscript collections.

C   Bern, Stadtbibliothek, manuscript 389
I   Oxford, Bodleian Library, manuscript Douce 308
K   Paris, Bibliothèque de l'Arsenal, manuscript 5198
N   Paris, Bibliothèque nationale, fonds français 845 (Cangé manuscript 67)
O   Paris, Bibliothèque nationale, fonds français 846 (Cangé manuscript 66)
P   Paris, Bibliothèque nationale, fonds français 847 (Cangé manuscript 65)
V   Paris, Bibliothèque nationale, fonds français 24406 (Chansonnier de La Vallière manuscript 59)
X   Paris, Bibliothèque nationale, nouvelles acquisitions françaises 1050 (Chansonnier de Clairambault)
a   Rome, Biblioteca Vaticana, 1490
i   Paris, Bibliothèque nationale, fonds français 12483

'PRIONS EN CHANTANT'

1

The Manuscript Sources of the Trouvère Songs as Visual Records

Before embarking on a thorough exploration of the trouvère devotional songs in their social, literary, and musical contexts, it is necessary to establish their identity as palaeographic documents. The manuscripts in which the songs of this edition are recorded, designated X and V, are primarily secular chansonniers, manuscripts that contain collections of songs. Both manuscripts are of late thirteenth-century provenance and were acquired by the Bibliothèque nationale in Paris during the nineteenth century. They appear in descriptive catalogues and collections compiled in the late nineteenth and early twentieth centuries.[1] Most of the information given in these works, however, concerns the secular chansonniers to which the devotional songs are appended, and in no case has any attempt been made to analyse the musical palaeography of the manuscripts. Therefore, an attempt will be made in this chapter to deal with questions of scribal variants and transmission for the two manuscript sources.[2]

The two manuscripts differ markedly in appearance. Manuscript X is exquisitely copied and illustrated, and shows throughout a consistency of scribal hand for both text and music. It fits the description of a formal presentation copy, one that was compiled for the library of a noble family and designed to preserve copies of favourite songs heard at court. It shows no sign of wear, suggesting that it was not used by composers or performers as a working copy. It served the function of a formal chansonnier in providing a visual record of musical items, and it was perhaps notated from other written copies. Manuscript X is closely related to the trouvère manuscripts of the Cangé 'family,' N, O, and P.[3] Its music is in the standard square notation of the mid-thirteenth century, which was still in use for monophonic songs until much later in the century.[4]

Manuscript V, by contrast, was carelessly copied and abounds in omissions and metric irregularities. The entire manuscript is the product of three distinct scribal hands for the text and of three for the music, one of which is to be found only in the devotional section.[5] Staves are ruled for all thirty devotional songs, but musical notation was completed for only the first eighteen. The manuscript shows some indication of use and was apparently not a formal presentation copy. Its text is closely related in content to that of manuscript C, which contains no musical notation. The music of the devotional portion of V is written in a hybrid of the square and the later mensural notation, but the mensural forms are used without any consistent adherence to the rules of rhythmic notation. The manuscript may have been the work of a scribe who was trained in non-rhythmic monophonic forms but who was later introduced to the new Franconian mensural style which became common in France around 1260 for the notation of polyphony. Since the trouvère songs are not polyphonic, it is impossible to know how familiar the scribe was with correct mensural usage. It is also possible that the scribe was a performer accustomed to both mensural and non-mensural notation systems but fully comfortable with neither because his method of learning songs was primarily aural.

Although the details and significance of manuscript transmission in an essentially oral culture are complex and often bewildering, it is possible to derive some conclusions from the presence of errors and variant readings – identified through the comparison of manuscripts from the same family – in the notation of text and music. In the comparison of two manuscript versions of a text, two types of discrepancies are encountered. In some cases two versions differ in spelling or wording in such a way that both are equally plausible in the contexts of grammar, orthography, and metre, and in other cases one of the readings is obviously incorrect, having been garbled, truncated, or altered in a way that does not fit the demands of the context. Discrepancies of the first type are properly called 'variants,' whereas those of the second type are genuine errors. Variants, then, are legitimate versions of a text. The same distinction holds true for music, although errors in music are far more difficult to identify. It is only when a clef is misplaced or when notes are added or omitted in a song of syllabic structure (in which each note corresponds to one syllable of text) that one can say a melodic line is 'wrong.' Musicologist Hendrik Van der Werf cautions against any expectations of uniformity in trouvère melodies, although he does relate consistency in manuscript transmission to coherence of melodic structure:

It would be reasonable to assume that the degree of uniformity among the preserved versions would be commensurate with the coherence of the original melody, since one may expect singers to have little trouble remembering well-constructed melodies and to falter on those that do not seem to cohere.[6]

It is reasonable to assume that what was crucial to the transmission of a song in the thirteenth century was not necessarily the accuracy of a scribe but the memory of a singer. When the two were the same person, as must often have been the case, the alteration of a few words, notes, or ligatures in the process of copying would have been a matter of a musically literate individual putting a personal stamp upon a song received from someone else, who may or may not have been its originator. What seems to have been at work was a process of aural-visual transmission, the logic of which can be confirmed by any modern music copyist: one *hears* what one writes, and if what is heard differs from what is seen, discrepancies can result that are within the bounds of the musical style in question. In the case of separate scribes for text and music, the process might have been one whereby the visual mode of transmission was superimposed upon the aural, producing occasional discrepancies of phrasing and accentuation from one stanza to the next which required a performer to shape the melodic patterns according to the verbal patterns of each stanza. Such discrepancies are common in the notated folk-song literature of Europe as well as in the trouvère repertoire. Both genres involve mixed aural-visual transmission, and the lack of concern for individual authorship in folk-songs allows a number of variants to be accepted as equally legitimate. It is not unlikely that trouvère songs with sufficient recognition to merit a written record were performed by a number of individuals and in a variety of locations, and that performers regarded the text and music as somewhat flexible. By changing a phrase of text to suit the circumstances of a particular performance and by adding a melodic ornament here and omitting another there, singers could shape a song into a demonstration of their own creative skills.

The question of transmission is further complicated by the fact that many trouvère devotional songs are contrafacta of earlier secular works – songs composed of new stanzas of text written to fit pre-existing melodies, or songs consisting of approximations of both text and music of earlier songs. The most appropriate material for such alterations would have been the best known songs, which audiences would recognize immediately. Far from being regarded as plagiarism, the skill of contrafacting was greatly admired. It was derived from the rhetorical practice of troping, in which an orator embroidered a text with spontaneous descriptive and figurative passages. Tropes entered late medieval liturgical music in the form of text added to the wordless melodic passages, called melismas, which occurred in some types of plainchant. It later became a common practice in the crafting of secular songs to quote melodic lines from well-known works of one's predecessors and colleagues, as well as from familiar hymns. The imitation was regarded as a tribute to the author of the borrowed source and a demonstration of the imitator's skill. The word trouvère, along with its Occitan counterpart *troubador*, may have been associated with the Latin rhetorical term *tropare*. From the same root comes the modern French verb *trouver* (to find). The concept of invention – itself derived from a Latin word that implies discovery rather than creation – was regarded in the medieval period as a process of working variations on previously existing themes. Creation *ex nihilo* was a power unique to God, and the human artist was seen as a clever craftsman whose power lay in manipulating the recombinative elements of known material, in finding one more way to say what had been said before.

The notation of the music of trouvère songs may also have been a field for recombinative creativity. It shows far less consistency between sources than one might expect if the demands of modal or mensural performance are taken into account; this factor, more than any consideration of interpretation, may argue against consistently standardized application of modal rhythm to monophonic trouvère songs. For performers and scribes of music in a monophonic and secular tradition, notation may have served as a convenient lingua franca in which the meaning of individual forms was somewhat flexible: one paid more attention to what one wanted to write than to the way in which one wrote it, and if one changed a long to a breve or a *podatus* to a *plica*, it was not likely to confuse anyone who followed the same generally accepted guidelines. What is revealed to the modern scholar is not the system of strictures and regulations, but the freedom with which that system was practised outside of the monastic scriptoria in which it developed. If the trouvère manuscripts contain inconsistent and contradictory examples of notation, it is perhaps because the people involved in their production and use were more concerned with a good tune than with the precision of the symbols used to record it. In a culture still primarily oral, the ear had precedence over the eye.

The transference of musical items from sound to visual record, then, was in the late thirteenth century a rather flexible process. The manuscripts served a function different from that of musical scores produced in our time, which specify such details of performance as phrasing, speed of delivery, and variations in volume and tone colour. The trouvère manuscripts represent an effort to preserve songs in a visual medium, affording secular works the same access to permanence that had been given to sacred music for centuries. It is unlikely that they were regarded as official records of the way each song ought to sound. Considerable freedom in performance – with regard to tessitura, tempo, tone quality, and use or non-use of accompanying instruments – was probably the norm. What the manuscripts can convey to our time are clues to the parameters of performance practice and to the nature of music literacy in the time of the trouvères.

The structure of the manuscripts is also worthy of notice because it contains clues to the specific attitudes held toward devotional songs in a secular context. In both X and V the devotional song collections are separated from the secular collections, which suggests that they were regarded as separate repertoires by their compilers. This in itself is significant, as is the fact that the devotional songs are anonymous while the secular songs are attributed to specific authors. Furthermore, in V the devotional songs are written in a scribal hand that differs from those in the secular portions and that is of a more recent origin, which indicates that the devotional songs were probably appended to the chansonnier after the completion of the secular part. In X the same text hand is evident throughout both repertoires, but the devotional songs are set apart and preceded by a miniature painting of the Madonna and Child and the rubric 'Ja comencent les chançons de la mere dieu' (Now begin the songs of the mother of God). This rubric gives the first unequivocal clue to the nature of the trouvère devotional songs. They are primarily written about or addressed to Mary in her roles as mother, virgin, and protector of sinners. This focus, along with the vernacular texts, sets them apart as a distinct repertoire, one that differs in important respects from the Latin devotional songs and hymns of the medieval church as well as from the secular works of the trouvères. Unlike the Latin repertoire, the trouvère devotional songs were not primarily didactic or doctrinal works. They were products of a secular court culture, an aristocracy whose leadership was intimately connected to the political hegemony of the established Catholic Church.

Description and Contents of Manuscript V

Manuscript V measures 28.75 cm × 19 cm. The restored binding is red leather with gilt over boards, the pastedowns are of wave-patterned paper, and there are three paper flyleaves, on one of which a list of contents is added in a nineteenth-century hand. The manuscript is made of parchment, with pages edged in gold; each page is arranged in two columns. Capital letters are in red and blue with gold, the large ones being 4.5 cm square in size, and the small 1 cm square; capitals are discontinued from folio 120. Staves of four or five lines for music in the main (secular) chansonnier are in red ink; those in the portion containing the devotional songs (ff. 148–55) are in black ink that has faded to brown, and are somewhat carelessly drawn. The manuscript exhibits signs of use: a dark smudge is on the lower corner of each page, and there are signs of wear along the edges. It was acquired by the Bibliothèque nationale on 14 March 1895.

The main chansonnier (ff. 1–119v) contains one illustration, of a vielle player performing before two seated crowned figures, a man and a woman. Three crests are set under the figures: the first and the third are red with a central gold cross, and the second shows a double-armed cross in blue with red bars on a field of gold. On the verso of f. 1 is a coat of arms consisting of bell shapes of blue and gold across a field of red, bordered by a garland of brown and gold shells. A medallion of Apollo with a snake hangs from the crest, which was probably added in the fifteenth century as an indication of ownership. This crest, with its medallion, is identified in the catalogue of the Bibliothèque nationale as the arms of Claude d'Urfé.[7]

Manuscript V contains nineteen gatherings arranged as follows:

1) ff. 1–8v	6) ff. 41–8v	11) ff. 81–8v	16) ff. 120–32v
2) ff. 9–18v	7) ff. 49–56v	12) ff. 89–96v	17) ff. 133–40v
3) ff. 19–24v	8) ff. 57–64v	13) ff. 97–108v	18) ff. 141–5v
4) ff. 25–32v	9) ff. 65–72v	14) ff. 109–13v	19) ff. 146–55v
5) ff. 33–40v	10) ff. 73–80v	15) ff. 114–19v	

The secular chansonnier occupies gatherings 1 to 15; on 119v, its final folio, is written a notice of the marriage of Raoulet Berthelot and Perine de Fougerays, dated 1457. Gatherings 16 and 17 (ff. 120–40v) contain a 'Traitié de quatre necessaires' (Treatise on the four necessities) dated 1266.[8] The *Bestiaire d'amours* of Richart de Furnivall occupies ff. 141–8r in gathering 18 and in part of 19.[9] The remainder of gathering 19, consisting of ff. 148–55v, contains the thirty anonymous devotional songs. Staves are ruled for all of them, but only the first eighteen have the musical notation recorded.

In its description of manuscript V, the *Catalogue général* of the Bibliothèque nationale states that the scribal hand of the secular chansonnier is older than that of the devotional songs.[10] In fact, the manuscript as a whole is the work of three distinct scribes for the text and of three scribes for the music. An examination of the scribal hands may lead to further conclusions about the construction and history of manuscript V.

The three text hands are as follows: 1) ff. 1–64v in gatherings 1–8 have large, thick, round letters; 2) ff. 65–119v in gatherings 9–15 have small, angular, ornate letters; 3) ff. 120–55v in gatherings 16–19 have small, thick, vertically aligned letters, less formal than those in the other hands, and certainly from a later date.

The following is a description of the three music hands: 1) ff. 1–48v in gatherings 1–6 have solid square notes, long tails, wide staves, and oblique flat signs; 2) ff. 49–119v in gatherings 7–15 are characterized by small notes, short tails, wide staves, open-ended flat signs, and faded ink; and 3) ff. 148–52v in gathering 19 contain small sketchy notes, long tails, narrow staves, and rounded and closed flat signs; the music hand for this last gathering is less formal than the other two and is also certainly from a later date.

The first two scribal hands of both the text and the music appear only within the secular chansonnier. The third text hand, which is shared by the narrative works and the devotional song texts, is a later and less careful one. The later portions of the manuscript (beginning at f. 120) do not contain coloured initials: some capitals are drawn in but not painted, and many are missing. Likewise, the *Bestiaire* has spaces left for illustrations that were never executed. It is likely that the secular chansonnier was conceived as a discrete document, with the other portions appended to it at a later date, perhaps when it was first bound or during an early restoration of the original binding. The third text hand may date from as late as the first quarter of the fourteenth century, and the third music scribe's familiarity with mensural notation forms (see the discussion above and in chapter 4) argues for a date not earlier than 1260, the inception of the Franconian system, a view supported by the date of the 'Traitié de quatre necessaires.' If one takes into account subsequent changes in French musical notation occurring with the *Ars Nova* treatise of Philippe de Vitry (ca. 1310) and leaves a decade for the new fashions to establish themselves, it is likely that the devotional songs of manuscript V were compiled and copied between 1270 and 1320.[11] Trouvère manuscript C, with which V concords extensively, can be dated, according to Richard Allen Schutz, to 'the last decade of the 13th or the early 14th century.'[12] It is therefore plausible to narrow the dates for the devotional portion of V to the same period, ca. 1290–1310.

Families and Stemmata of Manuscript V

The devotional section of manuscript V, with thirty songs, has only one (no. 32) in common with manuscript I at the Bodleian Library in Oxford but twenty-four with manuscript C at the Stadtbibliothek in Bern, a source that contains no music notation.[13] Many of the texts in V are faulty and they abound in omissions and metric irregularities. The corresponding texts in C are often more complete, suggesting that V may be a descendant of C. The relation between the two sources is complex, however. Of the first twenty-five devotional songs in V, all but one appear in C, and that one, no. 45, 'Per vous m'esjau,' whose text is a polyglot of French and Provençal, is unusual. What further obscures the picture is that C contains three secular Provençal texts among its French contents, but does not include the only one in V. A common ancestor, one that included all four Provençal texts, is therefore suggested.

In addition, C shows a small number of obvious scribal errors, as distinct from variants, that are in common with V. In song no. 41, a line is missing in both sources, while the spelling of rhyme words is garbled in nos. 42 and 55. Apparent aural transmission is indicated in no. 49: in the seventh stanza, the *celle espée* of C becomes the less plausible *se l'espée* in V. A striking contradiction to the acceptance of C as a direct ancestor to V, however, comes in song no. 54, which obviously was regarded by the scribe of C as an appendage to no. 53 despite the fact that its metre and rhymes are different. The text of no. 54 is truncated in C, and its conflation with the preceding text is apparently the result of the use in both songs of the device of allegorical debate. Since the contents of C are arranged in alphabetical order by first word, there is no reason for nos. 53 and 54, which begin with different letters, to appear in succession unless the scribe of C copied from a source, like V, that had arranged them in a different sequence. The only evident solution to the puzzle, then, is to posit a hypothetical parent source arranged in the order V exhibits, and to assume that the scribes of both V and C altered the texts to some degree. A simple stemma for the transmission might look like this:

Description and Contents of Manuscript X

Manuscript X measures 25 cm × 17.5 cm. The restored binding is of red leather with gilt over boards; pastedowns are of marbled paper. The binding is now somewhat loose and the thongs used to sew individual gatherings are visible, as are two parchment flyleaves and a fragment of an old parchment cover. Seven paper folios containing an alphabetical inventory of the contents were added at some point after the final compilation. The manuscript is in parchment and consists of 272 folios plus eight folios in paper that were added at the end to replace a missing gathering (ff. 273–80). Folios 121, 126, and 136–54v are also later copies on paper written in an eighteenth-century hand and were supplied from manuscript N of the Cangé group.[14] Manuscript X does not show any particular signs of wear. It was acquired by the Bibliothèque nationale on 27 October 1876.

Each page is ruled in two columns. Capital letters are red with blue tracery, or blue with red tracery; the large ones are 5 cm × 3.5 cm and the small 2 cm × 1.5 cm. The large capitals are decorated with animal heads or geometric designs in shades of blue, green, rose, pink, and gold. At the beginning of the section containing the anonymous devotional songs at f. 257v is a miniature of the Madonna and Child in the initial letter V (*Virge des ciels*), along with the rubric 'Ja comencent les chançons de la mere dieu' (Now begin the songs about the mother of God).

With the inevitable exception of the eighteenth-century replacement folios, manuscript X appears to have been copied by one scribe, or by one for the texts and another for the music. The text hand is large and clear, and the notes are well squared. In the secular portion of the chansonnier a small number of songs are marked with a red drawing of a crown, in which is written the word *coronee* (crowned). These are apparently examples of the *cantus coronatus* (crowned song) form praised by thirteenth-century French theorist Jean de Grouchy as fit for kings and rulers.[15] The Marian devotional songs, although grouped together in a distinct section at the end of the manuscript, were obviously part of the original design for its compilation: they begin in the middle of a gathering and are in the same hand as the secular portion.

Families and Stemmata of Manuscript X

The correlation of manuscript X with manuscripts N, O, and P in the Cangé family has been amply detailed in earlier literary and palaeographic studies.[16] Because the concordances apply only to the secular portion of the chansonnier, they need not be examined here, with one exception. Of the thirty-one devotional songs in X, nine also appear in P, and a comparison of the two versions can serve to clarify the process of transmission. The songs that are common to both sources are nos. 2, 3, 6, 7, 9 to 12, and 15. The following is a description of selected comparative details among them.

Song no. 2: There are two minor musical variants, of which only the latter is significant: the final note of the song in X is the final of its scale, while in P the final note is the third degree of its scale.[17]

Song no. 3: In addition to minor variants in music and to one in the text, the refrain in X reads *qui sert ... la flor de paradis* (who serves ... the flower of paradise), but in P it is *qui sert ... li rois de paradis* (who serves ... the king of paradise). Because the song text is otherwise consistently Marian, the version in X seems more accurate.

Song no. 6: There are minor musical variants in the two manuscripts.

Song no. 7: Minor musical variants are found. In two cases, a ternary ligature that is plicated in X is not plicated in P. Notes written as longs in X are often breves in P. Finally, the text in X contains five stanzas, of which the first four appear in P with the addition of two unique stanzas. Thus, a hypothetical third parent source can be added to the stemma.

Song no. 9: Manuscripts X and P concur with only minor variants in text and notation.

Song no. 10: There are notational variants: longs in X are breves in P.

Song no. 11: There are several notational variants. A currentes ligature in X is a descending ternary ligature in P. The third stanza text is corrupt in X and P, which both give the same version, but the text is correct in manuscript a, which also contains two additional stanzas. The version of the third stanza in X and P is not a truncation of that in a, however, and seems to be taken from another source.

Song no. 12: Manuscripts X and P concur, with minor variants, in text and notation. The third stanza in both sources is truncated; the correct text appears in manuscript a. One variant line in the second stanza illustrates a complex connection among the three sources in a it is 'qui de nous print tel pité'; in P 'qui de nos prist grant pité'; and in X 'qui de nos ot grant pité.' In addition, manuscript a contains one additional stanza after the third, while manuscript i includes the first four stanzas that are found in the other three sources as well as four additional unique stanzas.

Song no. 15: Minor variants exist in notation. Longs in X are breves in P. In the second stanza, two lines missing in X are present in P. The text of the two-line refrain differs in the two sources: the version in X is consistent through all five stanzas, while the version in P remains consistent in the first four and changes in the fifth.

With the information derived from the comparison of the songs, it is possible to construct a stemma for the sources of the manuscripts X, P, a, and i. One must first posit two lost parent sources, β and Γ, such that: β contains fewer stanzas than a for songs 11 and 12; β contains a different final stanza than Γ and P for song no. 3; and β contains a different final stanza than Γ for song no. 7. Manuscript X follows the reading in β and P follows the reading in Γ. With the addition of a still earlier source α as the parent of β and Γ, the following stemma results:

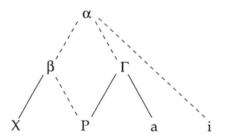

Manuscripts X and V, the work of living minds and hands in their time, were also products of a culture that valued their contents. Examining the trouvère devotional songs in the context of that culture is the next exploratory step.

2

The Trouvère Devotional Songs in the Context of Popular Culture

Among the extant corpus of approximately two thousand songs by the trouvères of thirteenth-century France is a small subgenre – some 10 per cent of the total number – with devotional texts. Their existence is not surprising: vernacular devotional songs were common throughout Europe, which was in the midst of what we now characterize as an 'Age of Faith.' The scene is easily set: crowds streaming through the portals of Notre-Dame de Paris on Easter morning, friars preaching in town squares, and housewives timing their recipes by the length of a paternoster. Preacher, priest, and poet, weaving tapestries of rhyme and song in praise of Mary, or in prayer for redemption. Who, then, wrote the devotional songs of thirteenth-century France, and what segments of society formed their audience? What relation did their contents have to the secular repertoire of the trouvères, to the vernacular devotional songs of other European cultures, or to the doctrines of the Catholic Church? If they are to be assigned to the realm of popular culture, to what segments of the populace do we refer, and what were the tenets of their collective faith? It will be the task of this and subsequent chapters to provide some plausible answers to these questions, as well as some speculations about the nature and purpose of the trouvère devotional songs. Let us enter the scene, then, and take a closer look.

The definition of popular culture in the medieval period is reminiscent of the Sufi fable of the blind men and the elephant:[1] the nature of the beast is entirely dependent upon what part of it you encounter first. Popular culture may initially be defined, for this period, as being outside the realm of the institutional church and its clergy, but what is then to be done with the entire genre of 'popular' vernacular devotional literature? For that matter, can a song performed for a select audience of nobles at court be called 'popular' in the same sense as a peasant's dance tune or even a liturgical hymn sung in procession by an entire village once each year? The problem is well stated by historian Pierre Boglioni:

The popular is, in its first approximation, the lay as opposed to the clerical, the episcopal, and the monastic; but it is also the lower clergy as opposed to the educated and university clerics ... It is the local, the peripheral, the specific as opposed to the centralized and uniform. It is oral culture and the values of the group as opposed to written culture and the values of the individual ... It is the charismatic and the unexpected as opposed to the institutional and to established standards ... Recent discussions on the notion of popular religion show that it is at the same time difficult and essential to define exactly these diverse stages of opposition.[2]

The first definite statement that can be made about the devotional songs of the trouvères is that they apparently were not associated with either the highly educated urban clerics or the plebeian elements of thirteenth-century society. Their presence in carefully copied and decorated manuscripts points to wealthy audiences, and their vernacular texts are not typical of university or monastic works. Having eliminated these ends of the spectrum, one is left with a rich middle ground of nobles, urban bourgeoisie, local and court clergy, and professional entertainers. It is not unlikely that all of these elements had some involvement in the process of creating or receiving the vernacular devotional songs, but for the true home ground of the trouvère *chanson* one must look to the courts of the nobility, at which were resident both the poets and musicians to perform the songs and the chaplains and clerks to record them.

Thirteenth-century French music theorist Jean de Grouchy, whose *Tractatus de musica* is the only extant contemporary treatise to include a discussion of secular musical styles, connects one form of song with the nobility. In describing the *cantus coronatus*, he states that: 'It should be composed by kings and nobles and be sung before kings and princes of the earth, that their souls may be moved toward boldness and fortitude, generosity, and liberality, all of which contribute to good government.'[3] He makes no specific mention of lyric songs with devotional texts, although his description of the related *chanson de geste* – the narrative song of deeds which recounts the actions of a heroic warrior – encompasses the vernacular lives of saints and *martyria*, the latter heavily mythologized accounts of martyrdom designed to inspire devotion. The material of the *cantus coronatus* may be equated with that of the trouvère songs in a general sense, however. The trouvère doctrines of *fin'amor* and *loiauté* – the idealized love and loyalty required of the courtly lover – may well have seemed in Jean de Grouchy's Aristotelian view to move the souls of princes toward virtuous government, and thus to fill the function he associated with the *cantus coronatus*. It is clear, in any case, that the devotional songs of the trouvères were formed according to the model of the secular works, although their contents differ in several important respects.[4] Like their secular counterparts, the devotional songs were written by and for the land-owning aristocracy.

The involvement of members of the French aristocracy in writing poetry and songs, as well as in listening to them, is well documented through the biographical sketches in troubadour *vidas*,[5] through descriptive appellations in the trouvère chansonniers, and through the vocabulary and thematic material appearing in many of the trouvères' texts. What holds true for the secular material may also be applied to the devotional works: the vocabulary of court manners and feudal society permeates many of the songs that are addressed to Mary. Among the trouvères who wrote both secular and devotional songs was Thibaut, Count of Champagne and King of Navarre. Among the anonymous authors of the works under examination here were, quite possibly, a number of landed nobles and knights.

Inextricably connected with the poetic activity of nobles were the *jongleurs*, professional entertainers whose talents included anything from singing *chansons de geste* to storytelling and acrobatic acts. A noble trouvère who sang his own compositions was a rarity, according to historian Edmond Faral.[6] It was far more common for a nobleman to hire a professional singer in order to make his work public, and a fair number of trouvère songs contain references to this practice by including an *envoi* addressed to the performer. One of the songs in manuscript V is a case in point:

> Or te pri je, Polidamas,
> si chier com ceste dame as,
> que dou chanter ne te soit gas
> ne painne ...
> > 52, st. 5

Much of the modern literature on the *jongleurs* is concerned with distinguishing those serving as court musicians from the *jongleurs de foire*, the public entertainers whose vagrancy and suspect morals drew the ire of the clergy. Faral dismisses the distinction as academic: 'The distinction between popular and courtly *jongleur* activities appears insufficient, and, in order to complete it one must establish an important subdivision in each of the two classes. It is at this moment that one begins to comprehend the vanity of this scholastic game and of these entirely theoretical divisions, for the castle gates were never closed to street entertainers.'[7] Whatever the truth of the matter, the *jongleurs* themselves were sometimes responsible for the composition of songs, both secular and devotional. As examples of the latter, Faral cites the vernacular Bible of Guiot de Provins and the moral narratives of the *menestrel* Robert de Blois.[8]

If our knowledge of the distinctions between the trouvère and the *jongleur*, between the amateur and the professional, and between the poet and the *dévot* remains somewhat blurred, what do we know of those whose profession was prayer? The involvement of the clergy in the composition of devotional songs is again a matter for conjecture. Recent scholarship has linked the nascent Franciscan order with the rise of vernacular devotional lyric in Italy and England,[9] and the educated class of court chaplains with the same phenomenon in France.[10] It is certainly probable that court clerics were responsible for much of the process of recording songs in late medieval Europe. It was common practice for them to serve the court chancery as scribes and notaries and the court chapel as scribes of music, tasks which few others would have been trained to perform. In the thirteenth century there occurred a swelling of the ranks in the lower clerical orders, resulting in a distinct class of *clercs vagants*, non-beneficed clergy who gravitated to the court milieu and who may have been responsible for much of the vernacular moral literature written at the time, as well as the occasional foray into political satire. Romance language scholar Michel Zink, discussing the rise of vernacular sermons in southern Europe, cites this phenomenon: 'Pierre Cardinal, tired of being a canon at Puy, threw his cassock in the nettles and made himself a troubadour. Without going as far as this conversion in reverse, several of our authors were able, while remaining within the bounds of religious literature as almoner, lector, or secretary to some wealthy devout layman, to put their training in Latin to the service of vernacular prose.'[11]

And also of poetry? It is appropriate, in the absence of direct attributions, to associate the composition of religious poetry with the clergy, and they may well have had a hand in some of the songs appearing in manuscripts V and X. However, there is little in common between the structure and imagery of these songs and those of the popular devotional works in Latin that might be expected to have served as models for vernacular material written by members of the clergy or by friars. The trouvère devotional songs more closely resemble secular songs than they do religious works from Latin or other vernacular traditions, and for this reason some caution should be taken in suggesting clerical authorship.

What, then, may be said about the religious views and attitudes of lay people in the thirteenth century? Song is by nature a public art form, shaped by audience as well as author; whatever the authorship of the vernacular devotional songs, they were certainly intended for performance among the laity. Before examining the texts themselves, therefore, it may be helpful to sketch a brief outline of late medieval Christianity as it appeared to those who practised it in the secular world.

A treatise in rhymed verse, written about 1400 by the English priest John Mirk (Myrc), contains instructions for parish priests on matters of behaviour, morality, and responsibilities. Among the subjects treated is the teaching of prayers to parishioners.

The pater noster and the crede
Preche thy paresche thou moste nede
Twyes or thryes in the yere.
To thy paresch hole and fere;
Teche hem thus, and byd hem say
Wyth gode entent every day,
'Fader owre that art in hevene ...'[12]

In addition to the Creed and paternoster, Mirk expected members of the congregation to know and practise the Hail Mary and the Fourteen Articles of Faith. Devotion to Mary was of particular importance during the late medieval period, and the thirteenth century gave rise to a burgeoning tradition of Marian literature and art that permeated popular as well as ecclesiastical culture.

Alongside the official doctrines of the church was a rich tradition of popular beliefs, often enmeshed with influences quite external to orthodox Christianity. Little is written about Mary in the Gospels, yet the late medieval legendaries and collections of devotional poetry are full of detail about her nature, her character, and the miracles attributed to her.[13] The late medieval cult of the Virgin Mary, which may stem from traditions developed in Byzantine Christianity during the course of the fourth and fifth centuries, seems to have been imported to the West during the Crusades. It crept into the devotional writings of French monastics and into the prayers of lay people before it was officially recognized by the established church, which appears to have been reluctant to grant it doctrinal status at first because it raised the spectre of pre-Christian goddess worship.[14] The cult undoubtedly represents a fusion of several parallel systems of belief. Among the monastic orders, Mary came to represent the essential feminine, made ethereal through her paradoxical attributes of virginal purity and maternal compassion. Among the secular clergy she was seen as an embodiment of divine mercy. The image of Mary as the gentle and forgiving advocate of repentant sinners could reassure parishioners that salvation was possible for them. To the devout laity, Mary was the mediatrix whose advocacy might secure their entry into heaven, and she was as well the queen of that heaven, a ruling figure whose position in the celestial hierarchy echoed and legitimized the hierarchy of their temporal aristocracy. In a society based on agriculture, Mary became a substitute for the pre-Christian earth goddesses, a symbol of fertility so generous it required no earthly seed: the Virgin, like her earlier counterparts, was celestially impregnated. If the devotional songs and the Latin hymns often stressed the unearthly quality of her pregnancy, as well as her giving birth in midwinter, it was undoubtedly in an attempt to combat the assumption so easily made by farming people that she was a personification of the fertile earth itself.

From these overlapping layers of belief, shaped by the needs and the logical associations of each segment of late medieval society, came a complex web of popular heterodoxy. Its development may be seen as a vital element in the history of Christian faith. Historian Carolly Erickson comments:

Heterodoxy – belief that goes beyond or varies from orthodox doctrine – had always existed in the western church as the unavoidable result of partial or faulty knowledge of doctrine joined to the rich religious imagination of Latin and

Germanic peoples. But where worship involves only the superficial observance of ritual it is unlikely for organized popular heterodoxy to develop; differing views emerge only when belief becomes a matter of inner conviction and meditation. By the mid-twelfth century the internalizaton of Christianity was sufficiently intense to promote the growth of alternative forms of belief.[15]

The nature of inner conviction is at best difficult to determine in historical circumstances, particularly when written records are scarce. We have in the vernacular devotional songs one form of historical record from which the shape of popular beliefs may be drawn. This aspect will be examined in detail in subsequent chapters. Another source, rich in both social and individual detail, is furnished by extant registers of the Inquisition.

The index to the registers of Jacques Fournier, bishop of Pamiers, lists the occupations of suspects and witnesses in the hearings of the Inquisition. Among them are a shepherd, a merchant, a notary, a student, an innkeeper, a tailor, a weaver, and a nurse. Many discussions of complex theological issues are described as having taken place in taverns and farmhouses, either at the instigation of self-styled local preachers or without the participation of any persons educated in a formal sense.[16] Fournier's records are from the south of France in the first quarter of the fourteenth century, and his object was to root out what remained of the Albigensian or Cathar doctrine, considered a heresy by northern Catholics, from its home ground. Given these extreme circumstances, it is risky to generalize by attributing the same conditions to an earlier period in the north. Still, one is left with the impression that people in all ranks of society, however ignorant of theological doctrine, knew the Creed and the Articles of Faith, held them in reverence, and were greatly concerned with issues pertaining to religion. Analogies have been made between the religious fervour of the late medieval period and the modern concern with political matters:

At the end of the Middle Ages, the spiritual world, the world contemplated by theology, was the real world, while the world of politics, over which we quarrel today, was the nominal world ... At the beginning of the fourteenth century the man in the street could be complacent about the political issues of the state, and even indifferent to them, whereas he had an opinion about the affairs of heaven and hell that did make a difference to him and he tended to belong loosely to the party whose doctrines best suited his taste or convenience.[17]

If the passion for opinionated discussion of religious matters held true among merchants, tailors, weavers, and their wives, it is likely also to have affected the atmosphere of the courts that gave rise to the trouvère lyrics. Relations between the landed aristocracy and the ecclesiastical hierarchy in thirteenth-century France were close, complex, and turbulent: it is probable that the political affairs of the church, as well as doctrinal issues, occupied a large place in the thoughts and conversations of the aristocracy. The views and beliefs of individuals are not easily traced, but an occasional glimpse is granted to the vigilant. The fourteenth-century poet and chronicler Jean Froissart describes the devotional practices of Gaston Phebus, count of Foix: 'He said plenty of prayers every day, a nocturn of the psalter, hours of Our Lady, of the Holy Spirit, of the Cross, and vigils for the dead. Every day he had five francs given in coin for the love of God, and alms at the door to all people.'[18]

Froissart describes the devotions of a literate man, a well-known patron of poets and musicians. It is among his counterparts in the thirteenth century that one may find trouvères and their patrons. Along with the formalized aspects of religion, the prayers, and charities, there are documented instances of personal revelation. The English knight Hubert de Burgh, a military man who held great political power in the first quarter of the thirteenth century, is described by the chronicler Matthew of Paris as encouraging his troops to pillage churches on enemy lands; the crucified Christ appeared to him in a dream, and the next day he stopped his troops from looting a church and restored its goods to the priest who confronted him with a crucifix identical to the one in the dream.[19] Whether or not the incident and its inspiration actually took place, the chronicler's mention of it bears witness to a particular frame of mind reflecting a context of devotion that was associated with the late medieval aristocracy and that was expected of it. If a king was king by the grace of God, it must follow that he was obliged to maintain some contact with the celestial powers and with their representatives in the temporal church. The same was held to be true of his underlings in the titled aristocracy, and their actions and habits – patronage of monastic houses, widespread public charity, having members of the clergy resident at court, lavish gifts to churches, and prayers recited daily and on the eve of battle – support the view. It is well to remember that the later stages of trouvère activity coincided with the reign of King Louis IX, a canonized saint who was renowned during his lifetime for piety and who expected a similar attitude from his nobles.[20] It should come as no surprise that among the *chansons de fin'amor* so popular among the aristocracy at the time were a number of *chansons de nostre dame*. To summarize contemporary views of the efficacy of such songs, one can do no better than to quote the thirteenth-century prior and poet Gautier de Coinci:

Qui l'anemi velt enchanter
de la grand dame doit chanter
dont jor et nuit li angle chantent.
Dyable endorment et enchantent
tout cil qui chantent son doz chant:
Or escoutez comment j'en chant.'[21]

3

The Texts

Doctrinal Content

Devotional literature is usually written for didactic purposes. The trouvère devotional songs are no exception, but their purpose is achieved by somewhat unexpected means. The songs contain few accounts of biblical events, few paraphrases of liturgical Latin, and almost no mention of the church as a temporal or symbolic institution. What most of the songs offer is praise of Mary in two specific roles: as the mortal medium for the Incarnation and as the mediatrix who intercedes for souls on the Day of Judgment. Nearly every song ends with a personal prayer for salvation, phrased in terms that, though often formulaic, are nonetheless highly emotional. The secular lover pleading with his unapproachable lady is mirrored in the songs by the penitent pleading with the mediatrix. It is easy to categorize the second as a derivation from the first. Yet the role of penitent that was so often assumed by the poet was a sociological reality as well as a literary type. The thirteenth century was a time of important doctrinal revisions within the church that were formulated and published by the Fourth Lateran Council of 1215. Among many areas affected by the council's decrees were the attitude and conduct of lay people who professed the Catholic faith.

Confession and communion began as matters subject to individual choice. The church required both but did not specify that they be done at particular times or with particular frequency. The twenty-first decree of the Fourth Lateran Council changed both to an annual obligation: 'All the faithful of either sex must confess all their sins alone, at least once per year, to a priest, and must take the sacrament of the Eucharist reverently, at least at Easter.'[1] A further refinement of the concept of confession is given in the twenty-second decree, which orders physicians to refrain from applying physical remedies until after the patient has confessed to a priest: 'Since infirmity of the body proceeds from nothing other than sin ... we state in this decree and strongly urge physicians of the body that when it happens that they are called to the infirm, they first warn and induce them to call the physicians of the soul.'[2]

Periodic examination of conscience and repentance were now specifically required of each individual who wished to remain a member of the
Catholic community and to be buried with its rites. Repentance was also
emphasized by the first chapter of the Lateran text, a gloss on the Creed
that describes explicitly the nature of evil and the process of salvation:

The devil and other demons were created by God as good, but became evil by
themselves: humanity sinned by suggestion of the devil. And if anyone after
[infant] baptism should fall into sin, they may be restored by true penitence. Not
only those who are virgin and continent, but even those who are married, may
by proper faith and good works pleasing to God become worthy of eternal
blessedness.[3]

The implication of this passage is that repentance is essential not only for
the restoration of the soul in God's grace after individual sin, but also for
overcoming the stain of original sin, inherited, according to Catholic
belief, by every human born since Adam and Eve's fall from grace. Thus,
every man and woman of Catholic faith was required to repent and to
demonstrate the state of repentance by confessing to a priest, not only for
the purpose of staying within the good graces of the temporal church but
also as a requirement for the eternal salvation of the soul.

The impact of the Lateran decrees was immediate. Bishops were
enjoined to inform their parish priests that sermons must be preached on
the theme of salvation through repentance. The Dominican and Franciscan
preaching orders, founded in the course of the thirteenth century, emphasized the same point, continually delineating the differences between
Catholic doctrine and Cathar heresy to audiences whose knowledge of
both was often based on rumour and vague memories from childhood.
The subtleties of faith and dogma became current issues, preached and
proclaimed with fervour, debated at domestic hearths and public inns. In
this climate, the vernacular devotional songs of Europe were born and
flourished. Just as sermons employed homespun examples and popular
imagery, the songs incorporated secular music, imagery, and structure.

The ways in which the devotional songs both resemble and differ from
secular and catechetic literature of the time are significant. One might
expect to find a majority of texts describing doctrine or paraphrasing
scriptural passages. In the trouvère repertoire, texts of this sort are a
minority. Examination of the song texts for evidence of distinct thematic
or structural tendencies reveals five categories, represented in each of the
manuscripts to quite different degrees.[4] These categories of texts can be
defined as follows.

Courtly (Co): Song texts in this category are modelled on the secular
   chanson. The first stanza typically evokes a pastoral setting or a personal

observation of the natural world and refers to the purpose of the song. Stanzas two and three are typically narrative or descriptive, referring to scriptural events or presenting laudatory passages in praise of Mary. Subsequent stanzas may be in the form of prayers or they may be pre-scriptive, offering advice and instruction on how to lead one's life in order to attain salvation. An *envoi* is generally included. This category is a mixed genre, combining elements of categories Ca, La, and Pr in a pre-scribed structure. The vocabulary and imagery are often similar to the secular songs, but there is no indication of parody except in the evoca-tion of setting in the initial stanzas. This is by far the largest category in manuscript V (two-thirds of the total content); it is less significant in manuscript X (20 per cent).

Laudatory (La): These song texts are praises of Mary, either in a descrip-tive mode (third person) or as a direct address (second person). They contain vivid imagery, sometimes drawn from Latin models. In manu-script X, this type of song text is associated with certain structural factors as well: refrain forms, artful wordplay, serpentine and other internal rhyme patterns, and strongly rhythmic music. One-third of the songs in X are of this type.

Political (Pl): Song texts in this category are complaints about the state of the temporal world, usually containing criticisms of the church as an institution.

Catechetic (Ca): In the narrative mode and the third person, the texts in this category emphasize doctrinal information or scriptural content. This group includes the Annunciation texts in dialogue form.

Personal (Pr): These song texts are intensely personal prayers, confes-sions, or contemplative experiences in either the first person or as a direct address or both. Emphasis is placed on the role of Mary in the process of salvation, and on the importance of individual effort. The serious nature of the texts is sometimes lightened by the effect of the melodic lines, and one example (no. 10) may be a parody of the genre. Another third of manuscript X belongs in this category.

The text categories suggest some of the purposes for which the devo-tional works in the two manuscripts were composed. If one combines the contents of manuscripts V and X (see table 1) the Courtly group proves to be the largest. It is also the category most closely associated with the struc-ture and vocabulary of secular court poetry. Next in frequency are the Laudatory and Personal types, the first associated with both secularized Latin models (hymns, sequences, and litany) and popular round-form dance songs, and the other with a Christian poetic tradition of confession and testament. Both categories present the author's personal statement of faith without direct reference to scriptural or doctrinal sources.[5]

The explicit promulgation of the doctrines of the Fourth Lateran Coun-

Table 1
Text categories for the songs (the numbers refer to those used in this edition)

Category	Song numbers
Co	4, 8, 9, 11, 12, 13, 18, 19, 29, 33, 35, 37, 38, 39, 40, 41, 42, 43, 45, 46, 47, 48, 50, 51, 52, 53, 55, 56, 57, 58, 59, 60
La	2, 3, 6, 7, 14, 15, 20, 22, 23, 44
Pl	26, 27
Ca	5, 28, 31, 32, 34, 36, 49, 54, 61
Pr	1, 10, 16, 17, 21, 24, 25, 30

cil does not seem to have been the primary purpose of these songs. They seem instead to be expressions of doctrine that had been received and assimilated into personal beliefs. As such, they may stand as evidence for the popular acceptance of doctrinal change among the aristocrats of thirteenth-century France, who regarded the Catholic faith as a deeply personal matter of conviction and believed that eternal salvation of the soul would depend upon a combination of one's actions, one's attitudes, and the grace of God as represented by Christ the judge, the final arbiter of actions and attitudes. The process of judgment resembled that of the legal courts, and the soul on trial could call upon the advocacy of saints to plead its cause. Chief among these advocates was Mary, whose motherhood embodied the mercy of God and whose remote perfection recalled the unapproachable noblewomen of the secular trouvère songs. To the penitent, however, Mary was eminently approachable.

The Poet to the Lady

Among trouvère songs, devotional and secular texts share much of their structure, vocabulary, and imagery. This is particularly true of the Marian texts, which combine praise and supplication in ways that seem at first glance interchangeable with the terms and concepts of the secular love songs. A number of questions are raised by the similarities: did the poet whose lover and lady were both representative literary creations regard his devotional poems in the same light as the secular poems, or were they accurate indications of his personal religious faith? What can the Marian songs tell us about the image that the poets and their audiences held of Mary?

In the literature of the Provençal troubadours, which predated and undoubtedly influenced that of the trouvères, Marian poetry was a relatively late development.[6] It began with vernacular hymns that paraphrased those in the Latin repertoire, and it soon employed the terms and conceits of amorous court poetry. The Marian trouvère songs, however, represent a distinct genre. There is little chance of confusing a trouvère love song with a Marian devotional song, even if one removes all the specific names or references to the object of love, because the entire conceptual framework of the song provides essential clues to the identity of its object. Certain phrases, images, and attitudes portrayed in the Marian songs are peculiar to the devotional genre, being derived from the language of Scripture and from the tenets of contemporary theology. Certain elements of the secular songs are also generic characteristics, indicative of particular medieval attitudes toward the social and emotional aspects of erotic love. In both the secular and devotional repertoires of the trouvères, we find, almost inevitably, the image of a man speaking in supplication to a woman. The words he speaks in each case may have similarities, but they are not the same.

The poet's tone of supplication itself bears examining. The lover in the secular songs usually complains of suffering in love: despite his loyal service, the lady does not acknowledge him. A common theme is unrequited love:

> Bien deussez, dame, garder raison
> en moi grever, qu'ai servi et proié
> tant longuement en bon entencion,
> n'onques un jor ne me feïstes lie.[7]

The lady, however much praised, is often blamed for the sorry state of her lover. In some texts, she may be proud and distant, or unfaithful. In others, the combined effects of *vilté*, *fierté*, and *jalousie* (villainy, pride, and jealousy) and the lover's rivals prevent her from recognizing or responding to him:

> Dex, se ne fust la cruautez
> a cele malparliere gent
> et la tres granz desleautez,
> je l'alasse veoir souvent.
> Mais tant redout lour fauseté![8]

Nor can the courtly lover be certain that his loyalty will bring about the desired reward:

> Cil doit bien d'amours joïr
> par droit jugement,
> que sanz repentir
> la sert bien et loiaument.
> Mais on voit souvent

que cil qui plus bonnement
ont servi
faillent a merci.[9]

One can make a case for courtly love as an elaborate literary and philo-
sophical game, in which the potential of unfulfilled love becomes more
significant than any genuine emotional state and the process of striving to
attain an object becomes more important than the object itself. It is also
possible to regard the contents of the secular songs as formal but genuine
emotional expressions from a culture that idealized erotic love. It is clear,
in any case, that the concepts and attitudes expressed in the songs were
well known and popular among the intellectuals and aristocrats of
thirteenth-century France. Had there been any desire to apply the concept
of unfulfilled striving to religious themes, some enterprising poet would
undoubtedly have done so. Yet there are no examples of such an application. However similar the devotional songs may at first appear to the secular repertoire, the fundamental premise from which they were written is
quite different: that divine love, unlike that of the world, is always
requited.[10]

Consider first the devotional songs addressed to Mary. Like the secular
court songs they are either descriptive or supplicatory. What differs, however, to an often surprising extent is the attitude taken by the poet – who is
also the supplicant – to the object of his attention. Descriptive and laudatory passages show no trace of the detailed accounts of physical beauty so
common in the secular songs. We are never told the colour of Mary's eyes
or hair, the size of her waist, the quality of her smile, or the straightness of
her posture – all those traits that inspire and fuel the devotion of a courtly
lover to his lady. The Virgin is simply *bele* or *de grant biauté* (lovely or of
great beauty). The laudatory poems and passages speak rather about her
symbolic roles and functions or about the qualities she exemplifies. In
temporal terms, she is *mere, pucelle, reine* (mother, maiden, queen). On the
level of allegory, she is *lumiere, fontenele*, or *estoile marine* (light, fountain,
or star of the sea). To the soul who calls upon her, she is the source and
summit of goodness and gentleness. Mary shares, to be sure, the title of
dame de tous biens pleinne (lady full of all goodness) with a large number of
court ladies, but to her alone belongs

cele par qui habonde
au monde toute bonté.   22, st. 2

An attempt at a controlled comparison between the vocabularies of the
secular and devotional repertoires can be made through an examination of
the works of Thibaut de Navarre, one of the few trouvères with attributed
songs in both genres.[11] Thibaut's devotional songs are often of the Cate-

chetic type, although laudatory passages to Mary are common: the latter are notable for the modesty of their content, in comparison with the extravagant praises that appear in the secular love songs. The poet seems often to be building a logical case for the worthiness of the court lady as an object of love by describing her in great and glowing detail. To the medieval Christian, no such proof was needed for Mary, and Thibaut speaks more about her powers than about her individual qualities. The lines

> Dame plaine de grant bonté
> de courtoisie et de pitié[12]

might have been written about any court lady, but they are followed by

> et par vous est touz raluminé
> li mondes,[13]

an image which is peculiar to Marian poetry.

The line between earthly love and faith is sharply drawn by Thibaut. However attractive the ladies of his songs may be, they do not inspire trust in the mind of the lover, who may alternate praise with such blunt criticisms as

> Douce dame, de franchise
> n'ai je point en vos trové.[14]

Furthermore, any comparison between the two levels of love is explicitly denied by Thibaut, as by other poets. In the devotional song 'De grant travail,' he states:

> Mout par est fox qui autre amour essaie
> qu'en cesti n'a barat ne fausseté
> ne es autres ne merciz ne manaie.'[15]

The tone of supplication in the Marian songs also differs from that of the secular love songs. The secular lover pleads with his lady for recognition and appreciation, swearing that he has been faithful in serving her and lamenting her lack of response. The penitent who pleads with Mary for grace gives emphasis to the fact that he has not always been faithful to her in the past and that his service has often been given to the world:

> Mainte chançon ai fait de grant ordure,
> mes, se Dieu plaist, jamés n'en avrai cure:
> en moi a petit eü
> bien et sens et mesure.   5, st. 1

or that he has been in a state of ignorance, often symbolized by blindness, until faith overtakes him:

> Avuegles, muëz et sourz
> ai esté tout mon vivant:
> or sui gariz et resours.
>
> 48, st. 1

It is precisely the relation of penitent to petitioner that sets the devotional songs of supplication apart from the secular songs of unrequited love, to which they are analogous on a structural level. The supplicant, unlike the courtly lover, has not been a faithful and persistent servant. He has erred personally or has shared the burden of sin placed on humanity since the time of Adam. His plea to Mary, unlike the lover's to his lady, is put forth with a certainty that it will be answered:

> C'est cele, se Dieu me voie,
> qui touz pechëor ravoie
> quant il li quierent pardon.
>
> 4, st. 2

Because the penitent knows that his prayer will be answered, his tone contains none of the courtly lover's bitterness or reproach and no suggestion that the lady is cruel or capricious. He is an unworthy suitor with a successful suit, while his secular counterpart remains a worthy suitor without success.

The role of repentant sinner is not the only one presented by the texts of the songs to Mary. Often the poet speaks as a feudal vassal pledging homage to her as *domina* or *regina* (reigning lady or queen), vowing to serve as her champion in the mortal realm if she affords protection to his soul:

> et je fais tout lige homaige
> li et son fil et son pere
> de cuer, de cors, et d'espir
> a touz jourz sanz repentir,
> et por iceste lijance
> suis en certaine fiance
> qu'ele en pitié me voudra regarder,
> a mes besoignz et de touz maus garder.
>
> 58, st. 3

Of what did service to Mary consist and how was it accomplished? There is little information from the thirteenth century about the devotional practices of lay people, but a few glimpses are afforded by contemporary theologians and by poetry in the vernacular. Veneration of Mary became progressively more intense throughout the twelfth and thirteenth centuries in both clerical and lay circles. Monastic establishments came to celebrate the Marian office every day of the week, and sculptures depicting the legend of Mary appear on the portals of all French cathedrals built during the thirteenth century, even those dedicated to other saints.[16]

In the tradition of scholastic theology, the Virgin Mary was equated with *Ecclesia* – the allegorical embodiment of the church – and with the bride of the Song of Songs.[17] Treatises and sermons were written to catalogue and interpret her attributes through the practice of scriptural exegesis, among them works by the Cistercian St Bernard[18] and the Franciscan St Bonaventure.[19] One of these was a seminal and widely read source of Marian literature, the treatise *De laudibus beatae Mariae virginis* by 'Pseudo-Albert' (Richard of St Lawrence),[20] written between 1239 and 1245. It is a compendium of information about Mary and Marian theology, including a list of some 240 names and attributes applicable to the Virgin by writers of sermons, treatises, and liturgical poetry.

The *De laudibus* contains forty reasons for service to Mary; the term used consistently is *servire*, the same word used by the trouvères in both courtly and devotional contexts. That the concept was also current in conventual writings lends additional validity to the feudal notion of service and reward as a social and moral bond between two individuals of unequal status. Among the reasons listed by Richard of St Lawrence for serving Mary is the protection she can give: 'For she most strongly protects those who serve her from the triple adversary, namely, the world, the flesh, and the devil.'[21] This theme is certainly among the most common in the vernacular Marian devotional songs, appearing in all categories of text, from playful lyrics to penitential prayers. Among the host of ways, all pertaining to the fabric of devotion, in which this service can be accomplished are: 'We must hope in her,' and also 'delight and confide in her, be humble, have compassion.'[22] In the third chapter of Book 2, the author states that one must serve Mary *de corde*, or from the heart: 'We should sigh to her with crying and weeping.'[23] One who serves Mary or Christ must also develop appropriate personal qualities: be 'clean, righteous, devoted, truthful, discreet, humble, pious, peaceful, just, patient, joyful, and zealous.'[24] These qualities, prescribed for the friar or the oblate, are directly analogous to the *loiauté, vaillance, souffrance, cortoisie, franchise, plaisance* (loyalty, valour, patience, courtesy, generosity, good humour) prescribed for the secular courtly lover.[25]

The *De laudibus* prescribes other methods to serve Mary. Service *de ore* (by spoken prayer) includes praise, vocalized prayer, confession, magnification, and prayer in song.[26] In his commentary upon sung prayer, Richard of St Lawrence states:

And notice that because the righteous man says to Christ or Mary 'My singing is always of you,' the righteous ought to be *jongleurs* of Christ, Mary, and the saints: for the *jongleurs* of the court are wont to compose songs for, and to appropriate existing songs to, those from whom they have received or hope to receive great gifts. We ourselves have received many gifts from Christ and Mary and hope to receive many greater rewards from them.[27]

This passage suggests that singing to and about Christ, Mary, and the saints was considered admirable, although the author's reference is more symbolic than literal: a righteous life was apparently the 'song' of those who had neither training nor talent in composing cantilenas. Still, the text shows an awareness of the activity of court *jongleurs*, and the reference to appropriating existing songs undoubtedly refers to the practice of con-trafactum, the setting of a newly written text to the tune of a song composed by someone else, as well as the dedication, *mutatis mutandis*, of an existing song to one's patron.

Returning to the songs of manuscripts V and X, we can see something of the relation of the trouvère, whether a *jongleur* or an aristocrat, to Mary and Christ as he perceived them. Couched in the formulaic language of the penitent, vassal, or courtier are images that are startling in the intimacy of the devotion they describe. Consider, for example:

En la vostre maintenance,
roïne dou firmament,
ont mis mon entendement,
desierriers et acoustumance,
si que seule remenbrance
de vos, quant plus suis plaignanz,
me sane si doucement
que mes cuers nuiés de pesance
de joie tresaut et dance.   60, st. 1

Or the following plea to Mary, called in liturgical poetry the *sancta radix* (the holy root):

hé, douce virge, doucement
esrachiés de mon cuer l'espine
de pechié, qui si durement
de poindre touz jors ne me fine.   21, st. 5

Or the striking compassion of one poet's view of the Crucifixion:

qu'amors me fait sospirer
et doucement desirrer
Jhesu, qui dou cors la lance
vout ouvrir por li entrer
et en s'amor reposer.   30, st. 3

These appear to be authentic and affective statements of religious faith from members of a society that took seriously the Catholic doctrine of salvation whereby any person whose faith was firm could aspire to paradise. It is neither surprising nor paradoxical that some trouvères wrote both religious and erotic poems, that the same music could set both prayer and *pastourelle*. To the segments of thirteenth-century society that formed the trouvères' audience, faith was a matter of unquestioned truth, and salvation could come as readily to a repentant sinner as to an untarnished saint. The popular devotional songs that appeared throughout Europe were intended to express precisely this concept.

The Lady to the Poet

We have examined some of the differences between the secular and devotional personae of the trouvère poets, the lover and the supplicant. But what of the qualities of the one to whom the poet's plea was addressed? At this point it becomes necessary to abandon the dichotomy between the court lady and Mary in favour of a tripartite comparison: the lady of the love songs, the image of Mary in the devotional songs, and the image of Mary in orthodox theology.

Table 2 presents a comparison of the qualities attributed to the secular lady and to Mary in three representative sources. Each list of terms may be divided into the categories of: (a) physical description; (b) personal manner; and (c) virtues. The sample from the Latin source, the *De laudibus Mariae virginis* by Richard of St Lawrence, contains only the third category: there is no mention of Mary's appearance or personality among the qualities attributed to her, although these subjects are treated in other portions of the work as implied rather than inherent qualities.

The list from the secular chansonnier includes five physical and five personal terms; that from the devotional songs only two physical and one personal. Thus, the vernacular view of Mary would seem to be derived from theology along with some coloration from the secular tradition, as may be seen by examining the qualities of the third category. The popular image of Mary shared with her theological counterpart the virtues of goodness, sweetness, virginity, glory, pity, humility, wisdom, worthiness, purity, power, and high status.[28] From the courtly and feudal vocabulary of the secular tradition, she was credited with valour, loyalty, bravery, honour, royalty, perception, and joyousness.[29]

Along with specific virtues ascribed to Mary by scriptural and theological tradition, there was in the Latin literature a host of images, roles, functions, and powers associated with her. Richard of St Lawrence lists some 240 terms in his compendium,[30] each substantiated by scriptural and patristic sources. The compendium given in books 5 to 12 of his work is classified into conceptual divisions that indicate some of the qualities

Table 2
Comparison of qualitative terms in secular, devotional, and theological vocabularies

The *dame* (secular)
   a) Physical description: beauté, cler vis, cors gent, bel semblance, blonde
   b) Personal manner: bel parler, douz ris, plaisance, amorouse, riant
   c) Virtues: pris, sen, valour, courtoisie, honour, bonté, franchise, vaillance, gentilesce, simplece, douceur, hautece, joie

Marie (vernacular)
   a) Physical description: beauté, cler vis
   b) Personal manner: avenance
   c) Virtues: bonté, douceur, chastité, virginité, splendeur, saintesce, pitié, pardon, santé, humilité, vaillance, clarité, purité, loiauté, raison, valour, joie, honour, roiauté, pris, puissance, hautesce, confort, finesse

Maria (Latin)
   c) Virtues: humilitas, simplicitas, excellentia, pretiositas, gloria, celsitudo, virginitas, fecunditas, verecundia, fides, spes, caritas, paupertas, divitia, largitas, misericordia, pietas, compassio, benignitas, suavitas, dulcedo, obedientia, omnipotencia, sapientia, subtilitas

Sources: For the *dame* (secular), the source is manuscript O in Beck, ed., *The Chansonnier Cangé*. For Marie (vernacular): BN, manuscripts X and V. For Maria (Latin): *De laudibus beatae Mariae*, book 4, in Albertus Magnus, *Opera omnia*, vol. 36.

which theologians of the thirteenth century attributed to the image of Mary; they are in each of the books as follows:

Book 5: Physical descriptions, drawn from the biblical *Canticum canti-corum* and allegorical literature;

Book 6: Familial and social roles of woman, including *mater, soror*, and *regina* (mother, sister, and queen);

Book 7: Celestial terms, such as *sol, luna*, and *aurora* (sun, moon, and dawn);

Book 8: Terrestrial terms, including *tellus, area, mons*, and *petra* (earth, field, mountain, and stone);

Book 9: Images of water, including *fons, lacus*, and *cisterna* (fountain, lake, and well);

Book 10: Architectural terms, among them *arca, cella, thalamus*, and *fornax* (arch, cell, bedchamber, and furnace);

Book 11: 'Fortified and navigable devices which may symbolize Mary,' *urbs, turris, ecclesia*, and *navis* (city, tower, church, and ship), as well as proper names of cities;

Book 12: Agricultural images, *hortum, secretus, nebulosus, clausura, flos*, and *arbor* (garden, hiding place, cloudy, enclosure, flower, and tree), along with names of trees and flowers and attendant adjectives, *agilis, levis*, and *aromatica* (agile, light, and aromatic).

Thus, the image of Mary was associated with womanhood, the heavens, the nourishing elements of earth and water, the safety of shelter and ordered society, and the ubiquitous mysteries of seed and flower. What may surprise the modern reader is the tone of familiarity: along with the roles of *regina, ministra,* and *stella maris* (queen, minister, and star of the sea) come the earthier images of *pratum, canalis,* and *gutta* (meadow, canal, and drop of water). In an agricultural society that depended on fertile soil and rain for its survival and saw the results of God's pleasure in abundant crops, Mary was seen as the provider of nourishment, safety, beauty, and nurture in physical as well as poetic terms. The biblical *hortus conclusus* – the walled garden, flourishing, protected, and cherished – was a symbol of her dual role as virgin and mother, representing the inviolable protection afforded by a benevolent deity to the life-giving properties of the earth and of mothers. It is within the charmed circle of these qualities that an infant God or a human soul can grow to maturity.

There is great emphasis placed on the concept of motherhood in the vernacular poems as well. Most of the songs in manuscripts V and X are concerned with the events of the Annunciation and the Nativity, as well as with the concept of incarnation. Mary is spoken of in her relation to Christ, the mother of all his varied manifestations, as the

> Mere a l'aignel, mere au lyon,
> mere et fille au vrai Salemon,
> mere si que nule ensement.   41, st. 5

As such, she becomes the nourisher and protector of all souls. Like the *De laudibus,* the trouvère songs contain a wealth of images related to the themes of nourishment and safety provided by Mary. She is the *fonteinne* and *froment* (water and bread) that sustain life, as well as the flowers and jewels that embellish it. She provides an island of safety in the confusion of worldly existence, the *estoile marine* (star of the sea) to guide navigating souls,

> dedenz haute mer salée
> fontenele de douçour,
> clere en tenebrour,
> joiouse en tristour,
> en flamme rousée.   44, st. 1

To the image of defence provided by castle and fortress is added the arsenal of *ecclesia militans* (the militant church). Mary is seen as lance and sword ready to protect the fragile soul from the enemy; the power of evil was believed to be lying always in wait for those who succumbed to temptation. A common theme in the songs is the assurance that those who pray and sing to the Virgin with sincerity are safe from harm:

De la mere Dieu doit chanter
chascuns qui set faire chançon,
qu'anemis ne puet enchanter
celui qui par devocion
la sert en bone entencion.
Qui de cuer la proie
ja ne sera proie
de doleur
a l'enchanteür
qui le mont guerroie.

50, st. 1

The terms applied to Mary in the devotional songs (table 3) fit neatly into the same classifications as those from the *De laudibus*, with the addition of categories for military terms and for precious ornaments. In the added categories the influence of secular court literature may again be seen. The terms give further clues about the nature of Mary as the trouvères and their audiences perceived her. Her social roles encompassed those of mother, maiden, and queen derived from liturgical tradition. To these the vernacular songs added the courtly *amie* (beloved lady-friend) to the trouvère,

De li me covient chanter
et mon chant renouveler
et faire de li m'amie,

12, st. 1

and to Christ himself:

Dame, de qui Jhesu Crist fist s'amie,
si m'aït Diex, il ne vos gaba mie;
de bon cuer vos ama
quant mere vos clama:
en vos bon dame a
cil qui vos a chierie.

6, st. 2

The list of architectural terms includes the fortresses and dungeons of thirteenth-century society, as well as the biblical metaphors of chamber and tower. If the thought of a *deffensables donjons* (defensible dungeon)[31] conveyed to an audience a better sense of safety than the splendid palaces of Latinate tradition, then there was apparently nothing to prevent the trouvère from using such rough metaphors for the mother of God. She is also a bridge, the means by which souls might be transported from earth

Table 3
Names, images, and roles of Mary in the vernacular songs

Category	Terms
Descriptive	bele, avenant, cler vis
Social	mere, pucelle, roine, dame, fille, empereriz, amie
Celestial	solaus, lune, estoile, lumiere
Terrestrial	terre, mont, rive
Water	fonteinne, fluns, vessiaux
Architectural	chambre, porte, chastel, tor, palais, ponz, planche, forteresce, donjons, verrierre
Flora and Fauna	flor, rose, lis, violete, verdure, ierre, herbe, racine, grainne, froment, buisson, fenix, columbe, panthere, tigre
Ornamental	or, esmeraude, diamanz, jaspe, saphirs, rubiz
Military	estandarz, escuz, espée, monjoie, lance, hauberz
Powers	garantir, saner, garir, mediciner, aleger, aider, conduire, mener, defender, guerredonner, garder, recouvrer, ravir, rachater, resplendir, secorrer, conforter, concorder, raccorder

to heaven. Mary is further equated with a stained-glass window, *verrierre*, an image representing the Incarnation, since the conception of her child was explained by theologians as analogous to light passing through glass. In this way, the doctrines of Catholicism were reinforced and ornamented through the use of vocabulary familiar to the trouvères' audiences.

In the flora and fauna category are several images unique to the trouvère devotional songs. Floral metaphors are ubiquitous in Marian poetry of all languages, but the *ierre* and *verdure* (ivy and greenery) are unusual. Both are given as examples of constancy, the flowers and plants that never change their colours.[32] The *buisson*, the burning bush of Moses, appears in a pair of images designed to explain the process of the Incarnation, spoken by Gabriel to Mary:

> Douce dame droituriere,
> je te vieng dire et noncier
> qu'ausi con par la verriere
> entre solaus en mostier,
> ausi con ça en arieres
> ardoit sanz amenusier
> li buissons en la bruiere,
> concevras nete et [en]tiere
> par parole.[33]
>
> 28, st. 4

Several of the bird and animal images associated with Mary in the devotional songs are also somewhat unusual.[34] The phoenix, symbol of resurrection, is more commonly applied in theological writings to Christ than to his mother, but here she becomes

> la gloriouse fenix,
> mere et fille au douz pellicant,   37, st. 1

presumably because her dual role as mother and daughter parallels that of the bird which gives birth to itself. The pelican, which was believed to nourish its nestlings with blood drawn from its own breast, becomes a metaphor for Christ, while the image is drawn into further complexity by associating maternal nurture with both mother and son. Mary is also seen as the *columbe de relegion* (dove of the faith) (no. 50, st. 4), usually a depiction of the Holy Ghost, but equally resonant with its Old Testament attributes of peace and prosperity. According to the tradition of the bestiaries, the dove was remarkable for its chastity and for the affectionate care it bestowed on its young. Maternal zeal was ascribed to the tiger, as well. The *tigre en mirëour* (tiger in the mirror) (no. 44, st. 4, and no. 53, st. 2) refers to the belief that a hunter who wanted to steal tiger cubs could prevent the mother from pursuing him by casting a mirror in her path: mistaking the small reflection for a lost cub, she would stay to care for it. In another version, it is the sight of her own supreme beauty that arrests the tiger and renders her powerless to leave the mirror. In either case, the application of the image to Mary compliments her beauty and maternity through reference to a symbol intelligible to anyone exposed to the popular literature of the time.[35] So does the image of the panther, again more commonly associated with Christ than with Mary. The *panthere d'odour plus qu'embausemmée* (panther of odour sweeter than balsam) (no. 44, st. 3) refers to the belief that the panther, having slept for three days, would arise from its lair with a melodious roar, emitting on its breath a sweet odour of spices to which all other animals were attracted; only the dragon, a symbol of the devil, was supposed to be repelled by the breath of the panther. Thus, the panther was often used to symbolize the Resurrection, Christ's ministry as a preacher, and the enmity between divinity and evil. Its application to Mary might be termed a metaphor-once-removed, and the text in which it appears merits closer examination.

The song begining 'Rose cui nois ne gelée' (no. 44) contains a vernacular litany of Marian metaphors, none of which is drawn directly from the liturgical litany, which it resembles in structure. The qualities of Mary are presented in the form of a rhetorical opposition; she is

> santéz en languor,
> repos en labour,
> et païs en meslée.   44, st. 2

In addition to the panther and tiger of the bestiary, the song's third stanza contains a group of lapidary images:

Fine esmeraude esprouvée
de graciouse vigour,
diamanz, jaspe alosée,
saphirs d'Ynde la majour,
rubiz de valour.

According to lapidary treatises of the late Middle Ages,[36] the emerald could heal and stimulate vision and was a symbol of faith. The diamond, or *adamant*, the hardest of stones, could protect an unborn child in the womb, while jasper was an aid to childbirth and to the virtues of faith, hope, and charity. Sapphires were said to come in several hues, of which the finest, *le plus ynde*, was the colour of violet or of the sky. It was supposed to prevent foolish desires, promote accord among people, and symbolize prophecy, hope, and joy.[37] The ruby, symbol of the light of Christ, could comfort, heal, and illuminate all things. Thus, the stones associated with Mary were symbols of faith, hope, birth, and illumination.

The view of Mary given in 'Rose cui nois ne gelée' is of a being who provides unchanging peace, comfort, and security amid the turbulence of the mutable world. So might an infant, become articulate, describe its mother. The text is delicately crafted to combine symbols that a thirteenth-century audience could find both colourful and familiar: the exotic gems and animals that stand for known virtues, the unfading rose, closed door, and sweet fountain of scriptural tradition, and the crowned empress who provides the care and compassion of a mother. Some images are drawn from Scripture and liturgy, but only in a general sense because there is no direct translation or paraphrase. Others come from what might be termed popular literature and tradition: legends about the natural world that derived from and contributed to the learned treatises on natural science. Finally, there is a layer of church doctrine, the bedrock of the text, that appears in the final stanza:

Empereriz coronnée
de la main au creatour,
a la crueuse jornée
quant li ange avront päour,
prie au sauvëour
que ton chantëour
maint en sa contrée.   44, st. 5

The prayer is exemplary. Almost without exception, and regardless of their content in earlier stanzas, the Marian songs end with a prayer for salvation. The gentle mother, the simple maiden, the rose, all become in the end the empress with power over all souls, just as Christ the child becomes the king sitting in judgment. In the doctrine of the church, Mary was the mediatrix who could intercede on behalf of deserving individuals on the Day of Judgment through prayer to her son. Christ was depicted in sculptures on innumerable church portals in his role as judge, with power over saints and angels as well as mortals. The imagery of Day of Judgment sculptures, showing Christ attended by John and Mary, is brought to mind in the final stanza of one song:

> Dame, a ce jor dou jugement
> vos soiés en aïe:
> la ou li saint iront trenblant
> de päour, n'en dout mie.
> N'est nus qui por nos prie,
> ne apostre ne innocent
> fors Saint Jehan seulement
> et toi d'autre partie.
>
> 13, st. 5

Thus, Mary was seen as a protector and defender of souls even in the celestial court; those who, through virtue or repentance, showed themselves apt for salvation could count on her advocacy. Words that convey the concept of defence abound in the Marian songs. Just as she provided sword and shield against evil, the queen of heaven could shield a soul from the harshness of a judgment that might, without the element of mercy which she symbolized, result in condemnation. To the medieval Catholic, her role as a symbol of divine clemency was in keeping with her feminine nature: the word *mulier* (woman) was associated in popular etymology with *mollis* (soft, pliable, or easily moved).[38] As Eve's susceptibility to persuasion led to the fall from divine grace, the same quality in Mary was seen as leading to its restoration:

It is to be noted that Eve waged a triple war, through pride ... avarice ... and gluttony. But Mary, Eve's daughter, made peace through humility ... charity ... and virginity ... for if man fell because of woman, he cannot be raised except by woman.[39]

In addition to the roles of protector and advocate, Mary was seen as the healer of spiritual ills. In the list of powers attributed to her (table 3) are verbs associated with comfort and healing: *saner, garir, mediciner, aleger,* and *conforter* (restore to health, cure, heal, assure, and comfort). The diseases she cures are those of sin:

> Ja nus n'iert si enmaladis

que maintenant ne soit gueris,
se de bon cuer vos prie:
Or nos aidiez
et conseillés,
douce virge Marie.   23, st. 5

She is also described as a guide or beacon to direct the faithful on the path to salvation. The *estoile marine*,[40] a French translation of the liturgical *stella maris*, the pole star that guided navigators, is one such image. Another involves the notion of providing safe conduct to a distant realm:

Aiez dou monde pité,
qui s'en va de mal en pis,
et moi, qui vous aim et pris
d'enterine volenté,
en vostre riche païs
conduisiez a sauveté.   35, st. 5

The use of celestial terms (see table 3) is part of a larger complex of images concerned with light and splendour. Paradise is described as a place of clarity and beauty:

Lors sui raviz a mon gré
en un desir de cuer fin
de remirer la clarté
qui est et sera sanz fin.

de cel païs honnoré,
gloriousement ourné
par artefice devin.   36, st. 1 and 3

The summit and source of its luminosity is the queen of heaven:

Tant est bele que paradis
de li enlumine et resplent.[41]   37, st. 3

A particularly vivid picture of Mary's imperial role, reminiscent of innumerable paintings of the Coronation of the Virgin from the late medieval period, again refers to her as the source of celestial clarity:

Pardesus le firmament,
plus haut c'on ne puet cuidier,
pour paradis esclairier,
se siet honnoréement

e'l plus glorious estage
la saintiesme empereriz
de qui nasqui Jhesu Criz.[42]   39, st. 2

Her radiance is also seen as a source of light in the darkness of the mortal world,

la dame, par sa biauté,
tout le monde renbeli
qui estoit hors de clarté
au main et a la vesprée,   4, st. 3

and hence as a rival to the sun, a presence so bright that she cannot be safely regarded:

Toute biautéz qu'en lui s'amoncelle
la fet si resplendir
qu'envers li sont li solaus et la bele
tenebrous a vëoir.
Tout l'estouvroit avugler ou guenchir,
qui son douz vis, qui de joie estancelle,
oseroit a loisir
remirer et choisir.   33, st. 3

The images of light, clarity, and beauty all play upon the symbolic connection between *illuminatio* (vision), and *intellectio* (understanding or rational belief). To the authors of the songs and their listeners, seeing was believing; in a neo-Platonic world, one perceived what was holy by the radiance of its beauty, and blindness was a sign of the unbeliever. In the secular poetry of the trouvères it was through the eyes that the arrow of love entered the lover's heart. In their devotional works, the inner vision of understanding is seen as a gateway to faith.

In summary, then, the powers of protection, guidance, nurturing, healing, and illumination are ascribed to Mary. All of these attributes have the effect of speeding the souls of believers on the path to salvation. Mary is also seen in the role of mediatrix, the intermediary of divine mercy in the process of judgment. It is the conception of this role that provides a point of comparison between the vernacular songs and the established doctrine of the church.

The Poet, the Preacher, and the Priest

In the thirteenth century it was an established point of Catholic doctrine that salvation is accomplished through the sacraments, as it still is now.

The priest, qualified to administer the sacraments, facilitates the process, and the temporal organization of the church provides a conducive environment. One searches almost in vain, however, for any mention of sacraments, priest, or church in the devotional songs of the trouvères. While it is beyond the scope of this study to go into detail on the development of medieval thought concerning the various sacraments, it should be noted that local custom in the thirteenth century might have permitted variations on the official doctrine, that the doctrines themselves were not always clearly understood by rural parish clergy who were far from the urban centres of theology, and that lay parishoners might not have had as clear a comprehension of the process of salvation as their priests might have wished. When the new doctrines of the Fourth Lateran Council were announced, information on these matters was spread among the general public by the preaching orders. What seems to have resulted, if one can judge from the vernacular texts, was an increased attention to the matter of salvation as it concerned the individual. The operative question was 'What can I, however unworthy, do to assure my soul a place in paradise?'

The process envisioned was both active and receptive. First, there was repentance for past misdeeds and mistaken attitudes. The confession, with its attendant plea for help, is usually addressed to Mary as the mediatrix, asking her to intercede for the penitent and to provide safety from the power of sin or the devil. However, some of the texts imply a belief that the outcome of the final judgment depended upon the actions and decisions of individuals during their lifetime, and that conscious service to Mary was a valuable effort:

> Las, et ma mort ert si dure
> se de pechié et d'ordure
> ne puis m'ame resclarcir;
> mes qui sert sans repentir
> par raïson et par dure
> le fait pitiés esjoïr
> et a bone fin venir.   1, st. 2

There is also an implication that the righteous person must battle the natural tendencies of the flawed human condition:

> Tres grant force ne biauté
> ne me plest pas, bien sai por quoi:
> por ce qu'en honte et en vilté
> nest hom et muert hom, bien le voi.
> Por c'a droit qui en charité
> et en huevre d'umilité
> est touz jors, et en veraie foi.   27, st. 2

Nonetheless, the majority of texts emphasize the concept of grace bestowed equally upon the worthy and the repentant unworthy, with Mary as its principal means of transmission.

The preponderance of songs addressed to Mary is certainly a point to be considered in light of the theology of the time. In the culture of the trouvères, devotional songs were primarily Marian songs, and one senses the poets' intimacy with the image of Mary and her role in the celestial hierachy. She is often addressed as one who holds the power of salvation, without direct reference to mediation. It is tempting to infer from this omission that the vernacular devotional songs contain a kind of homegrown heresy. Heresy was a harsh word, however, and one unlikely to apply to the beliefs of the aristocratic audiences of the trouvères, who were fully educated in the catechism of the laity. Omissions of doctrinal detail are far more likely to have evolved from close familiarity with doctrinal teachings – so close that the obvious did not need to be explicitly stated and the oft-repeated could be abbreviated or allegorized.

What appears in the vernacular songs is not a deviation from established doctrine but rather a personalized and slightly secularized interpretation of the teachings of Catholicism, moulded to fit its audience as were the sermons of the preaching orders that were delivered in public situations. If the distinctions between prayer to Christ through Mary and prayer to Mary herself were sometimes blurred, it was possibly because the image of the mediatrix was so firmly instilled in the minds of both the poet and the audience as to need no explicit definition. If Mary represented the mercy of God, it was to her that one addressed pleas for mercy, particularly if the audience was composed of courtiers accustomed to hearing songs addressed to noble women.[43] Popular religion was neither so rigorous nor so sharply defined as that of monks and clergy:

It was not composed of professions of faith or by norms and prescription fixed once and for all. What sufficed for it were a few texts learned mechanically by heart, a few essential facts of the life of Christ, the symbol of the apostles and the ten commandments, a combination which one cannot always see clearly to what extent it was understood and applied. But around this tiny kernel of stable elements was gathered an entire collection of other elements, transmitted by word of mouth, constantly modified according to time and place with the variations and changes necessary to their being heard and accepted.[44]

What, then, were the tenets of faith expressed in the songs and how were they related to the official doctrines of Catholicism? Let us look first at the texts that can be specifically called Catechetic, those that set out to explain a facet of the teachings of church doctrine. The three of these that are in manuscript X (nos. 5, 28, and 31) present the story of the Annunciation in the form of a dialogue between Mary and the archangel Gabriel,

with introductory reference to the sin of Adam or to the poet's past misdeeds and present repentance. The dialogue is sometimes embellished
with fine dramatic detail:

> Marie a ses euz baissiés
> quant entent la novele,
> et puis les a rehauciés,
> saint Gabriel apele:
>
> 'Amis, di moi coment enfanteroie
> ne coment fruit en mes flans porteroie
> quant nul home ne conois
> ne nul n'en prenderoie?
> Mout sembleroit grant ennuis
> se sanz home engendroie!'   5, st. 2 and 3

The Catechetic songs in manuscript V have a broader focus than do
those in X, and they range over a series of doctrinal points that are
expanded like miniature sermons with illustrative metaphors. One song
gives an inviting description of paradise:

> Tuit li deduit enterin
> sont en cel riche regné:
> autant prise on le vin
> comme l'eue dou fossé.   36, st. 2

It goes on for two stanzas and then proceeds to a telescoped account of
history from Adam through to the Crucifixion in one stanza. Another song
(no. 49) presents a detailed account of the Crucifixion; it is written as a
lament on the death of Christ and is similar in tone and structure to
laments written for court funerals. The days of creation are described in
no. 54, which also presents the judgment of Adam and Eve in the form of a
debate between the allegorical figures of Justice and Truth for the prosecu-
tion, and Pity and Mercy for the defence. The trial resolves with the birth
of Christ:

> Quant Diex ot oï le contenz,
> les deus parties accorda
> si bien et si tres doucement
> que l'une et l'autre s'en loä.
> Dedenz la verge s'aömbra
> et en nasqui tres dignement,
> puis morut por sauver sa gent
> et revint et les delivra.   54, st. 6

The two others in V are more diverse. Song no. 3 is concerned mainly with the Incarnation and ends with a prayer to Mary. The doctrine of Christ's resurrection in the flesh is treated in no. 61:

En son cors fu humanitéz unie
a deité, [por] homme rachater:
si loiaument fu la chose establie
que quant la char couvint mort endurer,
la deitéz duranz sanz violer
ou sepucre li porta compaignie.
N'onques de lui ne fu l'ame guerpie
dedenz enfer, ne en toute la voie,
n'au resartir le laz d'or et de soie.[45]

61, st. 3

The Catechetic songs, then, are treatments of the basic framework of Christian faith: that Christ was the son of God, born as a man to save humanity from the sin of Adam, that he was crucified and resurrected in the flesh, and that he will judge all souls at their time of death. The texts that deal with the life of Christ are more inclined to be descriptive than laudatory, whether or not they fall into the category designated as Catechetic. There is a factual tone to them that stands in contrast to the delicious embroidery of the Marian songs. The list of names and images given for Christ (table 4) is far less elaborate than the one given for Mary, and all the terms have precedence in Latin ecclesiastical poetry.[46] The same can be said of terms for God the creator and for the devil; one finds the same terms that are in the songs also used for them in sermons or hymns, whereas the *fenix, tigre, espée, donjons,* and *ierre* (phoenix, tiger, sword, dungeon, and ivy) of the Marian songs are specific creations of the vernacular poetic imagination. There seems to be a difference in attitude: statements about Christ follow the pattern given in the Gospels and the teachings of medieval Catholicism, while statements about Mary have less information to draw upon and tend to be made from the standpoint of metaphor and personal expression, thereby absorbing the extravagance of secular court poetry. This difference is entirely consistent with the laity's concept of Mary as the essential feminine element that is missing from Catholic doctrine, the Mother brought in to complement the Trinity of male Father, male Son, and disembodied Holy Spirit. The borrowed secular imagery, which emphasizes the themes of fertility, maternity, and mediation, appears to be contrasted with the scriptural and liturgical vocabulary that is applied to the figures of the Trinity, as well as with the descriptive vocabulary that is applied to the court lady in the secular songs (see table 1). Such consistency implies that the writers of the devotional songs were consciously distinguishing among discrete categories of descriptive style and that it was an established rhetorical practice to do so.

Table 4
Names and images of God, Christ, and Satan in the vernacular songs

	Names and images
God	creator, pere, sire, Dieux, Damedieux
Christ	Jhesu Crist, rois, pere, sauvëor, Salemon, glorieus, soleil, seigneur, flor, fruit, prime florete, pellicant, rossignos, aignel, lyon
Satan	anemi, aversier, deable, Lucifer, serpent, soudoianz, traitour, trichierre

Many of the authors of vernacular devotional lyrics may have been court chaplains or their assistants in minor orders, men trained in the subtleties of Catholic doctrine. Even the poets of the laity, however, would have had some familiarity with the events in the life of Christ, the circumstances of the Last Judgment, the genealogy of Christ and Mary, and those portions of the Old Testament seen by theologians as prefiguring the birth of Christ and the salvation of humanity, namely the stories of Adam, Noah, Samson, Moses, David, Solomon, and Jonah, and parts of Prophets, Psalms, and the Song of Songs.[47] This information, available through sermons and legends to the illiterate and through popular devotional literature to those literate only in the vernacular, forms the foundation of the scriptural knowledge transmitted by the vernacular songs. Most of it is stated indirectly through paraphrase, through absorption of imagery from Scripture and liturgy, or through illustrative allusion. The authors occasionally demonstrate their familiarity with scriptural sources. For example, one oblique image in a Catechetic song unites the Old and the New Testaments:

Virge conçut au tesmoing d'Ysaÿe,
et enfanta sanz dolour endurer
celui par cui en deus fu departie
la Rouge Mer pour son peuple sauver.   61, st. 2

Such learned display is not the rule, however, and may indicate that the author came from the more educated end of the spectrum. The majority of the songs, which fall into the Courtly and Laudatory categories, show little influence from scriptural or liturgical sources (see tables 2 and 3).

Many of the Marian images in the Laudatory songs may stand as examples of absorbed imagery. The association of Mary with earth, water, light, architecture, and flowers came into the vernacular poetic tradition from the Latin, and into the Latin tradition from the interpretation of the Song of Songs by the late medieval practice of biblical glossing or exegesis.[48] In the scriptural glosses of Scholastic theology, the Bride of the Song was held to be a symbol of *Ecclesia*, the personification of the church wedded to Christ, and hence of Mary, the foundation of the church. All the imagery

Table 5
Proper names in the songs

Source	Proper names
Biblical (O.T.)	Adam, Eve, Evain, Kaïn, Ysaÿe, Salemon, Jonas, Pharäon
Biblical (N.T.)	Gabriel, Judas, Longis, Magdaleinne, Marie
Saints	Jehan, Gregoires
Historical	Alixandre, Omer, Vaspasien
Mythological	Merlin, Theofilus, Ysengrin, Iseut, Alaine

of garden, city, and royal bedchamber thus passed into the vocabulary of Marian poetry, to result in the *chambre, tor, porte,* and *flor* (chamber, tower, door, and flower) of the vernacular.

A list of the proper names, both biblical and from other sources, that are mentioned in the songs appears in table 5. The first five of the Old Testament names are associated with the Fall of Man and the genealogy of Christ, the remaining three with individuals said to have predicted or prefigured Christ in the exegetical glosses. Of the New Testament names, Gabriel is associated with the Annunciation, and the rest with the Crucifixion. It is perhaps surprising to find so few references to saints and to see them outnumbered by figures of myth and literary creation; this serves to underscore the conclusion that the trouvère devotional songs were concerned more closely with the individual's relation to the Saviour and the mediatrix than with the doctrines and structures of the established church. While there are frequent references to both the scriptural events and incidents that were familiar to the laity and the most basic matters of doctrine, there is very little reference or allusion to liturgy.[49]

Two images from the Latin repertoire of Marian hymns and antiphons, drawn from liturgy rather than Scripture, appear in the vernacular songs, the *stella maris* (star of the sea) in nos. 8, 9, 15, and 31, and the *sancta radix* (holy root) in no. 22. The use of these images is vastly outnumbered, however, by scriptural, courtly, and purely imaginative images. Again, the rarity of liturgical references is consistent with the notion among the preaching orders of suiting a text to an audience. Lay listeners, untrained in the mysteries of theology, were addressed in terms that were crafted to fit their education, experience, and memories of childhood catechism. In addition to the Incarnation and Nativity themes of the Marian songs, the trouvère devotional songs refer to a few specific events in the life of Christ and to the central doctrines of the Fall of Man and the Day of Judgment. All of the latter themes pertain to the concept of individual salvation, newly reformulated by the Fourth Lateran Council of 1215.[50]

The Day of Judgment was crucial to the doctrine of salvation. It was the moment at which all individuals would follow the pattern of Christ and be resurrected. Efforts to lead a good life would be rewarded, and misdeeds either pardoned or used as evidence for damnation. Thirteenth-century portal sculptures show souls being weighed against their sins on balance scales, and then either escorted by angels to heaven or pushed and pulled by devils to hell. One of the trouvère devotional songs gives an unusually graphic description of the day's events :

> Quant le filz Dieu nos vendra reprouver
> la destrece qu'il vint por nos soffrir,
> que nos verrons ciel et terre crouler,
> l'air corrompu et le monde bruïr,
> cors relever et buisines tentir,
> pierres partir, soloil descoulorer.
> Les plus hardiz fera mult redouter
> le jugemenz qu'il devront oïr.   32, st. 6

Most of the texts, however, mention the Last Judgment in the simpler and more personal terms of the penitent asking for forgiveness and protection. The graphic imagery of the sermon and the portal sculpture was well known to the listeners and did not need to be described in great detail. Typical of the Laudatory Marian songs is this stanza:

> Or prions la mere Dieu tuit hautement
> qu'ele deprit son chier fiz prochennement
> qu'allons tuit en paradis comunaument
> au grant jor dou juïs.   3, st. 5

This almost light-hearted approach is peculiar to the Laudatory category. More typical of the Personal songs, with their confessional tone, is the following:

> Por ce li proi doucement
> qu'ele soit a m'ame rendre,
> car mes cuers grant doleur sent,
> tant redout mon jugement.   1, st. 5

The reference here is more to the judgment of the individual soul at the time of death than to the apocalyptic Day of Judgment, but in either context the word *jugement* would have resonated strongly in the minds of devout listeners.

The doctrines of Original Sin and of the Fall of Man are also treated in a large number of texts, always with reference to the redemption inherent in the birth of Christ. This is sometimes presented in detail:

... fors nos mist de la tormente amere
ou mis nos ot Adans, no premier pere.
Le fruit manja par Evain sa moillier
que Dex li ot desfendu a mangier;
s'en cheïmes trestuit en grant misere,
quant de li fist li douz Jhesus sa mere.   31, st. 1

Sometimes it is presented by allusion:

Eve trestout le mont confondi,
je le vos di,
mes la mere Dieu respondi
por la nostre partie.   7, st. 5

The latter text emphasizes the role of Mary as the second Eve, who in bearing Christ redeems the wrong done by her predecessor. Known as the *felix culpa* (the fortunate fault or sin) this doctrine advanced the notion that the original sin of Adam and Eve was not an error but part of a divine plan since it gave God a reason for subsequently taking human form in order to demonstrate resurrection and redemption.

Of all the events in sacred history described in the vernacular songs, the one most frequently mentioned is the Incarnation. It is considered on both divine and human levels. On the one hand stands the image of the Madonna enthroned in glory and attended by angels, on the other of the mother giving birth and nourishing her child:

Mout l'ama Dex et grant honeur li fist
quant il l'eslut seur toutes damoiseles,
et char et sanc dedens ses costés prist
et aleta le let de ses mameles.   31, st. 2

Yet the greatest emphasis is put upon the process of the Incarnation, as if an audience might be inclined toward scepticism. A rich variety of images is used to describe the process of conception. There is the glass window that transmits light without breaking (no. 59), the gentleness of rain falling upon wool (no. 55), and the falcon that leaves no visible trace of its flight (no. 43), all designed to assure the listener that the Incarnation took place by miraculous means. The doctrine of virgin birth is further supported by emphasis on another miraculous aspect, that a woman should bear a child who was father of all:

Li fruiz planta l'arbre dont il issi,
et dou ruissel descendi la fontainne,
l'uevre l'ouvrier aleva et norri,

li solaus vint de la tresmontainne,
quant li filz Dieu vestuz en char humainne
en Bethleëm de la virge nasqui.   55, st. 3

It is a matter for some surprise, perhaps, that despite so many references to the Incarnation there should be relatively little attention paid to the Nativity as an event. One finds only one mention of Bethlehem in the songs and none of the manger, of visiting kings, of shepherds, or of Joseph. In fact, the birth of Christ is treated more as a symbol than as an event, precisely because it is seen in the context of individual salvation. The doctrinal facts of the birth and of Christ's life are not the central concern; what is of primary importance is the belief that God took on human form in order to save humanity. In most of the songs there is a leap from the Incarnation directly to Christ's role as judge of all souls and to Mary's as advocate of humanity. Only a few songs mention the Crucifixion, usually as just a brief reference. Nor is much attention given in the song texts either to the temporal church or to the symbol of *Ecclesia*. The clergy are mentioned in only three instances: twice in statements that the song may be heard and heeded by both clerics and laypeople (nos. 18 and 23), and once, more extensively, in a critical complaint about the state of the church and the world in general (no. 27).

While the complaint is the only extant piece of formal social criticism in the collection, it is certainly not a rare composition. The literature of thirteenth-century France abounds with complaint and satire, and political conditions concerning church and state were agitated. One may well surmise that the aristocracy, seeing its feudal rights eroded by new economic and political conditions and its coffers drained by the Crusades, was not on the best of terms with the institution of the church. If there are among the vernacular devotional songs few examples of outright criticism, neither is there much mention of confidence in the church; allegiance is pledged firmly and unequivocally to the celestial hierarchy and not to the ecclesiastical one. The poet does not say 'I may attain salvation if I take communion,' but rather 'I may attain salvation if I pray to Mary for guidance and forgiveness.'

Not surprisingly, the sacraments are rarely mentioned in the songs. The only reference to baptism (in no. 24), which occurs in a song of the Personal category, is problematic. Taken symbolically, the text may be seen as an exploration of the relationship between baptism as a formal ritual and the essence of Christianity bestowed upon its recipient. A more literal rendition suggests that the speaker has been denied the rite of baptism, but his complaint has more to do with his worthiness to receive the sacrament than with fear for his soul's salvation if he does not. In the two songs that contain specific reference to the Eucharist, it is presented in the full fragrance of mysticism. In the first, it is related to the 'flors ... vermeille et blanche,' the red and white flower that represents Mary.

Li blans est senefiance
de virginité garder,
li vermeus est remembrance
dou sanc Jhesu, qui sauver
vint touz ceus qui ont fiance
en li, sanz desesperance:
tel flor doit chascuns porter.   29, st. 2

In the context of this song the symbolism of the Eucharist enriches the
Marian metaphor by unstated association, linking the colours of the
flower with water and blood and with bread and wine. The second reference unites, with stunning integrity, the literal, ritual, and personal levels
of Eucharistic symbolism:

Dex, qui soi nos vout doner
le pain blanc et le vin cler
que nos espandi la lance
qui aprent a bien amer
cuer qui s'en puet enyvrer.   30, st. 5

This image, like the Crucifixion reference in the same song, is unusual and
does not alter the focal point of the devotional songs as a group. Both the
life of Christ and the sacraments are seen through the lens of personal
emotion. It is precisely this point that may mark the boundaries of a pan-
European trend in lay spirituality, which was expressed in devotional
poetry, in polyphonic and florid monophonic music, and in the expressive
faces and musculature of human figures in painting and sculpture. The
thirteenth century may be seen as a starting point for the growth of this
visceral approach, which is associated by Fleming with the Franciscan
styles of poetry and preaching,

in which the conscious manipulation of vicarious emotional experience has
become an important element ... [I]ts principal aim was ... the arresting engage-
ment of the visceral and the emotional, in the classic manner of the Bonaven-
turean *accessus*, to begin a spiritual assent [*sic*] beyond the realm of sensory
experience.[51]

The Trouvère Devotional Songs in the European Context

The literatures of Spain, Italy, England, Germany, northern France, and
the Occitan culture of southern France all produced comparable examples
of lyric song with devotional texts from the thirteenth to the fifteenth centuries.[52] The trouvère songs seem to represent a distinct category within
this larger repertoire. They do not, in general, closely resemble either the
Italian *laude* or the Galaico-Portuguese *Cantigas de Santa Maria*. The Italian

material[53] shows far greater concern for the events of the life of Christ, for themes drawn directly from the Bible, and for legends of the saints; its tone is primarily didactic and catechetic, not in the personalized sense of some trouvère songs, but in a way that accords well with the image of friars preaching in town squares – simple, direct statements, without the artful convolutions of phrase that characterize the French works. Many of the *laude* balance this simplicity of text with extremely florid melodic lines, musical embellishments that are unusual in the trouvère songs. Above all, the *laude* are not court songs. Associated with the Franciscans and with the penitential confraternities of urban Italy, they are religious works in accordance with the transmission of specific doctrines, rather than personal statements of faith.

The *Cantigas de Santa Maria*, which survive in the collection attributed to King Alfonso X of Castile, are specifically Marian songs and are arranged in a cohesive repertoire.[54] The majority recount miracles performed by the Virgin Mary in aid of individuals who have prayed to her; the variety and extremity of the transgressions and predicaments depicted is noteworthy and was undoubtedly intended to demonstrate the belief that Mary will protect even the most unworthy souls if they repent. Interspersed with the narrative songs are purely laudatory ones, whose structure and vocabulary are similar to the Laudatory trouvère songs. The complexity of the music in the *cantigas* is inversely proportional to the complexity of the information in the texts. Narrative texts are set to simply constructed syllabic melodies, while the less common laudatory texts are set to moderately florid music. What distinguishes all of them from the trouvère songs is a reliance on the narrative mode and the specific legends of Mary, while the rapport between the two repertoires is in their concern with the nature of personal salvation.

In Germany one finds indications of two separate types of devotional song. The *Geisslerlieder* proper, associated like the *laude* with public exhibitions of penance, dwell more on the fires of hell than on the delights of paradise, an aspect almost entirely lacking in the Romance language literatures. More closely analogous to the trouvère devotional songs is a small body of German court songs with devotional texts.[55] The theme of personal salvation appears in them frequently, as does the tone of direct address from the penitent to Christ or Mary, and the affirmation of trust in the powers of the mediatrix:

Sünder, du komst spot oder fru,
si begnodet dich und wil dir nit versagen.[56]

The German songs are far less likely than the French to convey their messages through such finely spun elegance of language as the serpentine rhymes of the trouvères. They rely instead on interpolated quotations from Latin hymns and sequences and on paraphrases of liturgical items. The emphasis on individual salvation, while present to a significant degree, is by no means omnipresent. The minnesingers were as likely to address the deity with exuberant affirmations of militant faith as with the plangent language of the penitent contemplating judgment.

The devotional songs of the troubadours come closest in content and technique to those of the trouvères; they are songs engendered by the currents of turbulent change in religion and society, and born in the haven of the secular court culture. The theme of personal salvation, the poet's assumption of the role of penitent, and the vocabulary of laudatory phrases are all similar to those of the French songs. Another similarity is the distinction between secular and devotional contexts, even within the works of individual troubadours. Giraut Riquier, the 'last troubadour,' author of a series of sly and witty *pastourelles*,[57] was also the author of these lines:

> Humils, forfaitz, représ e penedens
> entristezitz, marritz de revenir,
> so qu'ay perdut de mon temps per falhir.
> Vos clam merce, Dona, verges plazens,
> maires de Crist, filh del tot poderos,
> que no gardetz cum suy forfaitz vas vos;
> si.us plai, gardatz l'ops de m'arma marrida.[58]

The quickstepping spiral rhythms of the Laudatory songs in manuscript X are akin, as well, to these lines by Lanfranco Cigala:

> Aitals merces m'agrada,
> quar es secors
> Dels peccadors,
> Cui es razos loniada.
> Sia.m merces donata
> Maire de Dieu,
> Quar per merce fust nada.[59]

The inclusion in manuscript V of a song with a Provençal influence is further testimony to the cultural interchange between the troubadours and the trouvères. The text of 'Per vous m'esjau' (no. 45) is garbled beyond any certain linguistic classification: it may be a Provençal text that was copied and altered by a French scribe, a text in a Franco-Provençal dialect that was similarly altered, or an example of the bilingual technique of *descort* (in which a song is written in two opposing viewpoints that are often delineated by separate dialects or even languages) transplanted from a secular to a devotional context. Whatever its origins, the song's presence in a French manuscript may suggest an attempt by the compiler to collect songs on the same theme, whether the authors were recognized as trouvères or not.[60]

One final point of comparison comes from within the boundaries of the French material itself. The *Miracles de Notre Dame* by Gautier de Coinci, prior of Vic-sur-Aisne and later of St-Médard-de-Soissons, who died in 1236, is a collection of Marian legends in narrative verse.[61] The *Miracles*, which are now believed to be a source for the *Cantigas de Santa Maria* as well as for a host of French devotional songs, are interspersed with short lyric songs in praise of Mary. The legends that are presented are built on Latin models, and most of the music for the songs was borrowed from liturgical or secular sources. Gautier's lyric texts are often more erudite than those of most trouvère songs; they contain complex wordplay in the manner of the Laudatory texts in manuscript X, as well as quotations and paraphrases from Latin. Such techniques might well be expected from a writer exposed to daily liturgy and to the rhythmic and syntactical complexities of Latin sequences through his monastic training. The first lyric in the collection includes a passage that approximately concords with a stanza from one of the songs in X. It reads:

> Mere Dieu tant feiz aproisier,
> Ton pris ne puet langue prisier,
> Tant par soit bien aprise.
> Chascun te prise, je te prise;
> La rose es, la fleur de pris
> Char precieuse a prise.[62]

The trouvère equivalent is:

> De la virge ai tant apris
> que mout grant pris a;
> tout par tout doit avoir pris
> que Dex la prisa
> tant qu'o soi la prist,
> et Dex par ice m'aprist
> le sien grant pris.
> Puis que Diex la prise, je la pris.   2, st. 2

Both songs also contain similar puns on the word *confort*. Gautier's texts also include paraphrases drawn from the popular vein of liturgical chant (his *Hui enfantez* is based on the *Letabundus* sequence) and from courtly secular models, such as *Hui matin* and *S'amour dont sui espris*. In addition, he borrowed structure and imagery from the folk-based literary genre of the *reverdie*, in which a woman sings about her lover in simple formulaic stanzas; Gautier turned this form into a song of a nun joyfully wedded to Christ. These examples serve to clarify Gautier's intentions. The lyric interpolations of the *Miracles* were undoubtedly designed to approximate musical and literary genres familiar to an aristocratic lay audience in as wide a variety as possible, and to adapt the familiar elements to a devotional context. The trouvère songs of manuscripts V and X, both addressing the same audience, also employ a variety of familiar rhetorical tones (didactic, emotive, and laudatory) and devices (refrain forms, puns, litany, and dialogue) to express a central theme: the process of salvation and its meaning for the individual.

4

The Music

Melodic Styles

If the poetry of the vernacular devotional songs can reveal something of the faith shared by its authors and audience, the music is less easily read for signs of personal or cultural expression. The symbols of thirteenth-century musical notation yield few clues to the specific intentions of the composers at the time, nor can they indicate the emotional conditions that were evoked in audiences who listened to music of a particular style. The variables of performance – pitch, tempo, number of performers, improvisation, accompaniment or lack of it, age and gender of the singers, occasion and frequency of performance, and size and status of audience – are not indicated in the manuscripts, and these are the details that add flesh to the skeletal structures provided by notation. The music can nonetheless be read with an analytical eye and a receptive ear for the factors that define it as a discrete repertoire.

The music of the trouvère devotional songs is indistinguishable from that of the trouvère secular songs, however dissimilar their texts may be. The style presented in manuscripts X and V is essentially that of the Northern French court song, characterized by a stanzaic structure, by a largely syllabic declamation which may contain written ornamentation on the ends of phrases, and by a predominantly diatonic melodic motion.[1] It is a style crafted for declamation, to convey words: there are no florid melismas and few large intervallic leaps or melodic devices to draw attention to the music itself.[2]

The relation of music to text is evident in this declamatory style and more particularly in structural correlations between categories of text and of music. Just as similarities of theme, content, and structure link the song texts so that they fall into discrete categories, so too the music can be classified according to structural factors – presence or absence of repetition within a stanza, declamatory style, length of phrases, presence or absence of metric accentuation patterns in accordance with the text, and presence or absence of melodic rhymes in accordance with textual rhymes.

Table 6
Correlation of text categories with musical structures (the numbers refer to those used for the songs in this edition)

Musical structures	Text categories				
	Co	La	Pl	Ca	Pr
Ch	4	2		28	
	18	44		31	
	33			32	21/24
	35			36	
	38				
	40				
	42				
	47				
Th	12		26	49	
	39				
	41				
	45				
	46				
	48				
Rn	8	3	27	34	1
	13	7			16
	29				17
	37				25
	43				30
Se	9	6		5	10
	11	14			
	19	15			
		20			
		22			
		23			

Notes: Numbers 1 to 31 refer to songs in manuscript X; numbers 32 to 49 refer to songs in manuscript V. There is no extant music for numbers 50 to 61. Numbers 21 and 24 have the same melody with different words.

Table 6 presents an intersection of the text categories as defined in chapter 3 – Courtly, Laudatory, Political, Catechetic, and Personal – with the categories of musical structure that are observable in the devotional songs of X and V. The musical categories may be defined as follows:

Chanson (Ch): This is the most usual form for the secular trouvère song, with the first two musical phrases repeated and then followed by a series of unrepeated phrases. The structure is *ababcdef* ... for each stanza. Because this is the most common category, it may be regarded as the norm for trouvère composition. The declamation is largely syllabic with some ornamentation, usually at cadences.

Through-composed (Th): This category consists of freely composed phrases that are not repeated within the stanza and that are often embellished with melodic ornaments. The structure is *abcde* ... for each stanza. The declamation varies from syllabic to florid. Melodies of this type show less cohesion than other types, and the ornamentation and lack of repetition make them seem to wander. Trouvère melodies of this type resemble troubadour melodies and may represent either an early layer of composition or a conscious attempt to imitate the troubadour style.

Round-chanson (Rn):[3] Having tightly structured stanzas with short phrases and internal repetition within the stanza, these songs may include melodic sequencing or a refrain or both. Structures are, for example, *ababcdb*, *ababcdcefghb*, or *abacdefdeg* for each stanza. The declamation is usually syllabic; melodies are very cohesive and may sound 'folklike' or 'dancelike.'

Serpentine (Se): This is a more tightly knit subset of the Round-chanson category. The phrases are shorter and there is marked metric accentuation that is determined by the text. The category is primarily associated with Laudatory texts in which serpentine rhymes appear, imitating the internal rhymes of the text with musical rhymes. The structure for songs in this category is, for example, *ababcdbcdb* or $a_x a_x bcbc_x ddc_x bcbc_x$ for each stanza.

A few of the musical categories bear some relationship, whether close or general, to categories of text. The Courtly texts tend to be set with Chanson or Through-composed melodies if they are from manuscript V, or in Round-chanson style if in manuscript X. The three categories represent an adherence to the style of the formal court song, which is stately and graceful and carefully crafted to bring out each nuance of the text. The association of Catechetic texts primarily with Chanson melodies suggests that a system of imitation was at work and that these songs might have represented either an application of the formal court song to devotional purposes or the borrowing of well known secular melodies for devotional contrafacta. Certainly the Courtly texts that contain passages of description and praise of Mary are reminiscent in structure of secular songs that are directed to specific women. If, as was suggested in chapter 3, the Courtly texts represent purposeful attempts to alter and examine the tradition of amatory court songs, their music should also follow and reflect upon the models of the tradition.

The melodies of the Serpentine type, associated most frequently with Laudatory texts, may represent a subgenre of the court song that was derived from the influence of popular dance music and reflects its distinctive qualities in text as well as music.[4] The content of the Laudatory texts is almost exclusively Marian, and it is more light-hearted than that of the Courtly or Catechetic types. The texts contain little or no mention of penitence or apprehension about the afterlife, and they appear to be crowd pleasers, full of vivid images and repetitive phrasing. Their music is 'catchy': it is easy to imagine dancing to them or singing in a group with everyone joining in.[5]

The distinction between what may be called formal and popular styles can be further clarified by adopting Beck's distinction between *chanson* and *chansonnette*.[6] He defines the former, with its ornamented melodies and with little or no repetition of text or music within a stanza, as the formal art song of the trouvères. The *chanson* corresponds to the Chanson and Through-composed categories in this study. The *chansonnette*, on the other hand, is a 'light' form, with largely syllabic melodies, repetition of melodic lines within the stanza, and often a refrain. It corresponds to the Round-chanson and Serpentine categories.

It is also worth noting the occurrence of melodic types in each manuscript collection. The Courtly songs of manuscript X are primarily set to Round-chanson melodies, with a few in Serpentine style; only one is Through-composed. This text category in manuscript X stands in sharp contrast to that in manuscript V. Furthermore, all of the Serpentine melodies and all but one of the Laudatory texts[7] occur in manuscript X. Does X, with its predominance of Round-chanson and Serpentine melodies as well as of Laudatory texts, represent a 'popular' collection?[8] Does manuscript V, which contains a far greater number of Through-composed melodies than X, represent an earlier and more formal collection, one that was perhaps influenced by troubadour melodic style?

The stylistic distinctions are further supported by reference to the modalities of the repertoire.[9] It would be unwise to attribute to the composers of the trouvère songs any consistent use of modality for emotional expression or for association with the content of their texts. The association of modality with content was apparently foreign to the attitudes of their time. As well, the pitch, and hence the scale, at which a song was notated was probably a matter of convenience to the scribe and had little to do with the actual pitch of performance, which was determined by the individual characteristics of the performer's voice and the possible range of any accompanying instrument. Pitch was not standardized in the thirteenth century, and the notation of a monophonic song was a kind of code indicating intervallic relationships only. Perhaps most significantly, there is no clear expression of a specific scale in several of the songs; this is especially the case with those using melodic structures of the Through-composed type. Musicologist Hendrik Van der Werf warns against the assumption that the trouvères wrote in conformity with clearly defined scales, choosing one before beginning the process of composition.[10] Many songs in the Through-composed and Chanson styles seem to grow empirically from the nucleus of a brief melodic phrase, giving the impression that their heritage was a tradition of spontaneous improvisation in which

Table 7
Scales of songs in the secular repertoire of the Chansonnier Cangé

Modality			Number of examples
Major	final	C	11
		F	5
		G	15
Minor	final	D	14
		G/♭	1
		A	4

Table 8
Scales of songs in the devotional repertoire of manuscripts V and X

			Number of examples		
Modality			Manuscript V	Manuscript X	Total
Major	final	C	1	3	4
		c	1	2	3
		F	–	1	1
		F/♭	1	6	7
		f/♭	2	1	3
		G	2	9	11
Minor	final	D	8	5	13
		D/♭	–	2	2
		d	–	1	1
		G/♭	2	–	2
		A	1	1	2

a conjunct series of notes was shaped into a melodic line by the addition of ornaments.[11]

Such warnings notwithstanding, there does appear to be some correlation between melodic modality and the form, if not the content, of the texts. There is little correspondence on a specific level: one does not, for example, find that *pastourelles* with six-line stanzas are always set to melodies written in the scale with final g. However, in both secular and devotional groups there is a relationship between the genre of a song and the modality of its music.

Tables 7 and 8 give statistical profiles of the scales found in a sample of secular trouvère songs and in all of the devotional songs in manuscripts V and X. The songs are classified by their finals, and by the presence or absence of the b-flat. The songs in the devotional repertoire in the scales on c and d are further classified by octave, since both the treble (c, d) and tenor (C, D) pitches appear in the manuscripts as finals. The survey includes a sample of fifty secular songs and the forty-nine devotional songs from manuscripts V and X for which music is extant.

The secular sample drawn from the Chansonnier Cangé reveals a slight preference for the scale with final D in the *chanson* category, while scales with finals G and C dominate the *chansonnette* category. Both the secular and the devotional repertoires produce similar patterns of distribution with regard to the use of particular scales. Since many of the melodies in the devotional repertoire may be contrafacta of secular songs, this is not surprising. The greater part of the devotional songs in manuscript V, like their secular counterparts, employ the scales of D ('minor' modality) and G ('major' or 'minor' depending on whether the b-natural or b-flat is used; both were admissible in late medieval monophonic practice).[12] These songs fit primarily into the Courtly category of text and the Chanson and Through-composed melodic styles. The majority of songs in manuscript X employ the scales on C, F, and G containing the major third, a proportion which may be weighted by the influence of popular (or 'folk') styles on the Round-chanson and Serpentine types of devotional song, equivalent to the *chansonnette* as defined by Beck. The pattern suggests that there may have been purposeful use of particular scales to distinguish between formal and informal aspects of the repertoire.

It is likely that the *chansonnette* draws its simple, repetitive, and often vigorous melodies from the tradition of popular dance music. What little is known about this tradition links the nascent refrain forms of thirteenth-century song – the *ballade, rondeau,* and *virelai* – with the dance, along with the *estampie* for voices or instruments. That the popular refrain forms were also a part of the learned style of the court songs is evident by their subsequent development into the complex and mannered *formes fixes* of the fourteenth-century Ars Nova style. The *chansonnette* of Beck's definition may manifest the same phenomenon: the use of popular 'functional' music as a model for a type of 'artistic' song.[13] Do the songs of Laudatory and Serpentine type, then, represent a tradition of devotional *chansonnettes,* or perhaps even of songs used for processional dancing during court festivals in the Advent or Christmas season? An additional feature of this type is the use of closely structured rhymes, alliteration, and other wordplay. Two excerpts will serve as examples:

Dame en qui cors
toz bons acors
est, et toute concorde:
cors sans descors,
misericors
vostre misericorde.
Nos a de corde descordés

dont chascun estoit encordés:
cil qui a vos s'acorde
de lui ostés la corde
dont Adans touz nos encore. 23, st. 4

Dame, deffensables donjons
contre les deables dampnéz,
vos estes la planche et li ponz
ou mains pechierres est passéz. 51, st. 3

In this respect, the songs of the Laudatory and Serpentine category come reasonably close to imitations of late Latin devotional poems, which often contain similar linguistic artifices.[14] This type of court song is not a genuine 'popular' style, but one that employs elements drawn from both popular and learned traditions.

The influence of Latin liturgical tradition on the music of the trouvère devotional songs is less easy to define. The vernacular devotional songs do not follow the same rules or exhibit the same patterns as liturgical compositions.[15] They are not modal in the sense that the term is used for liturgical chant, and their melodies do not usually resemble those of monophonic liturgical compositions. They draw their melodic heritage far more from the models provided by amatory court songs than from antiphons, sequences, or hymns. There are, however, a few parallels in structure between the two genres that are worthy of mention.

One point of comparison between secular and liturgical melodies is in the structure of cadences. The vocabulary of the liturgical modes includes formulaic cadential figures that help to identify the mode and to determine its attendant reciting tone, indicating to the celebrant where to find the pitch of the next item in the liturgy. There is no system in the vernacular songs for such clearly defined formulas, but stereotypical cadences do appear in songs written in the scales with finals D and G. Of the sixteen examples in D, six end with the figure e-d-c-d and another six with f-e-d. Of the thirteen in G, six end with b-a-g and five with a-g-f-g. Whether this represents a conscious imitation of chant style is questionable; it might more easily be attributed to oral tradition in performance, and manuscript variants suggest that the cadential formulas could be changed by either individual performers or scribes. In both cases, however, the presence of formulaic cadences in the two genres suggests a shared aesthetic between church and court. Members of the aristocracy, familiar with liturgical chant formulas through their own devotions and their attendance at court chapels, undoubtedly regarded such standardized melodic phrases as desirable elements in their own songs or in those written for them.

In rare instances a trouvère melody will incorporate formulas drawn from liturgical practice or follow the outline of a well-known hymn or antiphon. A case in point is song no. 33, whose opening lines are reminiscent of the Marian hymn 'Ave maris stella' (Ex 1).

Ex 1

33, st. 1

Ave maris stella, opening phrase

The resemblance is not consistent enough to be called a parody, however, and the issue of liturgical melodic quotations in vernacular devotional songs is somewhat complicated by the many cases in which a secular model precedes the devotional contrafactum. At a certain level the distinctions become academic. The composer chooses, or is chosen by, the melodic vehicle most suitable to convey the poetic text, or finds words to adorn and concretize a well-loved melody. The process may have been then, as it is now, either laboured or spontaneous. If the songs resemble both liturgical and secular music it is because their composers heard both to varying degrees, regarded both as models for what music was about, and assimilated both into their own works.

Notation and Rhythmic Interpretation

The rhythmic interpretation of the devotional songs remains as ambiguous to the modern interpreter as that of any of the secular trouvère songs.[16] While the notation used for monophonic music of secular origin employs the same general vocabulary of visual symbols as that for liturgical polyphony, the symbols are apparently not assigned the same meanings in both usages. Even more problematic is the fact that while pitches are legible to the modern interpreter of the secular system, rhythmic duration and accentuation are not. If the notation of the trouvère manuscripts was intended to indicate specific rhythmic values distinct from the patterns established by the text, its meaning in this respect is now obscure. Given this circumstance, choices must be made with respect to rhythm.[17]

One option for performance and transcription is to assume that the notational symbols had the same meaning for monophonic song and for polyphony. In the polyphonic system of the thirteenth century, called early mensural ('measured') notation, individual notes and ligatures ('tied notes') are given specific rhythmic values according to patterns called rhythmic modes. Polyphony involves two or more lines of music sounding at the same time, and the parts must be aligned rhythmically in order to prevent the music from deteriorating into a tangle of individual interpretations. In the thirteenth century, modal rhythm apparently served not just this purpose, but also to express abstract numerical proportions that were considered symbolic of universal principles of hierarchy and harmony. No such regulation is needed for monophonic song, however, and the imposition of the inflexible rhythmic modes seems, at least to the modern interpreter's ear, to warp the texts unnecessarily.[18] There are, as well, conceptual distinctions between the two genres. Medieval polyphony was a vehicle for musical artifice, with or without textual content. In the thirteenth century many of its forms involved drawing out the syllables of a liturgical text on florid musical phrases, rendering the text largely incomprehensible, in order to portray the wordless jubilation of angels. Monophonic secular song was primarily a vehicle for conveying the meaning of text, as it had been for centuries.[19]

Another argument against the use of modal rhythm to interpret trouvère songs is that both manuscripts X and V – and indeed all of the trouvère manuscript sources – contain passages that are inconsistently notated if one is expecting adherence to a strict mensural pattern. In many of the songs that contain internal repetition, the second statement of a musical phrase is written differently from the first; the position of longs and breves may be reversed, or a descending ternary ligature used in place of *currentes*.[20] There is some indication that the scribe of manuscript V was familiar with the early forms of polyphonic mensural notation, including the ligature *cum opposita proprietate*, but he did not use them correctly or consistently in the recording of monophonic music. Mensural note forms seem, instead, to have been used loosely as general indicators of rhythmic phrasing. The interpretation of each phrase depends not only on the metric values of the note forms, but also on the syllabification and metric stresses of the text, as well as on the contours of the melodic line. The process is further complicated by the ambiguity of metric stress patterns in French verse; since the qualitative accentuation of any syllable depends on its context, the process of counting syllables in each phrase gives a more reliable indication of underlying patterns.

Thus, I have taken into account a number of factors in deciding on feasible transcriptions. Two examples of the process should serve to demonstrate the nature of the decisions involved.

Ex 2

De Yesse na-ï-stra / ver-ge qui flo-ri-ra, / c'a-vons nos d'Y-sa-ï-e:
'sains es-pirs i ven-ra, / qui se re-po-se-ra / en la rose es-pa-ni-e.'
Bien est la pro-fe-ci-e, / si m'est vis, a-com-pli-e:
la flor est Jhesu Criz, / si com dit li es-criz, / et la verge est Ma-ri-e.

20, st. 1

The song 'De Yesse naïstra' (Ex 2) is a clear example of a Laudatory text set to a melody of Serpentine type. At first glance, its initial phrases could fit into triple metre as well as duple: if one takes the first note as a downbeat, the first two phrases (*De Yesse ... florira*) appear to fit neatly into 3/4 bars. The next phrase, however, is problematic in triple metre, and the accentuation patterns of the text suggest a different solution. Here is the scansion of the first stanza:

De **Yes**-se na-ï-**stra** / ver-ge qui flo-ri-**ra**, / c'a-vons nos d'Y-sa-ï-e:
'sains es-pirs i ven-**ra**, / qui se re-po-se-**ra** / en la rose es-pa-**ni**-e.'
Bien est la pro-fe-**ci**-e, / si m'est vis, a-com-**pli**-e:
la **flor** est Jhesu **Criz**, / si com dit li es-**criz**, / et la verge est Ma-**ri**-e.

A pattern is established in the first line of six, six, and seven syllables; the main accent falls on the final syllable of the six-syllable phrases and the penultimate (also the sixth) of the seven-syllable phrases. Thus, in a piece with such clear declamatory rhythm, the sixth syllable of each phrase needs to be placed on a strong beat. The melodic line emphasizes this placement, since many of the sixth beats are given ornaments of two to four notes. Furthermore, accents occur on the second syllables of the first and ninth phrases, which are set to identical music. An arrangement of the six syllables of the two phrases that places the second and sixth syllables on strong beats produces the transcription given, with an upbeat leading to the strong second syllable in a 4/4 bar. The strong sixth syllable then becomes the first beat of the next 4/4 bar. It must be noted, also, that modern musical bar-lines are not always indicative of strong beats when applied to editing medieval monophonic songs; see, for example, phrases two, six, seven, and eleven, where an article or a weak syllable begins a bar.[21]

A more difficult challenge is presented by the song 'Mout sera cil bien norris,' a Catechetic text in Chanson style (Ex 3). Its initial phrases are clearly in duple metre, but no clear accent pattern is evident. The only strong accents are contained in the rhyme-bearing syllables.

> Mout se-ra cil bien nor-**ris** / et en bon cou-**vent,**
> et mout se-ra sei-gno-**ris** / tres bien et sou-**vent,**
> qui veut re-cla-**mer** / la me-re Dieu, et a-**mer** / tout son jou-**vent;** /
> et Dieu le nos a bien en cou-**vent:** /
> *Que cil a s'a-me ga-**ri**-e / qui sert la vir-ge Ma-**ri**-e.*

Here, however, the number of syllables in each phrase proves significant.

Ex 3

The pattern is seven and five, seven and five; five, seven, four, nine, eight, eight. The combination of odd and even-numbered groups suggests that rests must be used to fill out some of the measures. This proves to be the case for the first five phrases. The sixth and seventh are then connected by means of an upbeat on the syllable 'tout,' effectively producing a pattern of eleven syllables (seven plus four), followed by the next phrase of nine, and then the final two phrases are again connected because their final syllables are weak beats. The pauses (rests) between phrases can be regarded as delineating the patterns of rhyme and accentuation, calling attention to the rhyme-bearing syllables and preparing the ear to anticipate the next phrase of text. Following the syllabification patterns, placement of rests, and melodic contours produced the combination of 4/4 and 2/4 bars that is given.

The presence in song no. 2 of the phrase dividers, the small vertical strokes in the original notation, nearly corresponds to the positioning of the rests in the transcription. The correspondence is not exact, however, in this piece or elsewhere. We can only assume that such marks indicated a division of some sort to the thirteenth-century singer, who then worked out its exact nature by scanning the sense of the text and its accentuation. The vertical phrase dividers are only one example of the ambiguity of notation, and we can reasonably suppose that the primary mode of learning songs at the time was aural, with the notation serving only as an *aide-mémoire* .

The vocabularies of notation for both manuscripts are given in appendix 1. Some oddities appear in each. The oblique and plicated *currentes* (running) ligatures in manuscript V are unusual, and their meaning is sometimes unclear. Manuscript X contains a short-tailed single note (♩), that can be read as equivalent to both the long and the breve in syllabic passages. Its precise meaning is not clear from the context, but it may indicate an absence of the need to distinguish carefully between a long and a breve, i.e., an absence of strict mensural principles. The single oblique note (◆), usually associated with *currentes* figures, is also used on occasion as a breve. Finally, there is the single note with oblique ascending tail (✔), which seems to function as a plicated breve, perhaps a plicated form of the single oblique note.

The problem of rhythmic interpretation is compounded when two manuscript versions of the same song are extant and do not concur on notational details. An example is song no. 15, which appears in manuscripts X and P. Longs are the primary value in X, while breves or short-tailed notes predominate in P. An additional point of interest is the use of oblique single notes in both manuscript versions, but not in the same places. An example is in the following phrase in, first, source P, and then source X:

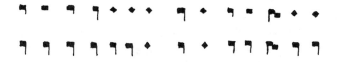

Fox est qui en fo-**li**-e / son tens met et em-**ploi**-e

One can conclude only that the syllable-bearing single notes, whatever their shapes, were in this case equivalent in metric value, or that different performers might interpret the same song with different metric patterns. The majority of songs common to X and P show minor notational variants of this sort, and the rules for notation appear to be somewhat flexible, particularly in manuscripts of secular origin. For that matter, such variants may also occur within a single stanza of one song, with identical melodic phrases having different ligature patterns. A case in point is song no. 29: the cadences at *amender* (measure 16 in the transcription) and *recouvrer* (measure 22), which are obviously parallel in content, do not appear to be so in the original notation.

Scribal errors or variants in the texts may also shed some light on performance practices. Because only the first stanza of each song in a given manuscript was provided with notation, it was left to the singer to align syllables with notes on subsequent stanzas. If a syllable of text is omitted from a line in syllabic texture, the singer (or editor) is faced with a decision: whether to eliminate a note, to join two notes on one syllable at the most unobtrusive point in the phrase, or to reconstruct the missing word. Song no. 14, a song appearing only in manuscript X, contains a problem of this sort. In the third stanza, a phrase, 'qui trestous a,' that usually contains five syllables appears with only four, probably through the omission of a word.[22] The corresponding melodic phrase is designed to carry five syllables, as is shown in the first stanza:

dou mal ou A-**dan**

If the first of the aforementioned alternatives is chosen, one can assume that some violence would be done to the metric balance unless a pause equivalent to the value of the missing note is inserted; there is nothing in the musical literature of the time to justify such impromptu 'rests,' but they remain within the realm of possibility. A more plausible solution would be to fuse the repeated note g at the beginning of the phrase into a note of double duration on the first syllable, thus:

qui trestouz a

Such lapses of one syllable on medial stanzas are not uncommon, and they are particularly puzzling because in most cases the 'incorrect' version is perfectly acceptable in grammar and content. These are not ordinary cases of scribal error, but legitimate variants that disregard the rules of metric consistency. Once again, the keyword is flexibility; it may at the time have been one of the tasks of a skilled singer to carry the melodic line smoothly over such rough terrain, or even to emphasize the aberrant phrases for the sake of introducing variety to a repetitive structure. Similar metric shifts can be found in stanzaic English-language folk-songs, and they are far less irksome in practice than in theory.

In taking a final look at the notational aspects of the devotional repertoire, it is well to remember that many of the songs are contrafacta, usually employing secular texts, which were in turn often modelled upon popular or liturgical melodies or both. Room was left at each successive transformation for changes of structure, metre, accentuation, and melodic detail, possibly resulting in a tradition that encouraged tampering with the version one was given. Where the manuscripts exhibit actual errors or inconsistencies, as distinct from variants, these flaws probably resulted not from ignorance on the part of the scribe but from the degree of familiarity that admits carelessness. This may be particularly true in the case of manuscript V, which is notated in a sophisticated but often inconsistent and inelegant hand. In learning the intricacies of notation, one absorbs an understanding of its function. One may then copy it carelessly, if the work in question is familiar to the aural memory, without loss of comprehension, just as one may choose to write down a familiar poem in an abbreviated personal shorthand that renders it illegible to anyone else.

The differences between manuscript copies that were intended for reference, for performance, or for presentation raise additional questions. Was there a professional hierarchy among music scribes, with master scribes hired to produce elegant presentation copies while their apprentices roughed out unadorned copies for everyday use? Were the professional scribes those who were considered most accurate in reproducing exact copies, or those considered most inventive in producing plausible variants? Were music scribes necessarily performers of music, and to what extent did their aural memories affect their accuracy? Did they necessarily learn their craft through clerical training, or was there a system – formal or informal – of apprenticeship in lay circles? And if clerical training was not involved, what, if anything, prevented lay scribes from inventing their own personal systems of notation, as the scribe of manuscript V may have done?

Performance Practices, Then and Now

Performance practices also provide a vast field for speculation. Because the trouverè songs are notated only as single-line vocal melodies, any evidence for accompaniment must be derived from other documents or iconographic sources. That instruments were played at European courts throughout the late medieval period is known from financial records listing payments to musicians. Pictorial evidence for the use of instruments in connection with monophonic lyric song in the thirteenth century can be inferred from the extensive collection of miniature paintings depicting musicians in a manuscript of the *Cantigas de Santa Maria*.[23] The instruments in the miniatures range from those of clearly Arabic origin that were employed at the royal courts of Spain to the harp, vielle, psaltery, and various forms of percussion that were found throughout Europe, including the courts of France. The bowed vielle is known to have been associated with performance of secular trouvère songs, apparently to provide a movable drone, to double and embellish melodies, or to play improvised interludes between the stanzas of songs. Plucked string instruments, including the harp, psaltery, and early lute, may also have been used. Percussion may have accompanied songs with clearly marked rhythm, particularly those of *chansonnette* type; it was, however, probably unsuitable for the more flowing lines of the Chanson and Through-composed melodies.

In any case, performance practices in the thirteenth century may have been quite flexible. There are no known rules specifying whether or not instruments are to be used or what kind are suitable for the performance of court songs. It is likely that the specifics of a given performance depended on the circumstances of the moment: who was involved, how large the venue, the audience, and the financial resources were, and whether professional singers were hired or talented members of a household were asked to demonstrate their skills. The only general rule was that although singers might be either professional or amateur, instrumental performance was almost entirely the province of professionals. It is probable that the more prominent festivals necessitated the hiring of trained singers, while amateurs would perform within their own households.

What the occasions were for performances is open to further conjecture. It is known that the trouvères and their *jongleurs* participated in competitive annual song festivals during Lent, when the courts abstained from entertainment. These festivals seem to have served as trade conventions, facilitating the exchange and spread of newly composed songs. At court it is probable that devotional songs of both formal and popular types were incorporated into lay devotional festivals at Advent and Christmas and at observations of the Annunciation and Assumption of the Virgin Mary. They may even have replaced songs with secular content if it was thought inappropriate at such times to entertain guests with love songs.[24] The variety of devotional song categories suggests that they may have been performed in a variety of circumstances. One can imagine a Catechetic song sung unaccompanied by a solo voice, a Courtly *chanson* performed to instrumental accompaniment by a pair of professional *jongleurs,* or a group of young girls singing and dancing a Laudatory *carole* to celebrate the beauty of Mary with their own grace.

The modern performer of trouvère songs is also free to determine the specifics of performance. In general, the songs are best regarded as chamber music, most suitable for fairly intimate venues. A solo voice will best carry the text and imitate the original conditions of performance, although songs of the *chansonnette* type may be sung by small groups. Accompaniment, when used, is best kept simple. Where there is access to reconstructed medieval instruments, strings are advisable. A recorder may be used to play improvised ornaments on the melody between stanzas of the song. If only modern instruments are available, suitable accompaniments may be crafted for the viola, flute, oboe, harp, or guitar. Percussion, in the form of a hand drum or tambourine, is suitable if the song has a precise rhythmic pattern.

Performers trained to present early music will find that the songs in this edition follow the same patterns for interpretation as any other trouvère songs. Some general musicians' ground rules for improvised accompaniment are provided here to make the songs accessible to classically trained performers.[25] These consist of the following:

- A movable drone may be provided at the unison or octave, moving to the fifth or fourth (with the second as a passing tone if appropriate) before cadences, and resolving again to the unison or octave.
- Common-practice tonal harmony is an anachronism and should be avoided. If a harmonic accompaniment is desired, it should be regarded as a countermelody, and it should be limited to the scale degrees found in the song itself. The seventh degree of the scale, if used at all, should generally be lowered to the minor seventh unless the major seventh is included in the song itself. Overly 'sweet' harmony should be avoided; parallel thirds are not characteristic of continental style in the thirteenth century.
- Heterophony – the approximate doubling of the melody with some ornaments added – is an effective technique for some of the songs. For models, one should listen to recordings of traditional Middle Eastern dance music. Brief clashes in the harmony from parallel seconds, sevenths, or ninths produced in passing are stylistically acceptable.

- Instrumental interludes may be added between stanzas of a song, or purely instrumental arrangements prepared. These are most effective when they employ not just a drone or a movable drone but also a melody instrument that paraphrases and ornaments the melody of the song. A pair of melody instruments in heterophony may also be effective. Each interlude may consist of a slightly different variation on the theme.
- With percussion, a 'four-square' beat should be avoided. More rhythmic interest is provided by leaving a beat or two out of the pattern or by adding anticipatory 'pickup' strokes before the accentuated beats or by doing both.

Folk musicians may also find the trouvère songs accessible. Unaccompanied singing is always an option, and a folk-singer's vocal style may be better suited to projecting these songs than a classical or operatic style. Instrumental arrangement is also a possibility: a pair of guitars (one to play melody and the other to provide a rhythmic drone), or of fiddles, or either one with dulcimer drone may be suitable. Such combinations are acoustically similar to the ensemble properties of reconstructed medieval instruments.

A few suggestions for singers are also appropriate. No indications of tempi are given for the songs, and so performers are free to choose their own. In general, the loosely structured melodies of the Through-composed type, as well as of many Chanson melodies, are best presented moderately and lyrically. The same holds true for any song with extensive ornamentation. The more dance-like and primarily syllabic pieces in the Serpentine category, as well as many of the Round-chanson type, are suitable for a fast tempo. Performers should let the contours of the melodic lines and the lengths of phrases guide their choices. The content of the text may give indications, as well; a lament is generally slower than a playful lyric, but a tempo should never be allowed to drag. Whatever the taste of thirteenth-century audiences may have been, a modern performer has a responsibility to a modern audience to keep the music interesting.

Bar-lines present another set of choices. In general, they are used to indicate the phrasing of a song, but there are instances where the accentuation pattern of the text does not fit the usual modern meaning of the bar-line as an indication of metric stress. This difference is especially common in portions of non-initial stanzas. A certain fluidity of approach will help solve such problems, as will a working knowledge of modern French. Those singers without training in French are advised to consult someone familiar with the basic principles of the language; the medieval texts differ from modern ones in many subtle ways, but the rudiments of grammar and syntax are similar enough to make modern French, along with the translations into English provided here, a reasonable guide for solving problems.

Performers may also wish to consult with scholars of medieval French, who are available at most universities and colleges that offer degrees in French literature. A basic guide to pronunciation is available in the recently published *Singing Early Music* by Timothy J. McGee.

Readers of this book should by all means try these songs – get acquainted, experiment, live with them. In doing so you will be reviving and continuing a tradition that inspired a distant culture and can still bring joy to audiences today.

Appendix A:
Notational forms

Manuscript V

single   *oblique*   *plicated*   *currentes*

binary

ternary

multiple and
compound

Manuscript X

single	oblique	plicated	currentes

binary

ternary

multiple and
    compound

Notes

1: The Manuscript Sources of the Trouvère Songs as Visual Records

1 See Schwan, *Die altfranzösische Liederhandschriften*; Jeanroy, *Bibliographie sommaire des chansonniers*; and Järnström and Långfors, *Recueil de chansons pieuses*, vol. 2.

2 The body of chapter 1 discusses general characteristics and comparisons. For codicological details and *stemmata* of transmission, see the 'Description and Contents' section at the end of this chapter, which is provided for readers seeking more technical information.

3 See Schwan, *Die altfranzösische Liederhandschriften*, and Beck, *Le Chansonnier Cangé* and *Le Manuscrit du roi*.

4 For the history of music notation, see Parrish, *The Notation of Medieval Music*, and Apel, *The Notation of Polyphonic Music*.

5 Unless the information is given by the scribe it is impossible to determine whether text and music were executed by the same person or persons. While it was apparently common for music scribes to be specialists who added notation to a previously prepared text, it would have been part of their training to prepare texts as well. Furthermore, the text layout for a song must be arranged according to the space needed for notation, so that the text and music scribes, if not the same person, must have had to work from the same copies or in close consultation with each other.

6 Van der Werf, *The Chansons of the Troubadours and Trouvères*, 46–7.

7 Paris, BN, *Catalogue général des manuscrits français*, compiled by Henri Omont (1902), 2: 345–6.

8 Incipit: 'Sel disanz ja soit ce que il ... de preciouse vertu de permanence.'

9 The work was written before 1260: see Segre, 'Li Bestiaires d'amours' di maistre Richart de Fornival e 'Li Response du Bestiaire.' It was copied through the mid-fourteenth century, and also appears in trouvère manuscript I.

10 Paris, BN, *Catalogue général*, 346.

11 For information on the history of music notation, see Apel, *The Notation of Polyphonic Music*, and Parrish, *The Notation of Medieval Music*.

12 Schutz, *The Unedited Poems of Codex 389*.

13 By comparison, the secular portion of V contains five songs in common with C, two with I, one with a, and two with the family consisting of K, N, P, and X.

14 See Spanke, *G. Raynauds bibliographie*, 1: 201–19.

15 See Rohloff, *Die Quellenhandschriften*, 130; Van der Werf, *The Chansons*, 153–5, and the Introduction to this work.

16 See Schwan, *Die altfranzösische Liederhandschriften*; Beck, *Le Chansonnier Cangé* and *Le Manuscrit du roi*.

17 For terms used in the discussion of the music, see chapter 4. Cadences of the third degree are not unusual in the trouvère repertoire, and both versions of the song are equally plausible in musical terms. It is nearly impossible to establish a 'correct' reading for monophonic music of this period, and I have not attempted to do so here.

2: The Trouvère Devotional Songs in the Context of Popular Culture

1 Cited by Shah, *Tales of the Dervishes*, 25–6.

2 Boglioni, *La Culture populaire au moyen âge*, 30–3: 'Le populaire est, en première approximation, le laïc par opposition au clérical, à l'épiscopal, au monastique, mais c'est aussi le bas clergé par opposition au clergé instruit et universitaire ... C'est le local, le périphérique, le particulier par opposition au centralisé et à l'uniforme. C'est la culture orale et les valeurs du groupe par opposition à la culture écrite et aux valeurs de l'individu ... C'est le charismatique et l'imprévisible par opposition à l'institutionnel et au juridiquement stable ... Les discussions récentes sur la notion de religion populaire montrent qu'il est à la fois difficile et essentiel de définir exactement ces divers paliers d'opposition.'

3. Rohloff, ed. *Die Quellenhandschriften ... Johannes de Grocheio*, 130. ('A regibus et nobilibus solet componi et etiam coram regibus et principibus terrae decantari, ut eorum animos ad audaciam et fortitudinem, magnanimitatem et liberalitatem commoveant, quae omnia faciunt ad bonum regimen.')

4 See chapter 3.

5 The vidas, or lives, are brief biographical stories of the troubadours in the manuscripts of their works. Modelled on contemporary lives of saints, they often contain apocryphal anecdotes designed to enhance dramatic effect.

6 Faral, *Les Jongleurs en France*.

7 Ibid., 79–80. ('La distinction d'une jonglerie populaire et d'une jonglerie seigneuriale apparaît ... comme insuffisante, et, pour la compléter, il faudrait établir dans chacune des deux classes une importante subdivision. C'est à ce moment qu'on commence à comprendre la vanité de ce jeu scolastique et de ces divisions toutes théoriques: car la porte des châteaux n'était pas fermée aux jongleurs de la foire.') See also Wright, 'Misconceptions concerning the Troubadours, Trouvères, and Minstrels,' *Music and Letters* 48 (1967): 35–9.

8 Faral, *Les Jongleurs en France*, 175.

9 See Fleming, *An Introduction to the Franciscan Literature of the Middle Ages*, and Jeffrey, *The Early English Lyric & Franciscan Spirituality*.

10 See Rakel, *Die Musikalische Erscheinungsform der Trouvèrepoesie.*

11 Zink, 'Le traitement des "sources exemplaires" dans les sermons occitans, catalans, piémontais du XIIIe siècle,' in Privat, ed. *La Religion populaire en Languedoc,* 171. ('Pierre Cardinal, las d'être chanoine au Puy, jeta son froc aux orties et se fit troubadour. Sans aller jusqu'à cette conversion à rebours, tel de nos auteurs a pu, en restant dans le cadre de la littérature religieuse comme aumônier, lecteur, secrétaire de quelque riche dévot, mettre sa formation latine au service de la prose romane.')

12 Peacock, ed. *Instructions for Parish Priests, by John Myrc,* 13.

13 See, for example, the *Cantigas de Santa Maria* of Alfonso X. An overview of the genesis of late medieval Marian devotion can be found in Arcangeli-Marenzi, *Aspetti del tema della Vergine nella Letteratura francese del Medioevo.*

14 For a number of plausible theories about the origins of Marian veneration, see Ashe, *The Virgin: Mary's Cult and the Re-emergence of the Goddess.*

15 Erickson, *The Medieval Vision,* 94–5.

16 Duvernoy, ed., *Le Registre d'inquisition de Jacques Fournier.* The Cathar system of religious education was undoubtedly responsible for much dissemination of doctrine through the ranks. However, a large number of the individuals who are cited in the Fournier records were orthodox Catholics called as witnesses to the heretical beliefs of others. The climate of concern with matters of religion as a facet of everyday existence seems to have applied to them as well as to the accused.

17 Blackney, ed., *Meister Eckhart,* xviii.

18 Froissart, *Voyage en Béarn,* ed. A.H. Diverres, 67. This edition consists of an excerpt from Froissart's lengthy chronicles. ('Il disoit planté d'oroisons tous les jours, une nocturne du psaultier, heures de Nostre Dame, du Saint Esperit, de la Croix, et vigilles de mors. Tous les jours faisoit donner V frans en petite monnoie pour l'amour de Dieu, et l'aumosne a sa porte a toutes gens.')

19 Matthew of Paris, *Chronica majora,* ed. H. Luard, 3: 290–1. See also F. Cazel, 'Religious Motivation in the Biography of Hubert de Burgh,' *Studies in Church History,* 15: 109–10.

20 See Labarge, *Saint Louis: The Life of Louis IX of France.*

21 Prologue to the *Miracles de Notre Dame* of Gautier de Coincy, ed. Koenig, lines 69–74. ('Whoever wishes to put a spell on the devil should sing of the lady of whom the angels sing day and night. Those who sing her sweet song will enchant the devil and put him to sleep: now listen to how I sing it.')

3: The Texts

1 Hefele, *Histoire des conciles d'après les documents originaux,* 8: 133. ('Omnis utriusque sexus fidelis ... omnia sua solus peccata confiteantur fideliter, saltem semel in anno, proprio sacerdoti, et ... suscipiens reverenter ad minus in Pascha eucharistiae sacramentum.')

2 Ibid., 134. ('Cum infirmitas corporalis nonnumquam ex peccato proveniat ...

decreto praesenti statuimus, et districte praecipimus medicis corporum, ut cum eos ad infirmos vocari contigerit, ipsos ante omnia mineant et inducant, quod medicos advocent animarum.')

3 Ibid., 119–20. ('Diabolus enim et daemones alii, a Deo quidem natura creati sunt boni, sed ipsi per se facti sunt mali: homo vero diaboli suggestione peccavit ... Et si post susceptionem baptismi quisquam prolapsus fuerit in peccatum, per veram poenitentiam semper potest reparari. Non solum autem virgines et continentes, verum etiam conjugati, per fidem rectam et operationem bonam placentes Deo, ad aeternam merentur beatitudinem pervenire.')

4 The distinctions are drawn along musical as well as textual lines. A discussion of these in full appears in chapter 4.

5 A survey of sixty-two additional devotional songs from other trouvère manuscripts (published in Järnström and Långfors, *Recueil*) reveals a similar distribution of thematic categories. The Courtly and Laudatory types each represent about 30 per cent of the repertoire. The Catechetic and Personal types are next in frequency (15 per cent each); the Political complaints are rare.

6 On the subject of the origins of trouvère and troubadour poetry, see Jeanroy, *La Poésie lyrique des troubadours*; Dronke, *Medieval Latin and the Rise of European Love-lyric*; Bezzola, *Les Origines et la Formation de la littérature courtoise en Occident (500–1200)*. A detailed bibliography is given in Taylor, *La Littérature occitane*.

7 Beck, ed., 2: *Chansonnier Cangé*, 227, song by the Chastelain de Couci (manuscript O, R.1872), st. 2. ('Lady, you must indeed have reason to torment me – I who have served and pleaded with you for so long in good faith – nor have you given me one day of joy.')

8 Ibid., 2: 37, song by Moniot d'Arras (manuscript O, R.863), st. 4. ('God! If it were not for the cruelty and disloyalty of these gossips, I would go to see her often, but I fear the lies they tell.')

9 Ibid., 2: 114, anonymous (manuscript O, R.1972), st. 3. ('He who serves love well and loyally, should rightly and without regret receive joy of it, but one often sees that those who have served best are given no reward.')

10 To suggest otherwise, of course, might have been regarded as heresy. However, popular beliefs about the efficacy of Mary as an intercessor derived from orally transmitted legends and from writings external to doctrine. The Catholic church was still uneasy about the matter, since the notion that Mary could influence divine will was too easily interpreted as granting superior power to her. For a full discussion see Ashe, *The Virgin: Mary's Cult and the Re-emergence of the Goddess*.

11 A number of Thibaut's works in both genres appear in Beck, ed., *Chansonnier Cangé*.

12 Ibid., 2: 87. ('Lady full of great goodness, nobility and pity.')

13 Ibid. ('and through you is light restored to the entire world.')

14 Ibid., 2: 50 (R.1620). ('Sweet lady, I have found no trace of generosity in you.')

15 Ibid., 2: 82 (R.1843). ('He who attempts to love any other is much like a fool: for in the one there is no treachery nor falseness, and in the other no mercy.')

16 Mâle, *L'Art religieux du XIIIe siècle*, 232–3.

17 See Smalley, *The Study of the Bible in the Middle Ages*.

18 Leclercq, ed., *Sancti Bernardi opera*, vol. 4, *Sermones in laudibus virginis Matris*.

19 Peltier, ed. *Sancti Bonaventurae opera omnia*, vol. 14, *Corona, Laus, Psalteria*, and *Speculum Beatae Mariae Virginis Matris*.

20 See Albertus Magnus, *Opera omnia*, vol. 36. The author has been identified as Richard of St Lawrence (d. ca. 1260); see Rigg, ed., *The Poems of Walter of Wimborne*, 21.

21 *De laudibus*, in ibid., 71. ('Quia potentissime protegit servos a triplici adversario, scilicet mundo, carne, et diabolo.')

22 Ibid., 89. ('Debemus etiam sperare in eam ... diligere, confidere, humiliare, compassionem habere.')

23 Albertus Magnus, *Opera omnia*, 36: 100. ('Ad ipsam cum fletu et gemitu debemus suspirare.')

24 Ibid., 126–33. ('mundus, rectus, devotus, verax, discretus, humilis, pius, pacificus, justus, patiens, hilaris, zelans.')

25 Terms extracted from a survey of fifty secular trouvère songs (nos. 101 to 150) from Beck, ed., *Chansonnier de Cangé* (manuscript O).

26 *De laudibus*, in Albertus Magnus, *Opera omnia*, 36: 103. ('laudatio, oratio, confessio, magnificatio, cantatio.')

27 Ibid., 117. ('Et nota, quod per hoc quod justus dicit Christo vel Mariae; *In te cantatio mea semper*, videtur quod justi debent esse joculatores Christi, Mariae, et sanctorum: solent enim curiales joculatores componere cantilenas, et jam compositas appropriare illis a quibus magna donaria jam acceperunt, vel sperant se accepturos. Nos autem jam multa beneficia a Christo suscepimus sive accepimus et Maria, et speramus multa majora percipere ab eis.')

28 In Old French: bonté, douceur, virginité, gloire, pité, humilité, raison, pris, purité, puissance, hautesce. In Latin: excellentia, dulcedo, virginitas, gloria, compassio, humilitas, sapientia, pretiositas, puritas, omnipotencia, celsitudo.

29 In Old French: vaillance, loiauté, valour, honour, roiauté, finesse, joie.

30 *De laudibus*, books 5–12, in Albertus Magnus, *Opera omnia* (vol. 36).

31 See song no. 51, st. 3. The term appears in a passage of alliterative wordplay.

32 See songs 56, st. 3, and 59, st. 1.

33 The use of the burning bush as a metaphor for the Incarnation probably derives from the sermons of St Bernard; see his *Opera*, ed. Leclercq, 4: 24.

34 Information is derived from the following editions of bestiaries: Randall, *Cloisters Bestiary*; Curley, ed., *Physiologus*; Alan Wood Rendell, *Physiologus of Bishop Theobald* (London 1925).

35 One well-known use of the image is in Adam de la Halle's 'De tant com plus aproche mon pais.' The association of the tiger with Mary also appears in some German vernacular sources; see Salzer, *Die Sinnbilder und Beiworte Mariens*, 63–5.

36 Information on the lapidary legends is drawn from the editions of Baisier, *The Lapidaire Chrétien*, and of Studer and Evans, *Anglo-Norman Lapidaries*.

37 Baisier, *The Lapidaire Chrétien*, 116, from the lapidary of King Philip in Paris, BN, fonds français 2008.

38 'Mulier vero a mollitie, tanquam mollier detracta littera, vel mutata, appellata est mulier.' ('Woman,' indeed, from 'softness,' with one letter taken out or changed, is called 'mulier.') Isidore of Seville, *Etymologiarum*, cap. 2, item 18, in *Sancti Isidori Hispalensis opera omnia* (Migne, *Patrologia Latina* 82: 417). It is worth noting that most of Isidore's etymologies are highly speculative. They do, however, give an indication of the simplifications given to an unlearned public in his time.

39 ('Notandum, etiam quod Heva triplicem guerram fecerat, supra se ... per superbiam ... avaritiam ... gulam. Sed Maria, Hevae filia, pacem fecit per humilitatem ... charitatem ... virginitatem ... quia ecce si vir cecidit per foeminam, jam non erigitur nisi per foeminam.') Albertus Magnus, *Opera omnia*, vol. 36, *De laudibus*, book 1, p.7. The doctrine of the *felix culpa* and of the parallel between Mary and Eve can also be found in numerous glosses by medieval commentators on Genesis 3; see, for example, the *Glossa Ordinaria* of Nicholas de Lyra.

40 See songs nos. 9 and 15.

41 The same image appears in songs nos. 4, 34, 35, 37, 39, 40, 45, and 47; all except the first are from manuscript V.

42 The scene described may owe its precision to an ecclesiastical pageant or a painting of the 'Virgin Enthroned.'

43 The use of imagery and vocabulary suited to the trade, profession, or social stratum of an audience was common to the preaching orders. See the *Communiloquium* of John of Wales, a thirteenth-century Franciscan manual for preachers (cited by Fleming, *An Introduction to the Franciscan Literature*, 156–8). The same concept appears in the Dominican *Beati Humberti de Romanis opera de vita regulari* (1265) of Humbert de Romanis, ed. Berthier, 2: 468: 'In consideratione vero modo loquendi, notandum quod varius modus est habendus secundum varietatem personarum, et juxta doctrinam Pauli dicentis (1. *ad Tim.* 5): seniorem ne increpaveris, sed obsecra ut patrem; juvenes, ut fratres; anus, ut matres; juvenculas, ut sorores in omni castitate.' ('In considering the modes of speaking, it must be noted that different modes should be used among different types of people, for according to the doctrine of Paul in 1 *Timothy* 5: "do not rebuke the elderly man, but address him as a father, young men as brothers, elderly women as mothers, and young women as sisters in all chastity."') The most extensive source for this concept is Alain de Lille, *Summa de Arte Predicatoria* (1190), which devotes ten chapters to the science of preaching to different types of audience: see *Opera omnia*, ed. Migne (*Patrologia Latina*), 210, columns 184–98.

44 Manselli, *La Religion populaire*, 32. ('Elle n'est pas constituée par des professions de foi ou par des normes et prescriptions fixées une fois pour toutes. Il

lui suffit de quelques textes brefs appris mécaniquement par cœur, de quelques faits essentiels de l'histoire sainte, du symbole des apôtres et des dix commandements, un ensemble dont on ne voit pas toujours clairement comment il fut compris et vécu. Mais autour de ce minuscule noyau d'éléments stables vint s'agglutiner tout un ensemble d'autres éléments, qui se transmirent de bouche en oreille, constamment modifiés selon les temps et les lieux avec les variations et retouches nécessaires pour être entendus et acceptés.')

45 The last line may refer to the garb of paradise; see the comment on this passage in the edition.

46 See Raby, *A History of Christian-Latin Poetry*, and the hymns and sequences collected in *Analecta hymnica*.

47 See Smalley, *The Study of the Bible in the Middle Ages*.

48 See ibid., and the *Biblia sacra cum glossa ordinaria* of Nicholas de Lyra.

49 Two of the Marian songs (nos. 8 and 44) contain long lists of metaphoric terms reminiscent of the litany of Mary; the latter also shows litanaic (i.e., repetitive) structure. The metaphors themselves, however, are not litanaic and the only similarity is in structural terms.

50 See chapter 1.

51 Fleming, *An Introduction to the Franciscan Literature of the Middle Ages*, 186–7.

52 For a general overview of the various types and their source manuscripts, see *The New Oxford History of Music*, vol. 1; Hoppin, *Medieval Music*; Harrison, *Music in Medieval Britain*.

53 See Liuzzi, ed., *La lauda e i primordi della melodia italiana*.

54 Their music has been edited by Anglès, in *Las Cantigas de Santa Maria*, and their texts by Mettmann, ed. *Cantigas de Santa Maria*.

55 A few examples appear in Seagrave and Thomas, *The Songs of the Minnesingers*.

56 Seagrave and Thomas, 123. ('Sinner, whether you come late or early, she blesses and will not forsake you.')

57 See Martin de Riquer, *Los Trovadores: Historia literaria y textos*, vol. 3.

58 Ibid., 3: 1618. ('Humble, downcast, penitent, saddened: I know that I have wasted my time in failure. I pray for mercy, gentle virgin, mother of Christ, daughter of the all-powerful, giving up all to you; if you please, protect my anguished soul.')

59 Branciforti, *Il canzoniere di Lanfranco Cigala*, 232–3. ('Such mercy is fitting, for she is the help of sinners, to whom reason is remote. May mercy be granted me, mother of God, because you were born for it.')

60 Lest it be thought that linguistic factors are the only distinction, the music of 'Per vous m'esjau' has the loose phrase structure, triadic melodies, and large *ambitus* associated with troubadour songs and easily distinguishable from the more tightly knit diatonic phrases typical of trouvère music. See chapter 4 for further explanation of the trouvère melodic style.

61 Koenig, ed., *Les Miracles de Notre Dame*. The lyric interpolations, with their music, were edited by Chailley in *Les Chansons à la Vierge de Gautier de Coinci*.

62 Chailley, ed., *Les Chansons à la Vierge*, 164. ('Mother of God, you are greatly

prized. No tongue, however articulate, can sufficiently praise your worthiness. Everyone prizes you, and so do I: you are the rose, the precious flower has taken precious flesh.')

4: The Music

1 For a detailed description of trouvère musical style, see Van der Werf, *The Chansons of the Troubadours and Trouvères.*

2 Such devices could, of course, have been improvised by performers without any trace being recorded in extant manuscripts. However, this is not likely: florid and dramatic melodic devices do appear in contemporary *Ars antiqua* liturgical manuscript sources.

3 This category is analogous to Gennrich's 'Rundkanzone.' See his *Grundriss einer Formenlehre des mittelalterlichen Liedes*, 245.

4 A detailed discussion of this concept is given below.

5 Experiments involving untrained amateur singers and music students support my contention. In general, both groups found the songs of the Laudatory and Serpentine categories easy to learn and to follow, the Chanson style less so, and the Through-composed songs very difficult. While late medieval people may have used very different criteria for determining which types of songs were participatory and which were for trained soloists and passive audiences, it can be argued that the human brain sets certain basic guidelines for ease of acquisition – the more repetition, the easier.

6 Beck, ed., *Chansonnier Cangé*, introduction.

7 See table 1.

8 And perhaps a later one? The repetitive refrain-form melodies in it show closer resemblance to the *formes fixes* (prevalent in the late thirteenth and the fourteenth centuries) than to the troubadour or troubadour-influenced early trouvère melodies.

9 The term 'modality' is used here simply to point out comparable intervallic structures in songs of various categories; it carries no implication of 'key' in the modern sense or of 'mode' in the medieval liturgical sense. There is no indication that the trouvère repertoire was based on the melodic modes of liturgical chant. There is, however, some suggestion that melodic modality based on the use of particular scale patterns was significant, although not consistently applied, as will be argued subsequently. This use of particular scales undoubtedly follows from the standard practices in music instruction at the time, in which singing was taught in ecclesiastical schools by means of intervallic relations within a scale. While this was not necessarily the way all trouvères or professional singers or both learned to structure melodies, it could not have been entirely unknown to them.

10 Van der Werf, *The Chansons of the Troubadours and Trouvères*, 46.

11 For examples, refer especially to songs nos. 33, 41, and 45. The last is clearly influenced by troubadour melodic style.

12 The use here of the modern terms major and minor is intended simply to indicate the presence of the raised (major) or lowered (minor) third degree of the
scale. Since the songs are monophonic and predate common-practice harmony
by several centuries, there is no implication of tonality; the classification of
scales is included solely to give a profile of the repertoire and to investigate
the question of *whether* the type of scale is significant to the form or content of
text. It is not known whether the third degree of the scale carried emotional
implications for medieval listeners as it does for modern ones, but it is
unlikely that such associations were systematized if they occurred at all. The
use of particular scales and scale degrees to carry emotional content in the
modern sense originated in the Baroque period.

  It should also be noted that the scale with final f was flexible with regard
to the fourth degree, which may be indicated by the presence in both manuscripts of songs using the b-flat only part of the time.

13 But is this an unusual situation? We know from narrative poems and chronicles that throughout the later Middle Ages aristocrats as well as peasants were
fond of dancing, and that clerics as well as courtiers wrote songs for entertainment at festivals. On the subject of clerical dances, see Rokseth, 'Danses cléricales du XIIIe siècle,' *Mélanges 1945 des Publications de la Faculté des Lettres de
Strasbourg*, 106: 93–126. For a contemporary reference on court and popular
dance music, see Rohloff, ed., *Die Quellenhandschriften ... Johannes de Grocheio*,
132–6.

14 See Raby, *A History of Christian-Latin Poetry*, and the sequences and rhymed
offices published in *Analecta hymnica*.

15 For the principles of plainchant composition, see Apel, *Gregorian Chant*.

16 For a survey of the problems, see Van der Werf, *The Chansons of the Troubadours and Trouvères*, and Hughes, *Medieval Music*, items 1160–72.

17 For a detailed account of my transcription practices, see the Preface to the
Edition.

18 I am aware that this assertion raises the question of whether a thirteenth-
century listener would have come to the same conclusion. Unless and until a
previously undiscovered theoretical treatise from that time is found, the question must remain moot. All modern interpretations of trouvère rhythm are
essentially educated guesses; mine results from the assumption that the monophonic song is a text-based genre.

19 In fact, lyric poetry and song were nearly inseparable throughout the medieval period, as is typical of oral cultures. As a result, lyric texts tended to be
formulaic in content. It was the poets of the early Italian Renaissance who
conceived of lyric forms as primarily written texts, creating the concept of
an *Urtext* and divorcing poetry from musical performance. In general,
written forms of poetry are less formulaic and more content-oriented than
sung forms.

20 For a vocabulary of thirteenth-century note and ligature forms, see Apel, *The
Notation of Polyphonic Music*.

21 For a discussion of this phenomenon, see the section on bar-lines on pages 63–5.

22 The phrase is emended in the Järnström and Långfors edition, *Recueil de chansons*, to 'qui trestous nos a.'

23 Edited by Anglès, *Las Cantigas de Santa Maria*, and by Mettmann, *Cantigas de Santa Maria*.

24 Or were they interspersed among secular texts? A modern parallel might be the inclusion of occasional gospel-type songs in concerts of pop, rock, and folk music.

25 These 'rules' are suggestions only, and are based on performers' experience with the acoustical properties of trouvère melodic structures. They are not certifiably authentic but represent probabilities.

Bibliography

Primary Sources

Bern, Stadtbibliothek, Manuscript 389, Manuscript C (microfilm)
Paris, Bibliothèque nationale, Fonds français 847 (Cangé manuscript 65), Manuscript P
– Fonds français 24406 (Chansonnier de La Vallière), Manuscript V
– Nouvelles acquisitions françaises 1050 (Chansonnier de Clairambault), Manuscript X

Selected Secondary Sources

Ahsmann, H.P.J.M. *Le Culte de la sainte Vierge et la littérature française profane du moyen âge.* Utrecht 1933.

Alanus de Insulis (Alain de Lille). *Opera omnia.* Ed. J.P. Migne. *Patrologia Latina,* vol. 210. Paris 1855.

Albertus Magnus. *Opera omnia,* vol. 36. Ed. Auguste and Émile Borgnet. Paris 1898.

Alfonso X. *Cantigas de Santa Maria.* Ed. Walter Mettmann. 3 vols. Coimbra 1959–64.

Analecta hymnica medii aevi. Ed. Guido Dreves and Clemens Blume. 55v. Leipzig 1886–1922.

Anglès, Higini. *Las Cantigas del rey Alfonso el Sabio.* N.p. 1952.

– *Scripta musicologica.* 3 vols. Ed. J. Lopez-Calo. Rome 1975.

Apel, Willi. *Gregorian Chant.* Bloomington, Ind. 1958.

– *The Notation of Polyphonic Music, 900–1600.* 5th ed. Cambridge, Mass. 1953.

Arcangeli-Marenzi, Maria Laura. *Aspetti del tema della Vergine nella Letteratura francese del Medioevo.* Venice 1968.

Arnould, E.J. *Le Manuel des péchés: étude de littérature religieuse anglo-normande.* Paris 1940.

Ashe, Geoffrey. *The Virgin: Mary's Cult and the Re-emergence of the Goddess.* London 1976. Repr. London 1988.

Aubry, Pierre, and Alfred Jeanroy. 'Une chanson provençale(?) à la Vierge.' *Annales du Midi,* 12 (1900): 67–71.

Baisier, Léon. *The Lapidaire Chrétien*. Washington, D.C. 1936.

Baker, Derek, ed. *Religious Motivation: Biographical and Sociological Problems for the Church Historian*. (Studies in Church History, vol. 15.) Oxford 1978.

Bec, Pierre. *La Lyrique française au moyen âge*. Paris 1977.

Beck, Jean, ed. *Le Chansonnier Cangé* (Corpus cantilenarum medii aevi, 2 vols.) Philadelphia, 1927.

– ed. *Le Manuscrit du roi*. (Corpus cantilenarum medii aevi, vol. 2.) Philadelphia 1927.

Bennett, R.F. *The Early Dominicans*. Cambridge 1937.

Berthier, Joachim Joseph, ed. *Beati Humberti de Romanis opera de vita regulari (1265)*. 2v. Rome 1956.

Bezzola, Reto R. *Les Origines et la Formation de la littérature courtoise en Occident (500–1200)*. 5v. Paris 1944–63.

Blakney, Raymond, ed. *Meister Eckhart*. New York 1941.

Boglioni, Pierre, ed. *La Culture populaire au moyen âge*. Montréal 1979.

Bonaventure, St. *Sancti Bonaventura opera omnia*. Ed. A.C. Peltier. Vol. 14. Paris 1868.

Branciforti, Francesco, ed. *Il canzoniere di Lanfranco Cigala*. Florence 1965.

Briffault, Robert. *The Troubadours*. Ed. Lawrence F. Koons. Bloomington, Ind. 1965.

Brooke, Rosalind and Christopher. *Popular religion in the Middle Ages: Western Europe, 1000–1300*. London 1984.

Bynum, Caroline Walker. *Jesus as Mother: Studies in the Spirituality of the High Middle Ages*. Berkeley, Calif. 1982.

Charland, P.T. 'Les auteurs d'*Artes Predicandi* au XIIIᵉ siècle,' in *Études d'histoire littéraire et doctrinale du XIIIᵉ siècle*. Paris 1932: 41–60.

Chaytor, Henry J. *From Script to Print*. Cambridge 1945.

Collins, R.G., and John Wortley. *On the Rise of the Vernacular Literatures in the Middle Ages. Mosaic* VIII, no. 4. University of Manitoba 1975.

Cuesta, Ismael Fernandes de la. *Las cancons dels trobadors*. Tolosa 1979.

Curley, Michael J., ed. *Physiologus*. Austin, Tex. 1979.

Delaruelle, Étienne. *La Piété populaire au moyen âge*. Turin 1975.

Deutschen Arbeitsgemeinschaft für Mariologie, ed. *Maria im Kult*. (Deutsche Archiv für Mariologie, vol. 3.) Essen 1964.

Dragonetti, Roger. *La Technique poétique des trouvères dans la chanson courtoise*. Bruges 1960. Repr. Geneva 1979.

Dronke, Peter. *Medieval Latin and the Rise of European Love-Lyric*. 2 vols. 2nd ed. Oxford 1968.

Du Manoir, Hubert. *Maria: Études sur la Sainte Vierge*. 8 vols. Paris 1949–71.

Duvernoy, Jean, ed. *Le Registre d'inquisition de Jacques Fournier, évêque de Pamiers (1318–1325)*. 3 vols. (Bibliothèque méridionale, sér.2, t. XLI.) Toulouse 1965.

Dygve, H. Petersen. *Trouvères et protecteurs des trouvères dans les cours seigneuriales de France*. Helsinki 1942.

Erickson, Carolly. *The Medieval Vision*. New York 1976.

Falvy, Zoltan. *Mediterranean Culture and Troubadour Music* (Studies in Central and Eastern European Music 1.) Trans. M. Steiner. Budapest 1986.

Faral, Edmond. *Les Jongleurs en France au moyen âge*. Paris 1910.

Fleming, John V. *An Introduction to the Franciscan Literature of the Middle Ages*. Chicago 1977.

Flinn, John. *Le Roman de Renart dans la littérature française et dans les littératures étrangères au moyen âge*. Toronto 1963.

Flutre, Louis-Fernand. *Table des noms propres ... dans les romans du moyen âge*. Poitiers 1962.

Foreville, Raymonde. *Latran I, II, III et Latran IV*. (Histoire des conciles oecuméniques, 6.) Paris 1965.

Frappier, Jean. *La Poésie lyrique en France aux XIIᵉ et XIIIᵉ siècles*. Paris 1963.

Gauchat, Louis. 'Les poésies provençales conservées par des chansonniers français.' *Romania* 22 (1983): 364–404.

Gautier de Coinci. *Les Chansons à la Vierge*. Ed. Jacques Chailley. Paris 1959.

– *Les Miracles de Notre Dame*. Ed. V. Frédéric Koenig. 3 vols. Geneva 1955–66.

Gennrich, Friedrich, ed. *Cantilenae Piae*. (Musikwissenschaftliche Studien-Bibliothek, vol. 24.) Langen bei Frankfurt 1966.

– *Die Kontrafaktur im Liedschaffen des Mittelalters*. (Summa musicae medii aevi, 12.) 1965.

– *Grundriss einer Formenlehre des mittelalterlichen Liedes*. Halle 1932.

Gerbert, Martin. *Scriptores ecclesiastici de musica*, vol. 2. Milan 1784. Repr. 1931.

Gilson, Étienne. *Les Idées et les Lettres*. 2nd ed. Paris 1955.

Greimas, A.J. *Dictionnaire de l'ancien français jusqu'au milieu du XIVᵉ siècle*. 2nd ed. Paris 1968.

Gripkey, Sr Mary Vincentine. *The Blessed Virgin Mary as Mediatrix in the Latin and Old French Legend prior to the Fourteenth Century*. Dissertation. Catholic University of America 1938.

Harrison, Frank Llewellyn. *Music in Medieval Britain*. London 1958.

Hefele, Karl Joseph von. *Histoire des conciles d'après les documents originaux*. Trans. Oden Delarc, vol. 8. Paris 1872.

Hoppin, Richard H. *Medieval Music*. New York 1978.

Hughes, Andrew. *Medieval Music: the Sixth Liberal Art*. (Toronto Medieval Bibliographies, 4.) Toronto 1974. 2nd ed. Toronto 1980.

Isidore of Seville. *Opera omnia*. Ed. J.P. Migne. *Patrologia Latina*, vol. 34, column 82. Paris 1850. 2nd ed. 1878.

Ives, Samuel A., and Hellmut Lehmann-Haupt. *An English 13th century Bestiary*. New York 1942.

Järnström, Edward, and Arthur Långfors, eds. *Recueil de chansons pieuses du XIIIᵉ siècle*. 2 vols. Helsinki 1910–27.

Jeanroy, Alfred. *Bibliographie sommaire des chansonniers français du moyen âge*. Paris 1918.

– *Poésie lyrique des troubadours*. 2 vols. Paris 1934.

Jeffrey, David. *The Early English Lyric & Franciscan Spirituality*. Lincoln, Neb. 1975.

Koran. Trans. J.M. Rodwell. New York 1918.

Labarge, Margaret Wade. *Saint Louis: The Life of Louis IX of France*. London 1968.

Leclercq, J., ed. *Sancti Bernardi Opera*, vol. 4: *Sermones*. Rome 1966.

Lemay, Richard. 'À propos de l'origine arabe de l'art des troubadours.' *Annales, Économies, Sociétés, Civilisations*, 21 (1966): 990–1011.

Leroquais, Victor. *Les Livres d'Heures manuscrits de la Bibliothèque nationale*. Paris 1927.

Le Vot, Gérard. 'Notation, mesure et rythme dans la "canso" troubadouresque.' *Cahiers de civilisation médiévale*, 25 (1982): 205–17.

Liuzzi, F. *La lauda e i primordi della melodia italiana*. 2 vols. Rome 1935.

Lommatzch, Erhard, ed. *Tobler-Lommatsch Altfranzösisches Wörterbuch*. 9 vols. Berlin 1925.

Lord, Albert B. *The Singer of Tales*. Cambridge, Mass. 1960.

McGee, Timothy J., ed. *Singing Early Music: The Pronunciation of European Languages in the Late Middle Ages and Renaissance*. Bloomington, Ind. 1996.

Mâle, Émile. *Art religieux du XIIIe siècle en France*. Paris 1931.

Manselli, Raoul. *La Religion populaire au moyen âge: problèmes de méthode et d'histoire*. Montréal 1975.

Marrou, Henri-Irenée. *Les Troubadours*. 2nd ed. Paris 1971.

Menendez-Pidal, Ramon. *Poesia juglaresca y juglares*. Madrid 1924.

Mirk, John. *Instructions for Parish Priests*. Ed. Edward Peacock. New York 1969.

Mushacke, W., ed. *Altprovenzalische Marienklage des XIII Jahrhunderts*. (Romanische Bibliothek, vol. 3.) Halle 1890.

Mussafia, Adolfo. *Studien zu den mittelalterlichen Marienlegenden*. Vienna 1886–98.

New Oxford History of Music. Vol. 2. Ed. Anselm Hughes. London 1955.

Nicholas of Lyra. *Biblia sacra cum glossa ordinaria*. 5 vols. Paris 1590.

Nova Vulgata Bibliorum sacrorum editio. Vatican 1979.

Palmer, Paul F. *Mary in the Documents of the Church*. Westminster, Md 1952.

Paris, Matthew. *Chronica majora*. Ed. H.R. Luard. London 1872–83.

Parrish, Carl. *The Notation of Medieval Music*. New York 1957.

Pope, Mildred. *From Latin to Modern French*. Manchester 1934. Repr. 1966.

Privat, Édouard, gen. ed. *La Religion populaire en Languedoc*. (Cahiers de Fanjeaux, 11.) Toulouse 1976.

Raby, Frederick James Edward. *A History of Christian-Latin Poetry from the Beginnings to the Close of the Middle Ages*. 2nd ed. Oxford 1953.

Rakel, Hans-Herbert. *Die Musikalische Erscheinungsform der Trouvèrepoesie*. Bern 1977.

Randall, Richard H. *Cloisters Bestiary*. New York 1960.

– *A Metrical Bestiary*. London 1928.

Raynaud, Gaston. *Bibliographie des chansonniers français des XIIIe et XIVe siècles*. Paris 1884.

Rigg, A.G. ed. *The Poems of Walter of Wimborne*. Toronto 1978.

Riquer, Martin de. *Los trovadores: Historia literaria y textos*. 3 vols. Barcelona 1975.

Rohloff, Ernst, ed. *Die Quellenhandschriften zum Musiktraktat des Johannes de Grocheio*. Leipzig 1972.

Rokseth, Yvonne. 'Danses cléricales du XIIIᵉ siècle.' *Mélanges 1945 des Publications de la Faculté des Lettres de Strasbourg*, 106: 93–126.

St Jacques, Raymond, ed. *The Virgin Mary in Art, Thought, and Letters in the Middle Ages and the Renaissance*. Ottawa 1975.

Salmen, Walter. *Die fahrende Musiker im europäischen Mittelalter*. Kassel 1960.

Salzer, Anselm. *Die Sinnbilder und Beiworte Mariens in der deutschen Literatur und lateinischen Hymnenpoesie des Mittelalters*. Darmstadt 1967.

Say, William. *Liber regie capelle*. Ed. Walter Ullman. London 1961.

Schutz, Richard Allen. *The Unedited Poems of Codex 389 of the Municipal Library of Berne, Switzerland*. Dissertation. Indiana University 1977.

Schwan, Eduard. *Die altfranzösische Liederhandschriften*. Berlin 1886.

Seagrave, Barbara Garvey, and Wesley Thomas. *The Songs of the Minnesingers*. Urbana, Ill. 1966.

Segre, Cesare. *'Li Bestiaires d'amours' di maistre Richart de Fornival e 'Li Response de Bestiaire.'* Documenti di Filologia 2.) Milan 1962.

Shah, Idries. *Tales of the Dervishes*. London 1967.

Smalley, Beryl. *The Study of the Bible in the Middle Ages*. Oxford 1941. 2nd ed. New York 1952.

Spanke, Hans, ed. *G. Raynauds Bibliographie des altfranzösischen Liedes*. 2nd ed. Leiden 1955.

Streng-Renkonen, Walter. *Les Estampies françaises*. Paris 1930.

Studer, Paul, and Joan Evans. *Anglo-Norman Lapidaries*. Paris 1924.

Taylor, Robert A. *La Littérature occitane du moyen âge*. (Toronto Medieval Bibliographies, 7.) Toronto 1977.

Tischler, Hans. 'The Performance of Medieval Songs.' *Revue belge de musicologie*, 43 (1989): 225–42.

– and Samuel Rosenberg. *Chanter m'estuet: Songs of the Trouvères*. Bloomington, Ind. 1981.

Van der Werf, Hendrik. *The Chansons of the Troubadours and Trouvères*. Utrecht 1972.

– 'Deklamatorischer Rhythmus in den Chansons der Trouvères.' *Die Musikforschung*, 19 (1966): 122–44.

– 'The Trouvère Chansons as Creations of a Notationless Culture.' *Current Musicology*, 1 (1965): 61–8.

– ed. *Trouvères-Melodien*. (Monumenta Monodica Medii Aevi, 11, 12.) Kassel 1977.

Wright, L.M. 'Misconceptions concerning the Troubadours, Trouvères and Minstrels.' *Music and Letters*, 48 (1967): 35–9.

Yates, Frances A. *The Art of Memory*. London 1966.

Yedlicka, Leo Charles. *Expressions of the Linguistic Area of Repentance and Remorse in Old French*. Dissertation. Catholic University of America 1945.

Zumthor, Paul. *Essai de poétique médiévale*. Paris 1972.

THE SONGS

Introduction to the Edition

Editorial Policy

This work is not a definitive critical edition. Its contents are drawn from only two sources, which are dissimilar; one, manuscript X, is apparently a presentation copy, the other, manuscript V, is a somewhat puzzling collection compiled as a miscellany and produced for unknown purposes. As well, variant readings in texts and music are provided in this edition only selectively; this policy deserves – indeed requires – some explanation.

No edition of music is complete within itself. It requires the efforts of a musician, at whatever level of skill, to bring its contents out into the air and make them audible, if only to the mind's ear. This edition is intended first and foremost for those readers who might be tempted to perform, or at least to read through, the music of the songs. For this reason, enough critical apparatus has been provided to satisfy the reasonably curious and to provide a basis for further investigation by the extremely curious. This edition does not duplicate or extend philological studies which can be found and followed elsewhere.[1] Its primary purpose is to make the music accessible – for the first time in the great majority of instances.

My reasons for limiting the edition to the two source manuscripts are explained in the Preface and can be further summarized here. Since there is no reliable way to determine a base text or standard version for the musical content of the songs, it seems pointless to establish a critical version of each text. To do so would in most cases either substitute one reading for another of equal plausibility, or upset the delicate accord of text with music so important to the genre of lyric song. The first and most obvious objection to this *laissez-faire* policy is likely to be voiced by readers of manuscript V: how can a manuscript that appears to have been so carelessly copied be taken as a definitive source? From the point of view of a modern editor, this is a legitimate question. What must be considered, however, is the fact that someone – a person thoroughly literate in music as well as French – used this manuscript at the time it was written. We do not know how it was used, how often, or whether the errors were given any notice, but the fact remains that it, like every other *chansonnier* of the period, is a document with its own logic and integrity. Each manuscript in this edition was written with much time and effort by one or more persons who knew by experience far more about its contents than we are ever likely to deduce. To alter their intentions by standardizing spellings, substituting words, changing melodic figures, or other editorial 'corrections' would seem to be both unfaithful and unnecessary. None the less, in places where the sense or metre of the text is obviously garbled by the omission of a word or words, passages from another source that allow the omitted words to be restored have been provided whenever possible. Additional stanzas found in other sources have also been supplied, since they will give the performer a wider range of options and the scholar a clearer sense of the text's story line.

Editorial Decisions

For the reasons stated above, as well as those mentioned within the discussions on form and style in earlier chapters, a number of editorial decisions have been applied.

Spelling: Each word appears as it does in the source manuscript. Abbreviations and numerals in the texts have been expanded according to the internal rules of each manuscript.

Punctuation: The comma, colon, and semicolon have been added when necessary to clarify the sense of a passage for the reader or its phrasing for the singer.

Accents: Thirteenth-century French made very sparing use of diacritical marks. Their original purpose was to clarify accentuation and pronunciation of the words in a text intended for reading aloud or singing, and their modern uses were developed much later. In this edition, the *accent aigu*, *tréma*, and *cédille* have been added only for clarification of grammatical sense and pronunciation. Because of the interchangeable use of *-ez* and *-es* endings for second-person plural verbs in the manuscripts, the *accent aigu* has been added to the latter group in order to indicate their proper accentuation for the singer. This policy preserves the spelling of the texts in their original forms.

Emendations: When a text is obviously in error and another source exists, corrections are provided in brackets. When a text is obviously in error and no other source exists, emendations are suggested in the footnotes. These are the only emendations provided.

Manuscript variants: These are given in footnotes only when the alternative version presents a reading equal (e.g., synonymous) or superior (e.g., more clear in sense) to the source manuscript. When additional stanzas for a song appear in another manuscript, these have been included in appendix B. Omissions of a single-syllable 'filler word' (e.g., *si*, *tres*, or *tel*) within a line, producing a metric shift, are common; these have not been regarded as errors but as legitimate metric variants (see chapter 3) which need no correction.

Music: Modern transcriptions are provided for the convenience of readers and performers who are not specialists in the period and its notation. Clefs have been modernized from the original c-clefs. Notation has been transcribed into rhythmicized versions.[2] These versions are not necessarily the only possibilities for transcription. They are intended to represent musically plausible choices, taking into account text accentuation, syllabification, phrasing as indicated by rhyme scheme and syntax, melodic patterning, ornamentation, cadential figures, and such subjective variables as 'musicality' and 'singer's intuition.' My decisions have been guided, whenever possible, by the declamation of the texts and the contours of the melodies, rather than by single-minded adherence to any established school of rhythmic interpretation. I do not believe that the notation of either manuscript gives unequivocal support to a single method of interpretation, and recent hypotheses suggest that flexibility in this matter, as in that of 'legitimacy' of variants, is advisable.[3] The ultimate justification for rhythmic transcriptions is, of course, their accessibility to modern performers. Readers with expertise in medieval notation will undoubtedly want to develop their own versions from the diplomatic transcriptions included along with the modern renditions. In a few cases, alternative transcriptions have been provided for the same song in order to demonstrate equally plausible artistic decisions (see appendix C). Since the original notation gives clues to phrasing and accentuation, it has also been included as a guide to the performer who wishes to convey the subtleties inherent in the melodic lines and as a research tool for the study of notational patterns in this repertoire.

Philology: Technical points of philology and rhetoric are beyond the stated province of this study and have not been included.

The text of each song is followed by a brief technical description, which includes the following categories.

Source: This section gives manuscript sources for each song. In addition, the 'Raynaud number' (R.)[4] is given in order to facilitate the work of literary scholars.

Text category: These are Courtly (Co), Laudatory (La), Catechetic (Ca), Political (Pl) or Personal (Pr), as described in chapter 3.

Music category: Identified as Chanson-style (Ch), Through-composed (Th), Round-chanson (Rn), or Serpentine (Se), as described in chapter 4.

Rhyme scheme: The pattern of rhymes and the number of syllables are given for each line of a stanza.

Musical scheme: A map of the melodic structure is provided for the song.

Editions: Earlier collected editions in which the songs appear, primarily those by Järnström and Långfors[5] and by Gennrich,[6] are listed.

Contrafacta: These are given by the number in the Raynaud-Spanke system.[7] The contrafacta are not necessarily literal models, but songs with similar metric or musical structure which may or may not have been directly related to the songs in this edition. Thus, the number of songs actually modelled on earlier sources may be much smaller than the number of contrafacta would suggest.

Remarks: This section is included only when there is something unusual to be noticed or explained.

Notes (to diplomatic transcriptions of the music): Where notation changes in the manuscript between the first and second occurrences of a repeated musical phrase, I have given the alternative forms in footnotes labelled 's. occ.' (second occurrence).

Translations: The translations of the texts are my own, and I have attempted to follow a middle ground between literal and poetic renditions. Where the syntax of the Old French would produce awkwardness in a literal translation, the phrasing in English has been smoothed out. Where an English idiom exists that renders the sense of an Old French idiom which would otherwise be incomprehensible, it has been used. In other circumstances, I have attempted to follow the original as closely as possible. In some cases a single word in the Old French has been given different English equivalents in different circumstances. An example is *clarté*, which is given as 'clarity' in no. 35, stanza 2 and as 'light' in no. 36, stanza 1. In other cases, a single word has been given two equivalents when it has a secondary meaning that amplifies or explicates the primary one. An example is *mastin* (no. 36, stanza 4), which has the meanings 'large dog' and 'servile.' Thus I have rendered it in context as 'servile dogs.'

Footnotes: These present manuscript variants to both text and music when necessary. The variants in musical notation that occur between the first and second statements of a melody in abab ... structure have been included in the notes to the songs in order to illustrate problems of rhythmic reconstruction; see chapter 4 for a discussion of their significance.

Notes

1 For more complete textual apparatus, see the text edition, *Recueil de chansons*, by Järnström and Långfors.
2 For a discussion of the placement of modern barlines, see chapter 4.
3 For a comparable approach, see Gérard Le Vot, 'Notation, mesure et rhythme dans la "canso" troubadouresque,' *Cahiers de civilisation médiévale*, 25 (1982), 205–17. Le Vot concludes that some troubadour verse forms were performed in metric rhythm while others were declaimed in 'free' (non-metric) phrases. It seems reasonable to apply the same assumption to the trouvère material.
4 Raynaud numbers are taken from the original catalogue of trouvère songs compiled by Gustave Raynaud in 1884 and still in use today. See Raynaud, *Bibliographie des chansonniers français*.
5 Järnström and Långfors, eds., *Recueil de chansons*.
6 Gennrich, ed., *Cantilenae Piae*.
7 Spanke, ed., *G. Raynauds Bibliographie des altfranzösischen Liedes*.

Songs

THE DEVOTIONAL SONGS OF MANUSCRIPTS X AND V

1 Virge des ciels clere et pure

1 Virge des ciels clere et pure
   dont Dex se vout espanir
   et nestre selonc nature
   sanz virginité maumir,
   mout desir
   vostre amor a deservir,
   car d'autre amie n'ai cure
   que grant joie m'asseüre
   de vos amer et servir.
   Por ce me covient guerpir
   la mauvaise voie oscure
   et touz les pechiés haïr
   qui font joie[1] faillir.

2 Roïne de grant mesure,
   por Dieu doint vos souvenir
   de ma lasse creature
   qui sanz vos ne puet garir,
   car morir
   doi, et en terre porir.
   Las, et ma mort ert si dure
   se de pechié et d'ordure
   ne puis m'ame resclarcir;
   mes qui sert sans repentir
   par raïson et par dure
   le fait pitiés esjoïr
   et a bone fin venir.

3 Dame des ciels coronnée,
   dolens et plorans vos di
   qu'en vie desordenée
   ai mon las cors envielli.
   Si vos pri,
   se trop tart vos cri merci
   que penitence doublée
   me soit enjointe et donnée
   tant que j'aie deservi
   que cil qui de vos nasqui
   l'ait en pitié regardée,
   si que li angre esbaudi
   soient de m'ame sesi.

4 Virge de gloire honorée
   ou tant bien sont aconpli,
   fontaine si savorée
   que tuit en sont repleni,
   vostre ami
   et pechëor autresi
   que Dex a grace donée,
   que leur ame en a lavée
   en lermes plaines de cri:
   ne metez, dame, en oubli
   ma volenté esplorée
   si qu'a m'ame aient failli
   et par vos li anemi.

5 Chançon, va moi sanz atendre
   a la rose de jovent
   qui puet et doner et prendre
   toute joie a son talent:
   di briement
   ...[2]
   qu'ailleurs ne puis mesentendre
   ainz me faut s'amor desfendre
   touz maus et les biens m'aprent.
   Por ce li proi doucement
   qu'ele soit a m'ame rendre,
   car mes cuers grant doleur sent,
   tant redout mon jugement.

Sources: BN, Manuscript X, ff. 257v–8;
   R. 2112
Text category: Pr
Music category: Rn
Rhyme scheme: 8a 7b 8a 7b 3b 7b 8a 8a 7b
   7b 8a 7b 7b
Musical scheme: a b a b' c d b" e e' f b''' e" e'
Editions: Järnström and Långfors, 2: 112;
   Gennrich, no. 1
Contrafacta: R. 2107 (Raoul de Soissons);
   R. 2091; *O constancie dignitas* (Adam de la
   Bassée), in *Analecta hymnica*, 48, no. 313

1 Emended by Järnström and Långfors to
   'qui font a joie.'
2 The line is missing in the manuscript.

1 Shining and pure virgin of the heavens

1 Shining and pure virgin of the heavens,
   in whom God wished to expand
      himself
   and be born according to nature
      without harming your virginity,
   I greatly desire to merit your love, for I
      care for no other,
   and to love and serve you will bring
      me great joy.
   For this reason, it suits me to renounce
      the evil dark path
   and hate all sins that cause deprivation
      of happiness.

2 Queen of great worth,
   for God's sake may you remember my
      weak nature
   which cannot be healed without you,
   for I must die and perish on this earth.
   Alas, my death will be hard if I cannot
      clear my soul of sin and filth;
   but he who serves without hesitation,
      through reason and [rectitude],
   evokes pity and comes to a good end.

3 Crowned lady of the heavens, I tell
      you, grieving and weeping,
   that my weak body has grown old in
      disordered living.
   Thus I pray you, if I call too late for
      pity,
   that you assign me doubled penance,
      as I have deserved,
   so that he who was born of you might
      look mercifully on it
   and the joyous angels be satisfied with
      my soul.

4 Glorious honoured virgin
   in whom such good was accomplished,

fountain so flavoured that all are
   refreshed there,
both your friends and also sinners
   whom God has graced,
who have washed their souls therein
   with tears and pleading:
Lady, do not cast my plangent wish
   into oblivion,
so that, through you, my soul may not
   be cheated,
   and the enemy may.

5 Song, go for me without delay to the
      rose of youth
   who is able both to give and take all joy
      at her desire.
   Say briefly ...
   so that nowhere can I misunderstand:
   Thus will it be if her love defends me
      from all evils
   and teaches me all goodness.
   For this I pray softly, that she be
      restored to my soul,
   for my heart feels great pain, so much
      do I fear the judgment that will be
      made of me.

1 Virge des ciels clere et pure

Virge des ciels clere et pure · dont dex se vout espanir
et nestre se — lonc na·tu·re · sanz vir-gi — ni — té maumir

mout desir · vostre amor a deservir · car d'autre amie n'ai cu-re

que grant joi-e m'asse-ü-re · de vos a-mer et ser-vir

por ce me covient guerpir · la mauvaise voie oscure

et touz les pechiés ha-ïr · qui font a joi-e faillir.

1 S. occ.: ♩
2 S. occ.: ♪

Vir - ge des ciels   cler - e_et   pu - re   dont Dex se vout
et nes - tre se - lonc   na - tu - re   sanz vir - gi - ni -

1.
es - pa - nir

2.
té   mau - mir,   mout de - sir

vost - re_a - mor a   de - ser - vir   car d'au - tre_a - mi - e n'ai   cu - re

que grant joi - e   m'as - se - ü - re   de   vos   a - mer

et   ser - vir.   Por ce me co - vient guer - pir

la   mau - vai - se   voi - e_o - scu - re   et   touz   les   pe -

chiés ha - ïr   qui   font   a   joi - e   fail - lir.

2 Mout sera cil bien norris

1 Mout sera cil bien norris
   et en bon couvent,
   et mout sera seignoris
   tres bien et souvent,
   qui veut reclamer
   la mere Dieu, et amer
   tout son jouvent;
   et Dieu le nos a bien en couvent:
   Que cil a s'ame garie
   qui sert la virge Marie.

2 De la virge ai tant apris
   que mout grant pris a;
   tout par tout doit avoir pris
   que Dex la prisa
   tant qu'o soi la prist,
   et Dex par ice m'aprist
   le sien grant pris.
   Puis que Diex la prise, je la pris:
   Que cil a s'ame garie
   qui sert la virge Marie.

3 En li sont tuit bon confort,
   mout bon confort a:
   nus ne set dire con fort
   touz nos conforta.
   Qui veut fortement
   avoir son confortement,
   tot son effors
   por li bien servir doit metre fors:
   Que cil a s'ame garie
   qui sert la virge Marie.

4 C'est cele qui a droit port
   nos fist raporter;
   mis nos a en grant deport
   por nos deporter.
   Mout grant deport a
   la dame qui Dex porta:
   ses portemens a rendu a touz
      deportemens.

Que cil a s'ame garie
qui sert la virge Marie.

5 Quant li mons fu desconfiz
   et mors et desfés,
   Dex nasqui de li con filz
   qui nos a refés.
   Ensi faitement
   par son saint afaitement
   touz nos mesfés
   nos a deschargiés et nos griés fez:
   Que cil a s'ame garie
   qui sert la virge Marie.

Sources: BN, Manuscript X, ff. 258r–v;
   Manuscript P, f. 197; R. 1570
Text category: La
Music category: Ch
Rhyme scheme: 7a 5b 7a 5b 5c 7c 4b 9b : 8d
   8d
Musical scheme: a b$_x$ a b$_x$ c d e f$_x$ g h
Editions: Järnström and Långfors, 2: 115;
   Gennrich, no. 2
Contrafactum: R.1573 (Robert de la Pierre
   or Guillebert de Bernevile)

2 He who will be well fed

1 He who calls upon the mother of God
  and loves her throughout his youth
  will be well fed and in good estate, and
    treated as well as a lord,
  for God keeps us all in good estate.
  For he who serves the Virgin Mary has
    protected his own soul.

2 I have learned much about this virgin
    of such great worth.
  She ought to be prized above all things,
  for God so prized her that he took her
    for his own,
  and God by this has taught me her
    great value.
  Because God so prized her, so will I:
  For he who serves the Virgin Mary has
    protected his own soul.

3 In her are all good comforts, she has
    many;
  none can tell how greatly she comforts
    all of us.
  He who strongly wishes to have her
    comfort must put all his effort
  into serving her well.
  For he who serves the Virgin Mary has
    protected his own soul.

4 It is she who has brought us to a safe
    haven;
  she has put us in a state of joy in order
    to gladden us.
  The lady who bore God has great
    delight:
  her actions have brought joy to all.
  For he who serves the Virgin Mary has
    protected his own soul.

5 When the world was discomforted,
    and dead, and at an end,

God was born to her as a son who
  restored us.
Thus, in this manner, by his blessed
  arrangement,
he has relieved us of all our misdeeds
  and heavy burdens.
For he who serves the Virgin Mary has
  protected his own soul.

2 Mout sera cil bien norris

Mout sera cil bien norris · et en bon cou-vent
et mout sera seig-no-ris · tres bien et sou-vent

qui veut reclamer · la mere dieu et a-mer

tout son jouvent, et dieu le nos a bien en couvent:

Que cil a s'ame gari-e · qui sert la virge Mari-e.

1 S. occ.: ♩

Mout se - ra cil bien nor - ris et en bon cou - vent,
et mout se - ra seig - no - ris tres bien et sou - vent,

qui veut re - cla - mer la me - re Dieu, et a - mer tout

son jou - vent; et Dieu le nos a bien en cou - vent:

Que cil a s'a - me ga - ri - e qui sert la vir - ge Ma - ri - e.

3 De la tres douce Marie

1 De la tres douce Marie vueill chanter
qui porta le sauvëor por enchanter
celui qui nuït et jor nos veut tenter
por faire son devis.
Cil doit bien estre esbaudis
qui sert touz dis
en fes et diz
la flor[1] de paradis.

2 Qui la tres douce Marie servira
et qui de bon cuer merci li proiera,
ja li anemis seur lui pooir n'avra,
de ce sui je touz fis.
Cil doit bien estre esbaudis
qui sert touz dis
en fes et diz
la flor de paradis.

3 Rose, violete, plaine de deport,
a vos sont tuit mi solas et mi deport:
la rive es aus pechëors et le droit port,
roïne, flor de lis.
Cil doit bien estre esbaudis
qui sert touz dis
en fes et diz
la flor de paradis.

4 [L]a[2] char Dieu, qui fu enclose en vos
     sains flans
et qui en la crois soufri si grans ahans,[3]
si fu feru el costé que li clers sans
corut aval son piz.
Cil doit bien estre esbaudis
qui sert touz dis
en fes et diz
la flor de paradis.

5 Or prions la mere Dieu tuit hautement
qu'ele deprit son chier[4] fiz prochenne-
     ment
qu'allons tuit en paradis comunaument
au grant jor dou juïs.

Cil doit bien estre esbaudis
qui sert touz dis
en fes et diz
la flor de paradis.

Sources: BN, Manuscript X, ff. 258v–9;
    Manuscript P, f. 197; R. 835
Text category: La
Music category: Rn
Rhyme scheme: 11a 11a 11a 6b: 7b 4b 4b 6b
Musical scheme: a b a b   c d e c f f e
Edition: Gennrich, no. 3
Contrafactum: R. 1362 (Richart de Semilli)

1 The line is 'li rois de paradis' in manu-
    script P.
2 'Fa' in manuscript X
3 'Enhans' in manuscript P
4 'Son tres chier' in manuscript P

3 Of the most sweet Mary

1 I wish to sing of the most sweet Mary,
    who bore the Saviour
to cast a spell upon the one who, night
    and day, wishes to tempt us
in order to do his will.
He ought to be strong and joyful, who all
    his days, in deed and word,
serves the flower of paradise.

2 He who serves sweet Mary, and prays
    for her mercy with good heart,
the enemy will never have power over
    him, of this I am confident.
He ought to be strong and joyful, who all
    his days, in deed and word,
serves the flower of paradise.

3 Rose, violet, full of delight, in you are
    all my solace and my joy:
you are a river bank for sinners to rest
    on, and a true haven,
queen, flower of the lily.
He ought to be strong and joyful, who all
    his days, in deed and word,
serves the flower of paradise.

4 The flesh of God, which was enclosed
    in your holy flanks,
and which suffered on the cross such
    great pain,
was struck so in the side that the clear
    blood ran down his breast.
He ought to be strong and joyful, who all
    his days, in deed and word,
serves the flower of paradise.

5 Now let us all pray to the mother of
    God aloud,
that she pray her dear son immedi-
    ately,
that we might all go to paradise
    together
on the great Day of Judgment.
He ought to be strong and joyful, who all
    his days, in deed and word,
serves the flower of paradise.

3 De la tres douce Marie

de la tres douce Mari-e vueill chanter
qui por-ta le sau-véor por en—chanter

celui qui nu-it et jor nos veut tenter por faire son devis.

Cil doit bien estre esbaudis· qui sert touz dis·en fes et diz·

la flor de pa-ra-dis.

1 S. occ.: ♩

De la tres dou - ce Ma - ri - e   vueill chan - ter   ce - lui qui nu -
qui por - ta le   sau - vĕ - or   por   en - chan - ter

ït   et jor nos   veut ten - ter por fai - re   son   de - vis.   Cil doit bien est -

re_es bau - dis qui   sert touz dis en   fes et diz la flor de   pa - ra - dis.

4 De la flor de paradis

1 De la flor de paradis
   voudrai dire une chançon,
   car de li doivent touz diz
   venir tuit li novel son.
   Nus ne puet estre esbaudiz
   ne ne puet avoir raïson
   qui ne sert en fes et en diz
   la dame sanz traïson
   et sanz nisun escondiz,
   car je m'esmerveilleroie
   coment porroie avoir joie
   nule ame se par li non.

2 Ele est la rose et le lis,
   le secors que nos avons,
   ce est trestouz li delis
   et li bien que nos savon.
   Par li est mout enbelis
   paradis que nos ravon.
   Ja mes n'iert par li faillis:
   se faisons ce que devon,
   nus de nos n'iert maubaillis.
   C'est cele, se Dieu me voie,
   qui touz pechëor ravoie
   quant il li quierent pardon.

3 Nos somes tout rachaté
   et tout honoré par li,
   qui estions mort et maté,
   destruit et enseveli.
   Adans avoit baraté
   tot le monde et maubailli:
   la dame, par sa biauté,
   tout le monde renbeli
   qui estoit hors de clarté
   au main et a la vesprée,
   et la roïne honorée
   nos aida par sa merci.

4 Mere Dieu, en enferté
   fûmes par Eve averti:
   or somes en grant chierté,

dame, par vos converti.
   Par vos avons aperté
   qui estïons amorti;
   fors somes de povreté,
   douce mere Dieu, parti.
   Ce sai je bien par verté
   que par vos nos ert donée
   grant joie et abandonée
   dont estïons departi.

5 Douce lune, douz solaus,
   dame plaine de biauté,
   mere Dieu especiaus
   plaine de grant loiauté,
   cil qui vers vos est loiaus
   et féaus sans cruauté
   n'i sentira james maus,
   ainz sera plains de santé
   sus en paradis touz saus
   en joie qui touz dis dure:
   cil avra male aventure
   qui envers vos sera faus.

Source: BN, Manuscript X, f. 259; R. 1581
Text category: Co
Music category: Ch
Rhyme scheme: 7a 7b 7a 7b 7a 7b 7a 7b 7a 8c
   8c 7b
Musical scheme: a b a b c d e f g h h i
Editions: Järnström and Långfors, 2: 117;
   Gennrich 4
Contrafactum: R. 1647 (Jaque de Cysoing)

4 Of the flower of paradise

1 I wish to present a song of the flower of
   paradise,
   for always from her should all new
   sounds come.
   No one can be happy, nor in the right,
   if he does not serve this lady in deed
   and word,
   without falseness and without any
   reservation,
   for I would be amazed if any soul
   could come to joy if not through her.

2 She is the rose and the lily, the help that
   we have,
   she is all the delights and the goodness
   we know.
   By her is greatly beautified the
   paradise which is ours.
   Never will anyone be disappointed by
   her:
   if we do what is expected of us, no one
   among us will be mistreated.
   It is she, as God helps me, who
   snatches up all sinners when they
   seek her pardon.

3 We, who would have been dead and
   vanquished, destroyed and
   entombed,
   were all ransomed and dignified by
   her.
   Adam had deceived everyone and
   been a poor guardian:
   the lady, by her beauty, restored the
   world to beauty and goodness
   when it had been far from such clarity
   both morning and evening;
   and the honoured queen aided us
   through her mercy.

4 Mother of God, we had been in a state
   of infirmity, turned that way by Eve:
   now we are well cared for, lady, turned
   around by you.
   Through you, we who would have
   been entombed have been set free:
   sweet mother of God, we have been
   severed from poverty.
   I know this well and truly, that by you
   we have been given great joy and
   freedom,
   from which we would otherwise have
   been excluded.

5 Gentle moon, sweet sun, beautiful
   lady,
   lovely mother of God full of great
   loyalty,
   he who is loyal to you and faithful,
   without cruelty, will never feel
   misery,
   for he will be in full health, safe up in
   paradise,
   in the joy that lasts forever;
   but he who is false to you will have a
   bad end.

4 De la flor de paradis

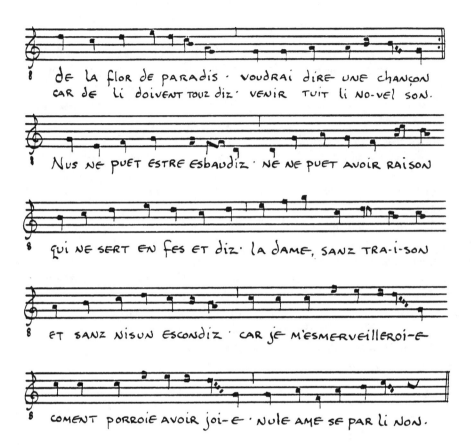

de la flor de paradis · voudrai dire une chançon
car de li doivent touz diz · venir tuit li no-vel son.

Nus ne puet estre esbaudiz · ne ne puet avoir raison

qui ne sert en fes et diz · la dame, sanz tra-i-son

et sanz nisun escondiz · car je m'esmerveilleroi-e

coment porroie avoir joi-e · nule ame se par li non.

De la flor de pa - ra - dis   vou - drai di - re_u - ne   chan - çon,
car de li doi - vent touz diz   ve - nir tuit li   no - vel   son.

Nus ne puet es - tre_es - bau - diz   ne ne puet a - voir raï - son

qui ne sert en   fes et diz   la da - me sanz tra - ï - son   et sanz ni - sun

es - con - diz,   car je m'es - mer - veil - ler - oi - e   co - ment por - roi -

e_a - voir   joi - e   nu - le_a - me   se   par li   non.

5 Mainte chançon ai fait de grant ordure

1 Mainte chançon ai fait de grant
      ordure,
   mes, se Dieu plaist, jamés n'en avrai
      cure:
   en moi a petit eü
   bien et sens et mesure.
   Or me tieng a deceü
   quant si lonc tens me dure.
   Bien ai mon cuer esmeü,
   car por chanter l'ai meü
   de la roïne pure
   par qui somes esleü
   en grant joie, et receü
   et fors de grant ardure.
   C'est la douce mere Dieu
   qui de dolor nos cure:
   rendu nos a le bon lieu
   ou joie toz jors dure.

2 Mout fu Marie et preciouse et bele,
   certes mout fu fine et nete pucele.
   L'angre li fu envoiés
   qui li dist la novele
   que Dex seroit alaitiés
   dou lait de sa mamele.
   Ne fu mie desvoiés
   l'angre, mes bien avoiés
   qui li dist 'Damoisele,
   ave Marie, or m'oïëz:
   Dex c'est a vos avoiés,
   car mere vos apele.'
   Marie a ses euz baissiés
   quant entent la novele,
   et puis les a rehauciés,
   saint Gabriel apele:

3 'Amis, di moi coment enfanteroie
   ne coment fruit en mes flans porteroie
   quant nul home ne conois
   ne nul n'en prenderoie?

Mout sembleroit grant ennuis
se sanz home engendroie!'
'Douce Marie, entent moi:
tu porteras Dieu neuf mois,
ne pas ne t'en esfroie.'
'Amis, quant vos en iroiz
a Dieu, de par moi dirois
que je sui toute soie:
de moi face li douz rois
ses voloirs, je l'otroie.
S'ancele sui, car c'est drois
et si en ai grant joie.'

Sources: BN, Manuscript X, ff. 259v–60r;
   R. 2111
Text category: Ca
Music category: Se
Rhyme scheme: 11a 11a 7b 7a 7b 7a 7b 7b 7a
   7b 7b 7a 7b 7a 7b 7a
Musical scheme: $a_x a_x$ b c b c_x d d c'_x d d c'_x b
   c b c_x
Editions: Järnström and Långfors, 2: 119;
   Gennrich, no. 5
Contrafactum: R. 987 (Moniot de Paris)

5 I have made many a song from the worst filth

1 I have made many a song from the
   worst filth,
  but – God be pleased! – I will never
   care any more for that:
  there has been very little good or sense
   or moderation in me.
  Now I recognize myself as one
   deceived, since it lasted such a long
   time.
  Well have I changed my heart: for I
   have moved it to singing
  of the pure queen by whom we are
   chosen in joy, and received,
  and kept far from the great burning.
  She is the sweet mother of God, who
   cures us of pain:
  she has brought us to the good place
   where joy lasts forever.

2 Mary was most precious and lovely,
  she was surely a fine and pure young
   maid.
  The angel was sent to her, who told her
   the news
  that God would be nursed from the
   milk of her breast.
  He was not led astray, this angel, but
   was well guided,
  when he said to her
  'Lady: hail, Mary, hear me now:
  God is sent to you, for he calls you
   mother.'
  Mary lowered her eyes when she heard
   the news,
  then raised them again and said to holy
   Gabriel:

3 'My friend, tell me how I am supposed
   to give birth,
  and how carry fruit between my flanks,

when I have known no man and will
   take none for that purpose?
  It would seem a great embarrassment if
   I were to conceive without a man!'
  'Gentle Mary, listen to me:
  you will carry God for nine months, do
   not be frightened.'
  'Friend, when you go to God, tell him
   from me that I am all his:
  through me will the sweet king carry
   out his wish, I consent to it.
  I am his handmaid, for it is right, and I
   have great joy in it.'

5 Mainte chançon ai fait de grant ordure

1 S. occ.: ⸜
2 S. occ.: ⸜
3 S. occ.: ▪
4 First occ.: ◆
5 S. occ.: ⸜
6 S. occ.: ▪

Main - te chan - çon   ai   fait de grant or - du - re,
mes,   se Dieu plaist, ja   més n'en a - vrai   cu - re:

en moi a   pe - tit e - ü   bien et   sens   et me -
Or   me tieng a   de - ce - ü   quant si   lonc tens me

su - re.   Bien ai mon cuer es - me - ü,   car por chan - ter
du - re.   par qui so - mes es - le - ü   en grant joie, et

l'ai me - ü de   la   ro - ï - ne   pu - re   C'est la dou -
re - ce - ü et   fors de grant ar - du - re.   ren - du nos

ce   me - re   Dieu qui de   do - lor nos   cu - re:
a   le bon   lieu ou joi - e   toz jors du - re.

6 Chanter vos vueil de la virge Marie

1 Chanter vos vueil de la virge Marie
qui mainte ame a et sauvée et garie.
Li doit on reclamer
et cherir et amer:
touz nos geta d'amer
et de grant vilainie.
Dame, ne demorés,
mes por Dieu secorrés
moi, qui sui devorés
se je n'ai vostre aïe.

2 Dame, de qui Jhesu Crist fist s'amie,
si m'aït Diex, il ne vos gaba mie;
de bon cuer vos ama
quant mere vos clama:
en vos bone dame a
cil qui vos a chierie.
Dame, ne demorés,
mes por Dieu secorrés
moi, qui sui devorés
se je n'ai vostre aïe.

3 Douce dame de touz biens raëmplie,
qui bien vos sert mout bien son tens
    enplie.
Cele fait bon servir
qui bien set deservir
de chascun le servir:
bien doit estre servie.
Dame, ne demorés,
mes por Dieu secorrés
moi, qui sui devorés
se je n'ai vostre aïe.

4 Douce dame, mere Dieu eschevie,
par vos ravon joie, solas, et vie.
Qui estïons despris
et tuit mort et tuit pris,
et par vos somes en pris
et en grant seignorie.
Dame, ne demorés,

mes por Dieu secorrés
moi, qui sui devorés
se je n'ai vostre aïe.

5 Douce dame plaine de vaillandie,
par vos ravon la riche manandrie
dont Adam nos osta
qui durement nos cousta.
Certes mout bon oste a
en ceste ostelerie!
Dame, ne demorés,
mes por Dieu secorrés
moi, qui sui devorés
se je n'ai vostre aïe.

Sources: BN, Manuscript X, ff. 260r–v;
    Manuscript P, f. 196; R. 1182
Text category: La
Music category: Se
Rhyme scheme: 11a 11a 6b 6b 6b 7a: 6c 6c 6c
    7a
Musical scheme: a a' b b' b" c: b b' b" c
Edition: Gennrich, no. 6
Contrafacta: R. 527 (Richart de Semilli);
    R. 538 (Richart de Semilli)
Remarks: The metre is somewhat unusual.

6 I wish to sing to you about the Virgin Mary

1 I wish to sing to you about the Virgin
   Mary
  who has both saved and healed many
   souls.
  One should call to her, and cherish and
   love her:
  she has delivered all of us from the
   bitter place and from all villainy.
  Lady, do not delay, but for God's sake help
   me,
  for I am devoured without your aid.

2 Lady, who Jesus Christ made his
   loving friend
  – as God aids me! – he did not mock
   you.
  With good heart he loved you when he
   called you mother:
  he who cherished you had a good
   lady.
  Lady, do not delay, but for God's sake help
   me,
  for I am devoured without your aid.

3 Sweet lady filled with all goodness,
  he who serves you fills his time very
   well.
  She commands good service
  for she well knows how to deserve
   service from everyone:
  she should be well served.
  Lady, do not delay, but for God's sake help
   me,
  for I am devoured without your aid.

4 Sweet lady, mother of God entirely,
  from you we take joy, solace, and life.
  We would have been despoiled, all
   dead and captured,
  but through you we are ransomed and
   in great lordship.

Lady, do not delay, but for God's sake help
 me,
for I am devoured without your aid.

5 Sweet lady full of valour,
  through you we recapture the rich
   residence
  from which Adam got us evicted,
   which cost us dearly.
  Surely we have a fine host at this
   hostel!
  Lady, do not delay, but for God's sake help
   me,
  for I am devoured without your aid.

6 Chanter vos vueil de la virge Marie

Chanter vos vueil de la virge Mari-e

qui mainte ame a et sauvée et gari-e

li doit on reclamer · et cherir et amer

touz nos geta d'amer · et de grant vilaini-e.

dame, ne demorés; mes por dieu secorrés

moi, qui sui devorés · se je n'ai vostre a-i-e.

Chan-ter vos vueil de la vir-ge Ma - ri - e qui main-te_ame

a et sau - vé - e_et ga - ri - e. Li doit on re - cla - mer

et che - rir et a - mer: touz nos ge - ta d'a - mer et de grant

vi - lai - ni - e. Da - me, ne de - mo - rés, mes por Dieu

se - cor - rés moi, qui sui de - vo - rés se je n'ai vos-tre_a - i - e.

See appendix C for alternative notation.

7 On doit la mere Dieu honorer

1 On doit la mere Dieu honorer
   sans demorer,
   et deseur toutes aörer,
   car ce[1] est nostre amie:
   Virge douce Marie,
   ne nos oubliés mie.

2 Il n'est nus, tant ait mesfait[2] de pechiés,
   tant soit bleciés,
   qui ne soit bien tost redreciés
   se de fin cuer la prie:
   Virge douce Marie,
   ne nos oubliés mie.

3 Par li avons tuit joie et honor,
   grant et menor,
   car ele porta le seignor
   qui tot a en baillie:
   Virge douce Marie,
   ne nos oubliés mie.

4 Certes quant Eve ot fait le forfait
   et le mal trait
   par quoi tuit estïons mort fait,
   ele nos fist aïe:
   Virge douce Marie,
   ne nos oubliés mie.

5 Eve trestout le mont confondi,
   je le vos di,
   mes la mere Dieu respondi
   por la nostre partie:
   Virge douce Marie,
   ne nos oubliés mie.

6 Tant a la mere Dieu de bonté
   c'est tout conté
   que par li soumes remonté
   de mort en haute vie:
   Virge douce Marie,
   ne nos oubliés mie.

Sources: BN, Manuscript X, ff. 260v–1r;
   Manuscript P, f. 196; R. 866
Text category: La
Music category: Rn
Rhyme scheme: 9a 4a 8a 7b : 7b 7b
Musical scheme: a b c d_x d_y d_x
Editions: Järnström and Långfors, 2: 121;
   Gennrich, no. 7
Contrafactum: R. 868 (Richart de Semilli)
Remarks: The metre is unusual, particularly
   the nine-syllable first line. Two addi-
   tional stanzas appear in manuscript P,
   which contains only the first four of the
   six stanzas in X:

5 Tuit estïon a Dieu descordé
   et mal cordé,
   tuit fusmes par li racordé
   et en grant seignorie:
   Virge douce Marie,
   ne nos oubliés mie.

6 Bien nos devon a li tuit corder
   et racorder,
   puis que le nos veut descorder
   de tote vilanie:
   Virge douce Marie,
   ne nos oubliés mie.

1 'Car ele est' in manuscript P
2 'Tant ai fet de' in manuscript P

7 One should honour the mother of God

1 One should honour the mother of God
      without delaying,
   and adore her above all women for she
      is our friend:
   Sweet Virgin Mary, do not forget us.

2 There is no one, no matter how many
      sins he has committed,
   nor how crushed he is, who will not be
      swiftly restored
   if he prays to her with gentle heart:
   Sweet Virgin Mary, do not forget us.

3 Through her all of us, great and small,
      have joy and honour,
   for she carried the Lord who has all
      things in his realm:
   Sweet Virgin Mary, do not forget us.

4 Surely when Eve had committed the
      crime
   by which we would all have been sent
      to death,
   she, Mary, helped us:
   Sweet Virgin Mary, do not forget us.

5 Eve confounded all the world, I tell
      you,
   but the mother of God answered on
      our behalf:
   Sweet Virgin Mary, do not forget us.

6 The mother of God has so much
      goodness
   that it was counted so that we were
      restored
   from death to life on high:
   Sweet Virgin Mary, do not forget us.

Alternative verses from manuscript P:

5 We would all have been in discord with
      God, and poorly accorded,
   but we were by her restored to great
      nobility:
   Sweet Virgin Mary, do not forget us.

6 We all ought to be in accord with her, and
      reconciled,
   since she wishes us to be in discord with
      all villainy:
   Sweet Virgin Mary, do not forget us.

7 On doit la mere Dieu honorer

On doit la me-re dieu ho-norer · sans demorer

Et de seur toutes a-ö-rer · car ce est nostre ami-e :

Virge douce Mari-e, ne nos oubli-és mi-e.

On doit la me - re Dieu ho - no - rer sans de - mo - rer,

et de - seur tou - tes a - ö - rer, car ce est nos - tre_a - mi - e:

Vir - ge dou - ce Ma - ri - e, ne nos ou - bli - és mi - e.

8 Quant voi le siecle escolorgier

1 Quant voi le siecle escolorgier,
le fiz apres le pere,
ne remaint clerc ne chavalier
n'autre qui nel conpere,
le mors Adam qui trabuchier
nos fist par Eve sa moillier,
ne nus a qui ne pere:
une chançon vueill comencier
de la saintisme mere,
de cuer entier.

2 Roïne de la roiauté,
dou ciel et de la terre,
chastel et tor de loiauté
en qui n'a point de guerre:
touz tens doit la crestïenté
por estre mise a sauveté
tel forteresce querre,
que son fiz nos a creanté,
se le volons requerre
pes et santé.

3 Virge pure, virge roial,
virge sans vilainie,
la plus bele et la plus loiau
qui onques fust en vie,
car en sa chanbre espirital
et en son ventre virginal
porta come hardie
nostre bon signor eternal
qui pardurable vie
done sanz mal.

4 Marie, estoile d'amer,
virge tres debonaire,
qui es grans perils de la mer
a ses amis esclaire;
por ce la devons reclamer
et li servir et honorer,
riens ne nos doit tant plaire.
Toute autre amor me semble amer,
et si doit ele bien faire
por li amer.

5 Douce dame sanz finement,
en gloire coronée,
deffendez moi d'enconbriement
et de male pensée,
et de tout pechié ensement;
et quant vendra au jugement
qu'el ne soit dampnée
m'ame, o les maus assemblemens
qui par leur destinée
vont en torment.

Sources: BN, Manuscript X, f. 261; R. 1276
Text category: Co
Music category: Rn
Rhyme scheme: 8a 7b 8a 7b 8a 8a 7b 8a 7b
    4a
Musical scheme: a b a c d e f d e′ g
Editions: Järnström and Långfors, 2: 123;
    Gennrich, no. 8
Contrafactum: R. 1484

8 When I perceive the world slipping away

1 When I perceive the world slipping
   away, the son following the father,
   so that there remains neither cleric nor
   knight nor any other who is worthy,
   and the bite of Adam, who caused us to
   fall by means of his wife Eve,
   so that there is no one who does not
   perish;
   then I wish to begin a song, from full-
   ness of heart,
   about the most holy mother.

2 Queen of all royalty, of heaven and of
   earth,
   castle and tower of loyalty, in whom
   there is no strife;
   Christianity should forever seek this
   fortress,
   which her son has promised us,
   in order to be put on the path to salvation,
   if we wish to request of him peace and
   well-being.

3 Pure and royal virgin,
   virgin without villainy,
   the most lovely and loyal who ever
   lived,
   for in her sanctified chamber and in her
   virginal womb
   she bore, with courage, our good Lord
   eternal
   who gives life everlasting without
   misfortune.

4 Mary, star of the sea,
   most good-natured virgin
   who lights the way for her friends in
   great peril on the sea;
   for this we ought to praise and serve
   and honour her,

nothing else should give us such
   pleasure.
Any other love seems bitter to me,
and it should be thus for love of her.

5 Sweet lady immortal, crowned in
   glory,
protect me from danger and from evil
   thoughts and all sins;
and when the time of judgment comes
protect my soul, so that it will not be
   damned
along with the crowd of evildoers
who will go to torment as their destiny.

8 Quant voi le siecle escolorgier

Quant voi le siecle escolorgier, le fiz apres le pere,

ne re-maint clerc ne chevalier · n'autre qui nel conpe-re.

Le mors Adam qui trabuchier · nos fist par Eve sa moillier

ne nus a qui ne pe-re, une chançon vueill comencier

de la saintisme me-re · de cuer entier.

Quant voi le sie - cle_ es - co - lor - gier, le fiz a - pres le pe - re, ne

re - maint clerc ne che - va - lier n'au - tre qui nel con - pe - re, le

mors A - dam qui tra - bu - chier nos fist par E - ve sa moil - lier, ne

nus a qui ne pe - re: u - ne chan - çon vueill co - men - cier de

la sain - tis - me me - re, de cuer en - tier.

9 Prions en chantant

1 Prions en chantant
la mere Jhesu,
qu'ele nos soit aidant,
ne soions perdu
envers son enfant
qui de li nez fu
qu'il nos soit garant
par sa grant vertu.
Bon fu onques née
la virge honorée,
la flor de bonté,
dame bien aimée,
roïne clamée
de grant roiauté.

2 Dex la salua
par l'ange, qui dist
'Ave Maria'
de par Jhesu Crist:
certes mout l'ama
quant en li se mist,
mout par l'onora
qui sa mere en fist.
Bien l'ost esprovée
et digne trovée
quant en li char prist:
corone rosée
d'or enluminée
el chief li assist.

3 A vos, pechëors,
ne vos quier celer!
Qui de bone amor
la veut bien amer,
et qui bien la sert,
sachiés sans douter
que mal et dolor
ne le puet grever.
La douce Marie
li donra s'aïe
et force et vigor,
car ele est amie
a ceus que folie
laissent por s'amor.

4 Flor de paradis,
mere et fille Dé,
pucele de pris,
rose de bonté,
vos avés conquis
la nostre herité
dont Adans jadis
nos avoit getés.[1]
Vos avés portée
la sainte ventrée
qui raïenst chaitis:
por nos fu penée
et a mort livrée,
dont nos somes vis.

5 Mere Dieu puissans,
de nos remenbrez:
proiés vostre enfant
qui de vos fu nez,
quant vendrons avant
por estre esprovéz,
de nos pechiés grans
ne soions dampnéz.
Estoile marine,
tres haute roïne,
car nos regardez;
par la vostre aïe
d'enfer la baïe,
dame, nos gardez.

Sources: BN, Manuscript X, ff. 261v–2r;
    Manuscript P, f. 195; R. 323
Text category: Co
Music category: Se
Rhyme scheme: 5a 5b 5a 5b 5a 5b 5a 5b 6c 6c
    5d 6c 6c 5d
Musical scheme: a b a b a b a b c d b' c d b'
Editions: Järnström and Långfors, 2: 125;
    Gennrich, no. 9
Contrafactum: R. 291 (Pierre de Corbie)
Remarks: The stanzaic and musical struc-
    tures are somewhat reminiscent of a litur-
    gical litany, although the text is not.

1 'nos out fors jeté' in manuscript P

9 We pray by singing

1 We pray by singing to the mother of
  Jesus,
  so that she will come to our aid and we
    will not be lost
  at the wrong side of her child, who was
    born of her,
  and so that he will be our guarantor by
    his great strength.
  This honoured virgin was born in good
    fortune,
  this flower of goodness,
  beloved lady, called a queen of great
    royalty.

2 God greeted her through the angel,
  who said 'Hail, Mary' on behalf of
    Jesus Christ:
  certainly he loved her greatly when he
    set himself within her,
  he honoured her greatly who made her
    his mother.
  She was well proven and found worthy
    when he took flesh of her:
  he placed a crown of roses, illumined
    with gold, upon her head.

3 From you, sinners, I do not try to hide!
  He who wishes to love her with true
    love, and to serve her well,
  will know without doubt that evil and
    misery will not be able to harm him.
  Sweet Mary will give him her help and
    force and strength,
  for she is the friend of those who leave
    foolishness for her love.

4 Flower of paradise, mother and daugh-
    ter of God,
  maiden of great worth, rose of good-
    ness,
  you have overcome our heritage, into
    which Adam cast us long ago.
  You have carried in your holy womb
    him who ransoms captives:

for us he was punished and sent to
  death, because of which we are alive.

5 Powerful mother of God, remember us:
  pray your child, who was born of you,
  when we come before him to be
    proven,
  that we be not damned for our great
    sins.
  Star of the sea, most high queen, since
    you notice us,
  protect us by your aid, lady, from the
    gaping mouth of hell.

9 Prions en chantant

Pri-ons en chantant · la me-re Jhe-su
qu'ele nos soit ai-dant · ne soi-ons per-du

En-vers son en-fant · qui de li nez fu
qu'il nos soit ga-rant · par sa grant ver-tu.

Bon fu on-ques né—e, la virge honoré—e,
Da-me bien ai—mé—e, ro-ï—ne clamé—e,

la flor de bon-té,
de grant roi—au—té.

1 S. occ.: ♪

Pri - ons en   chan - tant   la me - re   Jhe - su,
qu'ele nos soit ai - dant   ne soi - ons   per - du

en - vers son   en - fant   qui de li   nez   fu
qu'il nos soit   ga - rant   par sa grant   ver - tu.

Bon fu   on - ques   né - - - e   la virge ho - no -
da - me bien ai - - mé - - - e,   ro - ï - ne cla -

ré - - e,   la flor de   bon - té,
mé - - e,   de grant roi - - - au - - té.

See appendix C for alternative notation.

10 Lonc tens ai usé ma vie

1 Lonc tens ai usé ma vie
   en pechié et en folie.
   Las, chaitis, comment ai je char si
       hardie
   de tant dormir en pechié? C'est
       musardie!

2 Je sai bien que que nus die,
   que c'est aperte folie
   que m'ame soit en pechié tant
       endormie
   que mes anemis mortieus si ne dort
       mie!

3 Virge pucele Marie,
   a qui requerrai aïe,
   fors a toi, ma douce dame? Or me
       deslie,
   et me soiés au besoign veraie amie.

4 Liéz soi, car me deslie
   de pechié qui tout enlie,
   et me gete, s'il te plaist, de la baillie
   a cil qui la soë gent a malbaillie.

5 Dame de touz biens garnie,
   cest las qui de cuer vos prie,
   secor le par ta pitié,[1] que il n'en chie
   en ordure de pechié de glotonie!

Sources: BN, Manuscript X, f. 262; Manuscript P, f. 195; R. 1233
Text category: Pr
Music category: Se
Rhyme scheme: 8a 8a 12a 12a
Musical scheme: a a b c
Editions: Järnstrom and Långfors, 2: 128;
   Gennrich, no. 10
Contrafactum: R. 1499
Remarks: The final line of stanza five suggests that the song may have been
   intended for performance before or during a feast, either by an entertainer or
   perhaps by the entire group of partici-
   pants: its short stanzas and catchy
   melodic lines are suitable for communal
   singing. It is perhaps a parody of the traditional confession song, suggesting that
   – at least at one court – devotion could be
   gently parodied, as it occasionally was in
   monastic communities.

1 The phrase is 'secor le se il te plaist' in
   manuscript P.

10 For a long time I have spent my life

1 For a long time I have spent my life in
    sin and folly.
  Alas, miserable one! How could I have
    been so foolhardy as to sleep so long
    in sin?
  It is stupidity!

2 I know well enough what everyone
    says,
  that it is plain foolishness for my soul
    to have slept so long in sin
  when my mortal enemy does not sleep
    at all!

3 Virgin maiden Mary, to whom shall I
    beg for help,
  if not to you, my sweet lady?
  Now unbind me and be a true friend to
    me in need.

4 I am joyous, for you unbind me from
    sin which ensnares everyone;
  and throw me, if it please you,
  from the realm of the one whose ten-
    ants are badly treated.

5 Lady adorned with all goodness,
  help this miserable one who prays to
    you heartfully, for pity's sake,
  so that he may not fall into the filth of
    the sin of gluttony!

10 Lonc tens ai usé ma vie

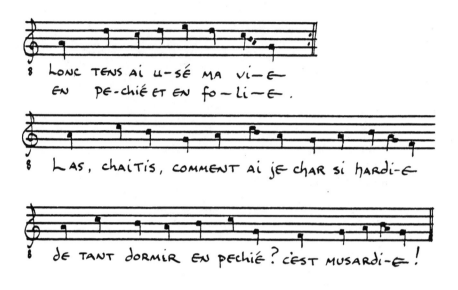

Lonc tens ai u-sé ma vi-e
en pe-chié et en fo-li-e.

Las, chaitis, comment ai je char si hardi-e

de tant dormir en pechié? c'est musardi-e!

Lonc tens ai u - sé ma vi - e
en pe - chié et en fo - li - e.

Las, chai - tis, com - ment ai je char

si har - di - e de tant dor - mir en pe - chié? C'est mu - sar - di - e!

11 Mere au roi puissant

1 Mere au roi puissant,
bon loier atent
qui vos sert:
l'amor vostre enfant
que vos amez tant
en desert.
Roïne honorée,
bone est la pensée
qui a vos s'aërt:
se ne fussiés née,
toute fust dampnée,
la gent qui sont
et qui seront,
tuit en somes cert.

2 Pieça qu'en disoit
c'un rainsiau[1] naistroit
de Jessé:
la flor qui en istroit
tout sormonteroit
par biauté.
C'est la profecie
que dist Ysaïe
mil anz a passés:
la verge est Marie,
la flor senefie
li rois Jhesu[2]
qui par vertu
a tout sormonté.

3 Hé, Dex! Que[3] feront
cil qui en enfer sont
sans retor?
Jamés n'en istront
ne joie n'en auront
a nul jor.
De cele compaigne
nos desaconpaigne
...[4]
cele qui est
et qui sera
jamés fin n'aura.

Sources: BN, Manuscript X, f. 262v; Manuscript P, f. 194; Rome, Manuscript a,
f. 122; R. 353
Text category: Co
Music category: Se
Rhyme scheme: 5a 5a 3b 5a 5a 3b 6c 6c 5b 6c
6c 4d 4d 5b
Musical scheme: a b c a b c d e f d e g g h
Editions: Järnström and Långfors, 2: 165;
Gennrich, no. 11
Contrafactum: R. 724
Remarks: The first two stanzas are found in
all three manuscripts. The third stanza is
truncated in both X and P. Additional
stanzas appear in manuscript a (the fifth
stanza is the same as stanza 3 in manuscript X). See appendix B.

1 'Que verge' naistroit in manuscript a
2 'Le dous Jhesu' in manuscript a
3 É las que' in manuscript a
4 A line is missing in both manuscripts X
and P, and the rest of the stanza is
corrupt.

11 Mother of the powerful king

1 Mother of the powerful king,
  he who serves you awaits a good
     reward:
  he deserves the love of the son you love
     so well.
  Honoured queen, he who attaches him-
     self to you has a good idea:
  had you not been born, we would all
     have been damned,
  those who are and those who will be,
  we are all certain of it.

2 It has been a long time since it was said
  that a little branch would be born from
     (the tree of) Jesse:
  the flower which came forth from it
     surpassed all in beauty.
  This is the prophecy which Isaiah told
     a thousand years ago:
  the branch is Mary; the flower signifies
     king Jesus
  who has surpassed all in power.

3 O God, what will they do,
  those who are in hell without hope of
     return?
  They will never get out, nor have any
     happiness ever.
  She who is and ever will be, without
     end ...
  separates us from such company.

See appendix B for additional stanzas.

11 Mere au roi puissant

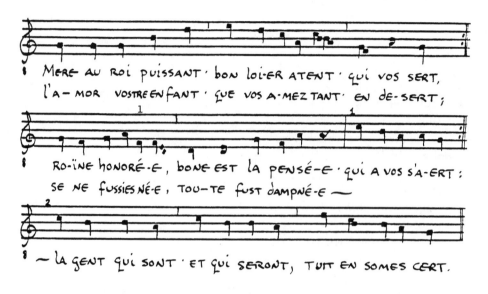

MERE AU ROI PUISSANT · bon loi-ER ATENT · qui VOS SERT,
l'A — MOR VOSTRE EN FANT · que VOS A-MEZ TANT · EN dE-SERT;

RO-ÏNE hoNORÉ-E , boNE EST la PENSÉ-E · qui A VOS S'A-ERT;
SE NE fussiES NÉ-E , TOU—TE fust dAMPNÉ-E —

— la GENT qui SONT · ET qui SERONT, TUIT EN SOMES CERT.

1 This note is missing on the first occurrence of the line; it is supplied here by analogy with the repetition.

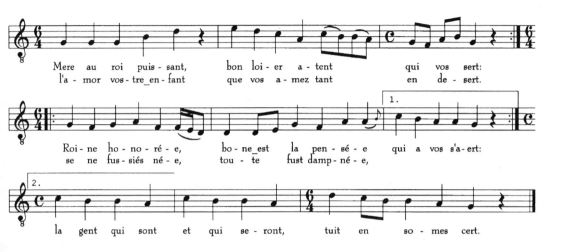

Mere au roi puis - sant,   bon loi - er a - tent   qui vos sert:
l'a - mor vos - tre en - fant   que vos a - mez tant   en de - sert.

Roi - ne ho - no - ré - e,   bo - ne est   la pen - sé - e   qui a vos s'a - ert:
se ne fus - siés né - e,   tou - te   fust damp - né - e,

la gent qui sont   et qui se - ront,   tuit en   so - mes cert.

12 'Qui bien aime a tart oublie'

1 'Qui bien aime a tart oublie':
  por ce ne puis oublier
  la douce virge Marie.
  De li me covient chanter
  et mon chant renouveler
  et faire de li m'amie,
  qu'ele me puisse acorder
  a celui qui ne faut mie
  ceus qui le vuellent amer.

2 C'est a Dieu, nostre douz pere
  qui de nos ot grant pité,[1]
  qui de la dolor amere
  d'enfer nos a toz getés.
  Percié en fu son costé
  et la char en fu navrée:
  bien nos entendist menbrer[2]
  d'icele dure jornée
  quant aillors devons penser.

3 Dame, per vostre proiere,
  me daigniés ensi user[3]
  ma jonesce et ma maniere
  qu'a vostre fiz honorer
  me puisse ensi concorder
  ...[4]
  sanz mentir[5] et sans fausser,
  que il m'i soit loiax mires
  a mes max mediciner.[6]

Sources: BN, Manuscript X, ff. 262v–3r;
  Manuscript P, f. 194; Manuscript i, f. 65;
  Rome, Manuscript a, f. 122; R. 1188
Text category: Co
Music category: Th
Rhyme scheme: 8a 7b 8a 7b 7b 8a 7b 8a 7b
Musical scheme: a b c a' e f g h i
Editions: Järnström and Långfors, 1: 140;
  Gennrich, no. 12
Contrafacta: R. 518; R. 1135 (Moniot);
  R. 1140a
Remarks: The opening line is proverbial,
  and occurs in other trouvère songs: see
  Järnström and Långfors, 1: 141. Stanza 3
  is truncated in manuscripts X and P;
  manuscript i does not include this stanza.
  Additional stanzas appear in truncated
  form in manuscripts i and a. See appen-
  dix B.

1 'Nos prist grant pité' in manuscript P,
  and 'nous print tel pité' in manuscript a
2 'Nous devroit ramenbrer' in manuscript i
3 'Ensi mener' in manuscript a
4 An additional line appears in manuscripts a and i: 'que j'aï s'amour entiere.'
5 'Sans tricier' in manuscript a
6 In manuscript a, the last three lines of this
  stanza are given as 'sanz tricier et sans
  fausser, / et me voille estre dous miere /
  pour mes maus mediciner.'

12 'He who loves well takes a long time to forget'

1 'He who loves well takes a long time to
      forget':
   For this reason I cannot forget the
      sweet Virgin Mary.
   I wish to sing of her and to renew my
      song, and to make her my
      lady-friend,
   so that she might be able to put me in
      agreement
   with the one who does not fail those
      who wish to love him.

2 That is with God, our gentle father,
      who had great pity on us,
   and who cast us out from the bitter
      pains of hell.
   His side was pierced, his flesh
      wounded;
   he intended us to remember this harsh
      journey,
   for we must think of other things.

3 Lady, please deign to use me, my
      youth and manner,
   in such a way that I can agree to
      honour your son without lie or false-
      hood
   so that he will be a loyal physician to
      me in healing my infirmities.

See appendix B for additional stanzas.

12 'Qui bien aime a tart oublie'

Qui bien aime a tart oubli-e: por ce ne puis oubli-er

la dou-ce vir-ge Mari-e; de li me covient chanter

et mon chant renouveler, et faire de li m'ami-e

qu'ele me puisse acorder · a celui qui ne faut mi-e

ceus qui le vuellent a-mer.

'Qui bien ai - me_a tart ou - bli - e': por ce ne puis ou - bli - er

la dou - ce vir - ge Ma - ri - e. De li me co - vient chan - ter

et mon chant re - nou - ve - ler et fai - re de li m'a - mi - e,

qu'e - le me puis - se a - cor - der a ce - lui qui

ne faut mi - e ceus qui le vuel - lent a - mer.

13 Je te pri de cuer par amors

1 Je te pri de cuer par amors,
   haute virge Marie,
   par ta pitié, par ta douçour,
   que ton chier fiz deprie,
   dame, que il n'oblie
   ces chaitis dolens pechëors
   qui metent leur ame a dolor
   ne se conoissent mie:
   perdu seront sanz nul retor
   se tu lor faus d'aïe.

2 Roïne, mere au sauvëor
   qui tout a en baillie,
   qui es de paradis la flor
   et la rose espanie,
   par toi, virge Marie,
   avront merci maint pechëor.
   Dame, qui te sert nuït et jor
   sa paine ne pert mie:
   n'avra garde d'entrer el four
   dont nus ne revient mie.

3 Haute dame, qui es es ciels
   roïne coronée,
   et des angres esperiteus
   servie et aörée,
   ...[1]
   vos qui portastes le fiz Dieu,
   le haute sire, le glorieus,
   qui t'a grace donée
   de delivrer qui que tu veus:
   ci ot digne portée.

4 Dame, qui bien te servira
   de fin cuer sans faintise,
   riche guerredon en aura
   au grant jor dou juïse,
   quant cil tendra justise
   qui en vostre cors s'aömbra.
   Ne haut ne bas n'espargnera:
   si est la chose enprise

selonc que chascun fait avra
l'en rendra le servise.

5 Dame, a ce jor dou jugement
   vos soiés en aïe:
   la ou li saint iront trenblant
   de päour, n'en dout mie.
   N'est nus qui por nos prie,
   ne apostre ne innocent
   fors Saint Jehan seulement
   et toi d'autre partie.
   Qui a ce penseroit souvent,
   melz en vaudroit sa vie.

Sources: BN, Manuscript X, f. 263; R. 1961
Text category: Co
Music category: Rn
Rhyme scheme: 8a 7b 8a 7b 7b 8a 8a 7b 8a
   7b
Musical scheme: a b a b' c d e c' d' e'
Editions: Järnström and Långfors, 2: 129;
   Gennrich, no. 13
Contrafacta: R. 837; R. 1919

1 A line is missing in the manuscript.

13 I ask you from the heart, for love

1 I ask you from the heart, for love,
   high Virgin Mary, for your pity and
      sweetness,
   that you beseech your son, lady, not to
      forget these wretched sinners
   who place their souls in pain and do
      not know themselves at all:
   they will be lost eternally if you fail to
      aid them.

2 Queen, mother of the Saviour who has
      all in his realm,
   you who are flower of paradise and
      full-blown rose,
   through you, Virgin Mary, many sin-
      ners will have mercy.
   Lady, he who serves you night and day
      will never waste his effort:
   he need have no fear of entering the
      ovens from which none ever return.

3 High lady, you who are crowned
      queen of the heavens,
   served and lauded by spirit angels ...
   you who bore the son of God, the high
      Lord, the glorious one,
   who has given you the grace to save
      anyone you wish:
   in this you had a worthy offspring.

4 Lady, he who serves you well with
      good heart, without falseness,
   will have a rich reward on the great
      Day of Judgment
   when he who shaded himself in your
      body will hold his court.
   Neither high nor low will be spared;
    the matter is so arranged
   that everyone will render service to
      him.

5 Lady, at this Day of Judgment, be our
      aid;
   there where even the saints will go
      trembling with fear, I have no doubt,
   there will be no one to pray for us, nei-
      ther apostle nor holy innocent,
   excepting only St John, and you at the
      other side.
   If one thinks of this often, one's life will
      be worth more.

13 Je te pri de cuer par amors

Je te pri de cuer par amors, haute virge Mari-e,

par ta pitié, par ta douçor, que ton chier fiz depri-e,

dame, que il n'obli-e . ces chaitis dolens pechë-ors

qui metent leur ame a dolor . ne se conoissent mi-e;

perdu seront sanz nul retor, se tu lor faus d'a-ï-e.

Je te pri de cuer par a - mors, haut - e vir - ge Ma - ri - e, par

ta pi - tié, par ta dou - çor que ton chier fiz de - pri - e, da -

me, que il n'o - bli - e ces chai - tis do - lens pe - chë - ors qui

me - tent leur ame a do - lor ne se co - nois - sent mi - e: per -

du se - ront sanz nul re - tor se tu lor faus d'a - ï - e.

14 Or laissons ester

1 Or laissons ester
   touz les chans dou monde,
   meillor fet chanter
   de la virge monde,
   de la mere Dieu
   qui trestouz nos monde
   dou mal ou Adan
   nos avoit poséz.
   Hé, mere Dieu,
   tres douce Marie,
   car nos secorrés!

2 Bien fait qui son cuer
   en cele marie
   qui est mere Dieu,
   qui a non Marie:
   c'est cele qui a
   mainte ame esmarie
   gerée et garie
   de grant enferté.
   Hé, mere Dieu,
   tres douce Marie,
   car nos secorrés!

3 Il fait bon chanter
   de cele pucele
   qui est mere Dieu,
   et dame et ancele.
   Or en chantons tuit:
   certes, ce est cele
   qui trestous a
   de dolor getés.
   Hé, mere Dieu,
   tres douce Marie,
   car nos secorrés!

4 Drois est que par tout
   sa bonté apere,
   car ele aporta
   Jhesu nostre pere:
   fox est qui a autre
   sa bonté conpere,

car ele a en li
trestoutes bontés.
Hé, mere Dieu,
tres douce Marie,
car nos secorrés!

5 Or prions la dame
   qui tant par est fine,
   la qui bontéz onques
   ne cesse ne fine,
   que noz ames si
   en la fin affine
   qu'il soient plus fines
   qu'or fin afiné.
   Hé, mere Dieu,
   tres douce Marie,
   car nos secorrés!

Sources: BN, Manuscript X, ff. 263v–4r;
   R. 1902a
Text category: La
Music category: Se
Rhyme scheme: 5+6a 5+6a 5+6a 5+5b:
   4+6+5b
Musical scheme: a b a b a c d_x e_x f g_x e
Editions: Järnström and Långfors, 2: 130;
   Gennrich, no. 14
Contrafacta: none

14 Now let us leave

1 Now let us leave all the songs of this
      world,
   it is better to sing of the pure virgin,
   the mother of God who cleanses us all
   from the sin which Adam imposed
      upon us.
   Mother of God, most sweet Mary, bring us
      succour.

2 He does well who marries his heart
   to this one who is the mother of God
         and has the name of Mary:
   it is she who has cured and healed
         many a troubled heart of its weak-
      ness.
   Mother of God, most sweet Mary, bring us
      succour.

3 It is good to sing of this maiden
   who is mother of God, lady and hand-
      maiden.
   Now let us all sing of her:
   surely she is the one who has snatched
         us all from misery.
   Mother of God, most sweet Mary, bring us
      succour.

4 It is proper that her goodness be
         apparent in all things,
   for she bore Jesus our father:
   he who compares her goodness to any
         other is a fool,
   for she has all possible goodness in her.
   Mother of God, most sweet Mary, bring us
      succour.

5 Now we pray the lady who is so fine,
   she in whom goodness will never cease
      nor end,
   that at the last she so refine our souls
      that they surpass fine gold in refine-
   ment.
   Mother of God, most sweet Mary, bring us
      succour.

14 Or laissons ester

Or laissons ester · touz les chans dou monde,
meillor fet chanter · de la vir-ge monde,

de la mere dieu · qui trestouz nos monde

dou mal ou A-dan · nos avoit posez :

hé mere dieu, tres douce Mari-e, car nos secorrés~!

Or lais - sons   e - ster   touz les chans dou mon - de,   de la me - re Dieu
meil - lor   fet chan - ter   de   la   vir - ge mon - de,

qui tres - touz   nos mon - de   dou mal   ou   A - dan   nos a - voit po - séz.

Hé   me - re Dieu,   tres dou - ce Ma - ri - e,   car nos se - cor - rés!

15 Fox est qui en folie

1 Fox est qui en folie
son tens met et emploie,
car l'ame n'est pas lie
quant li cors trop foloie.
Or me sui je aparceüz
que j'ai chanté folement,
por pou ne sui deceüs:
chanter m'estuet autrement,
de la roïne dou mont.
Sa grant bontéz mi semont
qu'a li soit mes chanz tornéz:
Mere Dieu, devotement
vos pri que me secorrés.

2 Virge douce Marie,
vrais pors, douce fontaine,
qui mainte ame esmarie
as geté fors de paine,
dame vos [estez]¹ li pors
[qui toz les biens aportez:
totes joies, toz depors,]²
a touz les desconfortéz.
Mout est cil en bon sentier
qui vos sert de bon cuer entier,
car mout bien li aiderés.
Mere Dieu, devotement
vos pri que me secorrés.

3 Virge tres pure et monde,
dame de bonté plaine,
par qui touz biens habonde,
dame de touz biens plaine,
dame qui Jhesu portas,
mout a en toi de bonté:
le haut lieu nos raportas
dont estïons desmonté.
Dame plaine de biauté,
qui de bone loiauté
vos sert, bien est assenéz.
Mere Dieu, devotement
vos pri que me secorrés.

4 Mere Dieu nete et fine,³
veraie estoile marine,
qui toz nos enlumine,
la qui bonté ne fine,
veraie lune sanz decors,⁴
vrais solaus sanz oscurté,
bone aïde, veraie secors,
bien puet estre assëuré
cil qui vos sert nuit et jor,
douce dame, bien sejor,
car mout bel⁵ li aiderés:
Mere Dieu, devotement
vos pri que me secorrés.

5 Mere Dieu, tant es douce,
tant saintisme et tant bele,
dire nel porroit bouche
tant fust de dire isnele.
Bien esprova sa biauté⁶
Theofilus li despris
qui estoit par sa folor
ja dou deable sorpris.
Dame, merci vos proia,
de cuer a vos souploia,
si en fu tost delivrés.
Mere Dieu, devotement
vos pri que me secorrés.

Sources: BN, Manuscript X, f. 264; Manuscript P, f. 198; R. 1159
Text category: La
Music category: Se
Rhyme scheme: 7a 7b 7a 7b 7c 7d 7c 7d 7e 7e 7f : 7d 7f
Musical scheme: a b a b c d c d e c d : c d
Editions: Järnström and Långfors, 2: 132; Gennrich, no. 15
Contrafactum: R. 1756 (Moniot de Paris)

15 A fool is he in folly

1 He is a fool who spends his time in
      folly,
   for the soul is not pleased when the
      body acts the fool.
   Now I realize that I have sung foolishly,
      and have almost been deceived:
   I wish to sing in another manner, about
      the queen of the world.
   Her great goodness incites me to turn
      my songs to her:
   Mother of God, I pray that you aid me.

2 Sweet Virgin Mary, true haven, sweet
      fountain,
   who has snatched many a troubled
      heart from pain,
   lady, you are the haven [which bears
      all good things,
   all joys, all pleasures] to all the discom-
      forted.
   He who serves you with his whole
      heart is on the right path,
   for you will help him.
   Mother of God, I pray that you aid me.

3 Most pure and clean Virgin, lady full of
      all goodness,
   through whom all good things abound,
      you who bore Jesus,
   there is much goodness in you:
   you call us back to the high place from
      which we were cast down.
   Lady full of beauty, he who serves you
      in good loyalty is wisely guided.
   Mother of God, I pray that you aid me.

4 Mother of God clean and fine,
   true star of the sea who enlightens us
      all,
   there where goodness never ends,
   true moon without discord, true sun
      without darkness,

good helper, true succour,
he who serves you night and day –
   sweet lady, true haven – can be well
   assured,
for you will aid him well.
Mother of God, I pray that you aid me.

5 Mother of God, you are so sweet, so
      holy and lovely,
   that no mouth could tell it all, however
      quick it was to speak.
   Theophilus the unworthy proved her
      beauty well,
   when through his folly he was sur-
      prised by the devil.
   Lady, he prayed for your pity, from the
      heart he beseeched you,
   and he was soon delivered.
   Mother of God, I pray that you aid me.

---

1 A missing word in manuscript X supplied from manuscript P.
2 Two lines are missing in manuscript X;
   text is supplied from P.
3 As in manuscript P; manuscript X reads:
   'Mere Dieu nete et pure fine.'
4 This is a reference to Aristotelian cosmol-
   ogy, the standard belief in the thirteenth
   century, which placed the earth at the
   centre of the universe. The moon was
   thought to be the boundary between the
   earth, where conditions were imperfect,
   discordant, and mutable, and the
   heavens, where conditions were perfect,
   concordant, and unchanging.
5 In manuscript P: 'mout bien li'
6 In manuscript P: 'ta bonté'
7 The final refrain of stanza 5 Manuscript P
   reads as follows: '*Douce mere Jhesu Cris, / a
   bone fin nos pernez.*'

15 Fox est qui en folie

Fox est qui en fo-li-e · son tens met et emploi-e,
car l'a-me n'est pas li-e · quant li cors trop fo-loi-e :

Or me sui je aparce-üz · que j'ai chanté fole-ment,
por pou ne sui de-ce-üs ; chanter m'estuet autrement

de la ro-ï-ne dou mont.

Sa grant bontéz mi semont · qu'a li soit mes chanz tornez :
Me-re dieu, de-vo-tement · vos pri que me se-corrés.

1 First occ.: ♦ ; in manuscript P this note and the two preceding it are ♦ .
2 First occ.: ♦ ; it is also found in manuscript P.
3 S. occ. is ♩ on the note B.

Fox est qui en fo - li - e son tens met et em - ploi - e, car
l'a - me n'est pas li - e quant li cors trop fo - - - -
loi - e.

Or me sui je_a - per - ce - üz que j'ai chan - té fo - le - ment,
par pou ne sui de - ce - üs: chan - ter m'e - stuet au - tre - ment,

de la ro - ï - ne dou mont. Sa grant bon - téz mi se - mont qu'a li soit mes chanz tor - nez:
Me - re Dieu, de - vo - te - ment vos pri que me se - cor - rés.

16 J'ai un cuer trop lent
[Thiebaut d'Amiens]

1 J'ai un cuer trop lent[1]
   qui souvent mesprent
   et pou s'en esmaie:
   et li tens s'en vet,
   et je n'ai riens fait
   ou grant fiance aïe.
   Lonc tens ai musé
   et mon tens usé,
   dont j'atent grief païe
   se par sa bonté
   la flor de purté
   son fil ne m'apaïe.

2 Mes cuers est trop vains,
   et vix et vilains,
   et gaïs velages:
   il n'est mie sains,
   ainz est faus et fains,
   plains de grans outrages.
   Il est hors dou sens,
   de povre porpens,
   de mauvés usages,
   uns chaitis dolens,
   pereceus et lenz,
   oscurs et onbrages.

3 Cil est fox adroit
   qui assez acroit
   et petit veut rendre:
   souvent me descort,
   telz presens recort
   qui me font mesprendre.
   Bien set en muser,
   en rire, en jöer,
   sa cure despendre:
   mes a bien plorer
   et a bien orer
   ne set il entendre.

4 Il veut pou veiller
   et pou travailler,
   et doute poverte;
   il veut pou proier,
   et uns grant loier
   avoir, sans deserte.
   Il veut sans semer
   assez messoner,
   c'est folie aperte:
   nus ne puet trover
   grant fruit sanz semer
   en terre deserte.

5 Thiebaut congié prent,
   la mort le sorprent
   qui le contralie.
   'Las, chaitif dolent,'
   se claime souvent:
   a Dieu merci crie.
   O, Thiebaut d'Amiens
   tant as eüs biens
   les jors de ta vie:
   or n'en portes riens,
   tant es plains de fiens,
   ta char est porie.

Sources: BN, Manuscript X, ff. 264v–5r;
   Manuscript i, f. 9; Paris, Bibliothèque de
   l'Arsenal, Manuscript 3517, f. 146;
   Oxford, Bodleian Library, Digby Manu-
   script 86, f. 3. Copies also in Dijon, Biblio-
   thèque municipale, Manuscript 526;
   Dublin, Trinity College, Manuscript
   D.4.18; Oxford, Bodleian Library, Douce
   252; BN, fonds français, 4929, 12581,
   24436; Paris, Bibliothèque de l'Arsenal,
   Manuscript 570. R. 202b
Text category: Pr
Music category: Rn
Rhyme scheme: 5a 5a 6b 5c 5c 6b 5d 5d 6b
   5d 5d 6b
Musical scheme: a b c a b c d e f e g c
Editions: Gennrich, no. 16; *Romania* 41: 217
Contrafacta: none

16 I have a heart which is too slow

1 I have a heart which is too slow, am
   often in error,
   and care little;
   time passes, and I have done nothing
   where I should have had great faith.
   For a long time I have wasted my time
   in idle amusement,
   for which I expect a painful reward
   unless through her goodness
   the flower of purity reconciles her son
   to me.

2 My heart is too vain and vicious and
   villainous,
   and a fickle unwanted thing;
   it is not at all healthy, it is foolish and
   false,
   and behaves outrageously.
   It is out of its mind, of poor consideration, and evil usage,
   a miserable wretch, lazy and slow, dark
   and shadowed.

3 This heart is indeed foolish
   which acquires much and wishes to
   give little:
   often I am at odds with it, recalling
   such incidents as made me do
   wrong.
   This foolish heart knows well how to
   amuse himself,
   to laugh and play around in order to
   disperse his cares:
   but he does not understand how to
   weep and to pray.

4 He does not wish to be watchful,
   he works little and fears poverty;
   he does not want to pray,
   but expects to have undeserved
   reward.

He wishes to reap much without
   sowing, which is obvious folly:
nobody can find fruit in a wasteland
   without planting seed.

5 Thiebaut takes his leave:
Death, his adversary, has surprised
   him.
Often he cries 'Alas, miserable wretch!'
   and calls out to God.
Oh, Thiebaut of Amiens, you have
   enjoyed the days of your life:
now you can take nothing of them with
   you,
you are full of filth, your flesh is
   rotting.

———

Remarks: This is the only composition in
   the edition that can be assigned to an
   author or a composer, one Thiebaut
   d'Amiens, about whom no information
   has survived. It is probable, however,
   that the two songs that follow this one in
   Manuscript X (nos. 17 and 18) are also by
   Thiebaut. My conclusion is drawn from
   musical evidence, because each of the
   three songs contains the same melodic
   signature phrase on a medial line of text;
   see the music of the phrases 'lonc tens ai
   musé' (no. 16), 'et me face acorde et pes'
   (no. 17), and 'Marie virge loiaus' (no. 18).
   Furthermore, all three songs are written
   on scales with final G, and nos. 17 and 18
   have nearly identical metric schemes, as
   well as final cadences on the second
   degree of the scale.

1 In some sources: 'cuer mout lait'

16 J'ai un cuer trop lent

J'ai un cuer trop lent · qui souvent mesprent
et li tens s'en vet · et je n'ai riens fait

et pou s'en es-mai-e
ou grant fi-ance ai-e,

Lonc tens ai musé · et mon tens usé

dont j'atent grief pai-e,

se par sa bonté · la flor de purté

son fil ne m'apai-e.

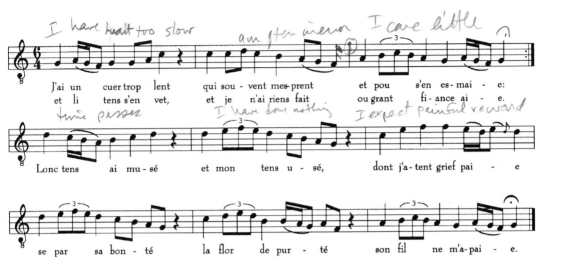

J'ai un   cuer trop lent   qui sou - vent mes-prent   et pou   s'en es- mai -   e:
et li   tens s'en   vet,   et je   n'ai riens fait   ou grant   fi - ance ai -   e.

Lonc tens   ai mu - sé   et mon   tens u - sé,   dont j'a-tent grief pai -   e

se par   sa bon - té   la flor   de pur - té   son fil   ne m'a-pai -   e.

17 Je ne vueil plus de sohier
[Thiebaut d'Amiens]

1 Je ne vueil plus de sohier[1]
  chanter, ne faire chançon:
  la mere Dieu vueill proier
  que me face vrai pardon,
  et me face acorde et pes
  vers son fil de mes mesfés,
  qu'anemis
  ne m'ait mort et pris.
  Tres douce Marie,
  ne m'oubliés mie.

2 Cil qui des pechiés oster
  se veut, et entrelaissier
  en bien dire, en bien penser,
  doit la mere Dieu proier
  qu'el nous get touz de torment.
  Je a mon comencement
  vos deproi,
  mere au puissant roi:
  Tres douce Marie,
  ne m'oubliés mie.

3 Dame plaine de pöoir,
  roïne de tout le mont,
  cil feront mout grant savoir
  qui de cuer vos serviront.
  Geté seront de pechié
  par vos, dame de pitié,
  douce riens,
  plaine de touz biens.
  Tres douce Marie,
  ne m'oubliés mie.

4 Virge plaine de douçor,
  roïne de paradis,
  getez moi de la dolor
  dont je sui si entrepris.
  Envers vos m'amenderai,
  et de cuer vos servirai
  nuit et jor,
  sanz faire folor.

Tres douce Marie,
ne m'oubliés mie.

5 J'ai au cuer un messagier
  ort et vilain et pulent,
  qui me fait souvent pechier,
  et metre m'ame en torment.
  Dame, c'est li vis maufés:
  envers li me defendez.
  Vrais saluz,
  soiés moi escus.
  Tres douce Marie,
  ne m'oubliés mie.

Source: BN, Manuscript X, f. 265; R. 1310
Text category: Pr
Music category: Rn
Rhyme scheme: 7a 7b 7a 7b 7c 7c 3d 5d : 6e
  6e
Musical scheme: a b a b c c d d' : e f
Editions: Järnström and Långfors, 2: 134;
  Gennrich, no. 17
Contrafacta: R. 1287 (Guillebert de Berne-
  vile)
Remarks: See those for no. 16 regarding
  attribution of authorship.

1 The word *sohier* appears quite clearly in
  manuscript X, but nowhere else in the
  known literature of the language. Its
  meaning has not been deciphered by
  previous editors. To hazard a guess, the
  term may be related to the verb *souiller*,
  to foul or contaminate. See Lommatsch,
  Tobler-Lommatsch Altfranzösisches
  Wörterbuch, vol. 9, c. 769.

17 I do not wish to sing of foulness any longer

1 I do not wish to sing of foulness any
      longer, nor to make songs:
   I want to pray to the mother of God,
   that she grant me true pardon
   and set me at peace and accord with
      her son
   regarding my misdeeds,
   so that the enemy might not kill and
      seize me:
   Most sweet Mary, do not forget me.

2 He who wishes to be carried from sin,
   and enmeshed in good words and
      thoughts,
   must pray to the mother of God
   that she cast us all from torment.
   I, at my beginning, pray to you,
      mother of the powerful king:
   Most sweet Mary, do not forget me.

3 Lady full of power,
      queen of all the world,
   those who serve you from the heart do
      a wise thing.
   They will be cast forth from sin by you,
      lady of mercy,
   sweet creature full of all goodness.
   Most sweet Mary, do not forget me.

4 Virgin full of sweetness,
      queen of paradise,
   cast me from the pain in which I am so
      entangled.
   I will reform myself for you,
   and serve you heartfully night and day.
   Most sweet Mary, do not forget me.

5 I have in my heart a messenger
   who is filthy and villainous and
      stinking:

he often causes me to sin and to put my
   soul in torment.
Lady, it is the vile devil:
   protect me from him!
True safety, be my shield.
Most sweet Mary, do not forget me.

17 Je ne vueil plus de sohier

Je ne vueil plus de sohier · chanter, ne faire chançon:
la me-re dieu vueill proier · que me fa-ce vrai pardon,

et me face a-corde et pes
vers son fil de mes mesfés

qu'a-ne-mis · ne m'ait mort et pris.

Tres douce Mari-e , ne m'oubli-és mi-e.

1 S. occ.: ⸲ (a)

2 Gennrich mistakenly 'corrects' the five final notes one step downward to end
on G.

Je ne vueil plus de so - hier chan - ter, ne fai - re chan - çon:
la me - re Dieu vueill proi - er que me fa - ce vrai par - don,

et me face a - corde et pes qu'a - ne - mis
vers son fil de mes mes - fés

ne m'ait mort et pris. Tres dou - ce Ma - ri - e, ne m'ou - bli - és mi - e.

18 De la mere au sauvëor
[Thiebaut d'Amiens]

1 De la mere au sauvëor
vodrai chançon comencier:
nus ne puet estre en dolor
qui merci li veut proier.
Marie virge loiaus,
pucele roiaus,
de cuer vrai
sans delai,
virge, vos proierai
qu'au jugement
nos desfendés de torment.

2 On doit bien tel dame amer
dont li biens puet venir,
en qui Dex vout reposer
et char humaine vestir.
Dame, qui vos servira
paradis avra
sanz esmai.
Bien le croi:
por ce doivent cler et lai
sanz redouter
de la mere Dieu chanter.

3 Marie de grant renon,
fontaine d'umilité,
ostéz nos as de prison
et de la desloiauté
ou Adans li desloiaus,
li nices, li faus,
nos laissa
quant manja
le fruit que li desvoia
le sauvëor,
par quoi perdismes s'amor.

4 Estoile resplendissant,
lune sans nule oscurté,
soleil grant clarté rendant,
Marie de grant beauté,
tres douce virge loiaus,

precieus vaisseaus,
je vos cri
et vos pri
qu'aiés pitié et merci
de pechëors
quant ert leur fin et leur jor.

Sources: BN, Manuscript X, ff. 265v–6r;
   R. 2013
Text category: Co
Music category: Rn
Rhyme scheme: 7a 7b 7a 7b 7c 5c 3d 3d 7d
   4e 7e
Musical scheme: a a$_x$ a a$_x$ b c de f gg$_x$
Editions: Järnström and Långfors, 2: 137;
   Gennrich, no. 18
Contrafactum: R. 1857 (Guillebert de
   Bernevile)
Remarks: See the remarks for no. 16
   regarding attribution of authorship.

18 Of the mother of the Saviour

1 I wish to begin a song about the mother
      of the Saviour:
   no one who prays for her mercy can
      remain in misery.
   Mary, loyal virgin, royal maiden,
   I shall pray to you with pure heart,
      without delay,
   that at the Day of Judgment you pro-
      tect us from torment.

2 One ought to love such a lady
   from whom all good can come,
   in whom God wished to rest and clothe
      himself in human flesh.
   Lady, he who serves you will attain
      paradise without difficulty,
   I believe it well:
   for this reason should clerics and lay-
      people sing without fear
   of the mother of God.

3 Mary of great renown, fount of
      humility,
   you have taken us from prison, and
      from the disloyalty
   in which Adam the disloyal, the igno-
      rant, the false, left us
   when he ate the fruit which the Saviour
      forbade him,
   for which we lost his love.

4 Resplendant star, moon without dark-
      ness,
   sun which renders great clarity,
   Mary of great beauty,
   most gentle loyal virgin, precious
      vessel,
   I cry out and pray to you
   that you pity and have mercy on
      sinners
   when they come to their end and their
      final day.

18 De la mere au sauvëor

De la mere au sauvë-or · vodrai chançon comencier :
Nus ne puet estre en do-lor · qui mer-ci li veut proi-er.

Mari-e virge loi-aus, pucele roi-aus,

de cuer vrai · sans delai, virge vos proi-erai

qu'au jugement · nos desfendés de torment.

De la me - re_au   sau - vë - or   vo - drai chan - çon   co - - men - cier:
nus ne puet es - tre_en   do - lor   qui mer - ci li   veut   proi - er.

Ma - ri - e vir - ge loi - aus,   pu - ce - le roi - aus,   de cuer vrai   sans de - lai,

vir - ge vos   proi - e - rai   qu'au ju - ge- ment   nos des - fen - dés   de   tor - ment.

19 Quant voi la flor novele

1 Quant voi la flor novele
  florir en la praële,
  lors chant chançon novele
  de la virge pucele
  qui dou lait de sa mamele
  li rois alaita
  qui de sa char digne et bele
  touz nos rachata.

2 Pucele digne et pure,
  qui de toz biens depure,
  qui de pechié nos cure,
  de moi te praigne cure:
  vers son chier fiz m'asseüre
  par tel covenant
  qu'es ciels en joie seüre
  soie parvenant.

3 Dame sainte Marie,
  de grace replenie,
  soiés nos en aïe,
  ne nos oubliés mie:
  qu'en iceste mortel vie
  puissons deservir
  qu'en la vostre conpaignie
  puissons parvenir.

4 Flor de misericorde,
  a ton chier fiz m'acorde,
  corde si bien la corde
  que jamés ne descorde,
  que deable ne s'amorde
  a moi descorder
  que me puisse par concorde
  a Dieu racorder.[1]

5 Marie, douce mere,
  onques ne fus amere,
  de roi es fille et mere,
  et si portas ton pere:
  or te pri, tres douce mere
  plaine de pitié,

que Dex qui est nostre pere
nos get de pechié.

Sources: BN, Manuscript X, f. 266; R. 598
Text category: Co
Music category: Se *serpentine-round*
Rhyme scheme: 7a 7a 7a 7a 8a 5b 8a 5b
Musical scheme: a b a b c d c e
Editions: Järnström and Långfors, 2: 138;
  Gennrich, no. 19
Contrafactum: R. 599

1 A musical play on words is implied by
  the vocabulary, presenting the believer as
  a musical instrument to be tuned by
  Mary. A literal translation of the second
  line would be 'tie the cord so well that it
  will never unravel.'

19 When I see the new flowers

1 When I see the new flowers blooming
    in the field,
 then I sing a new song of the virgin
    maid
 who nursed with the milk of her breast
 the king who came from her worthy
    and beautiful flesh
 to save us all.

2 Maiden worthy and pure, in whom all
    goodness is purified,
 who cures us from sin, take care of me:
 give me assurance through agreement
    from your dear son
 that I will be rewarded with certain joy
    in heaven.

3 Holy lady Mary, full of grace,
 be ready to aid us, do not forget us:
 so that in this mortal life we are able to
    merit
 the reward of a future in your com-
    pany.

4 Flower of mercy, put me in accord with
    your son:
 tune the string so well that it can never
    be made discordant,
 for the devil cannot apply himself to
    untuning me so well
 that I cannot be brought to concord by
    accord with God.

5 Mary, sweet mother, you were never
    bitter,
 you are daughter and mother of a king,
    and thus bore your father:
 now I pray, most gentle mother full of
    pity,
 that God who is our father will cast us
    far from sin.

19 Quant voi flor novele

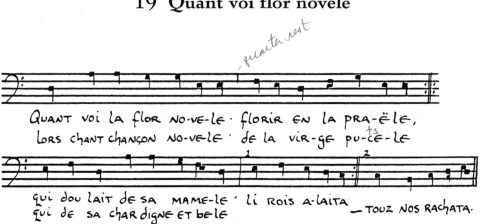

Quant voi la flor no-ve-le · florir en la pra-ë-le,
lors chant chançon no-ve-le · de la vir-ge pu-ce-le

qui dou lait de sa mame-le · li rois a-laita
qui de sa char digne et bele   — touz nos rachata.

Quant voi la flor no - ve - le flo - rir en la pra -
chant chan - çon no - ve - le de la vir - ge pu -

ë - le, lors ce - le qui dou lait de sa ma - me - le
qui de sa char dig - ne_et be - le

li rois a - lai - ta touz nos ra - cha - ta.

20 De Yesse naïstra

1 De Yesse naïstra
  verge qui florira,
  c'avons nos d'Ysaïe:
  'sains espirs i venra,
  qui se reposera
  en la rose espanie.'
  Bien est la profecie,
  si m'est [vis],[1] acomplie:
  la flor est Jhesu Criz,
  si com dit li escriz,
  et la verge est Marie.

2 Mout a plaisant desduit
  qui s'esbat et deduit
  en loer la roïne
  qui porta le douz fruit
  qui tout pechié destruit
  et tout mal medecine.
  Dex, tant est pure et fine
  et de loënge digne,
  tant a en li biauté
  et lumiere et clarté
  que touz nos enlumine.

3 Se li ciels orendroit
  parchemin devenoit,
  s'el vousist nostre sire,
  et se la mers estoit
  enke bon et adroit
  dont l'en peüst escrire,
  et la terre fu cire,
  ne porroit tant soufire
  qui escrire voudroit
  touz les biens qu'en porroit
  de la mere Dieu dire.

4 Qui porroit deviser
  les goutes de la mer,
  et fust chascune goute
  uns hons qui bien parlast,
  jusqu'au jor parlast
  que li mons tant redoute,

qui ma chançon escoute
...[2]
loässent la ades,
n'avroient il jamés
dite sa bonté toute.

Sources: BN, Manuscript X, f. 266; R. 7
Text category: La
Music category: Se
Rhyme scheme: 6a 6a 7b 6a 6a 7b 7b 7b 6c 6c
  7b
Musical scheme: a b c a b c d e a b c
Editions: Järnström and Långfors, 2: 140;
  Gennrich, no. 20
Contrafactum: R. 922 (Jaque de Hesdin)
Remarks: The source of the music is the
  conductus *Homo considera* (*Analecta hym-
  nica*, 21: 139). The image of unlimited
  praise that appears in the third and
  fourth stanzas, as well as in other songs
  in this collection, is discussed in Chapter
  3. Its earliest source seems to be the
  Koran.

1 Manuscript X reads: 'si m'est avis.'
2 The line is missing in the manuscript.

20 Born from the lineage of Jesse

1 'There will be born from the lineage of
     Jesse
   a branch that will flower,'
   we have this from Isaiah:
   'the Holy Spirit will come to it, and will
     rest in the open rose.'
   As far as I can tell, the prophecy has
     come to pass:
   the flower is Jesus Christ, as the
     Scriptures said,
   and the branch is Mary.

2 He has a happy task who takes
     pleasure in praising the queen
   who bore the sweet fruit that destroys
     all sin and cures all evil.
   God, she is so pure and fine and
     worthy of praise,
   there is such beauty in her, and light
     and clarity,
   that she illumines us all!

3 If our Lord wished for the heavens to
     become parchment right now,
   and the seas good ink, so that one
     could write with it,
   and the earth were wax, there would
     not be enough to suffice
   anyone who wished to write all the
     good things one could say
   about the mother of God.

4 If anyone were able to fashion drops of
     water from the sea
   so that each drop became a man who
     speaks well,
   and he spoke until the day which the
     world so fears,
   those who hear my song ...
   if they were to praise her now
   they would never tell all of her
     goodness.

20 De Yesse naïstra

De Yesse na-ï-stra · verge qui florira · c'avons nos d'Ysa-ï-e:
sains espirs i ven-ra · qui se re-po-sera · en la rose espa-ni-e.

Bien est la profeci-e · si m'est vis acompli-e:

la flor est Jhesu Criz · si com dit li escriz · et la verge est Mari-e.

1 S. occ.: ♩ (a)

De   Yes-se na - ï - stra   ver - ge qui flo-ri - ra,   c'a - vons nos d'Y-sa - ï - e: 'sains
es-pirs i ven - ra   qui se re - po-se - ra   en   la rose es-pa - - - -

Bien   est la pro-fe - ci - e,   si   m'est vis, a - com - pli - - e: la
ni - e.'

flor est Jhe-su Criz,   si   com dit li e - scriz,   et   la verge est Ma - ri - e.

21 Fine amor et bone esperance

1 Fine amor et bone esperance
me fait un noviau chant chanter
de cele qui touz ceaus avance
qui de cuer la vuellent amer.
Si vueil la mere Dieu loer
en la chançon que je comence:
en cele servir et amer
doit chascuns avoir sa baänce.

2 Ne doit chascuns bien sa puissance
en cele dame honorer
qui ne cesse sans recreance
de son chier fil por nos prier,
et merci por touz ciaus crier
qui ont en li ferme creance?
Ja nus n'iert si desconfortés,
se merci quiert, qu'el ne l'avance.

3 Dame, je sai bien sans doutance
que sans vos ne me puis sauver,
car je n'ai pas fait penitence
ou je me puisse assëurer,
n'a vostre chier fiz racorder
des pechiés dont sui en balance:
si ai grant päor de versier
se je n'ai de vos soustenance.

4 Douce virge, pure et entiere,
qui Jhesu Crist vout tant amer
qu'il fist de vos sa mere chiere
sans vos de noient entamer:
hé, virge qu'en doit äorer,
faites a vostre fiz proiere
qu'il nos get dou peril amer
dont Lucifer a la lumiere.

5 Douce dame qui nete et fine
fustes en cel concevement
et a l'enfanter enterine,
se l'escriture ne nos ment,
hé, douce virge, doucement
esrachiés de mon cuer l'espine

de pechié, qui si durement
de poindre touz jors ne me fine.

Sources: BN, Manuscript X, ff. 266v–7r;
   R. 222
Text category: Pr
Music category: Ch
Rhyme scheme: 9a 8b 9a 8b 8b 9a 8b 9a
Musical scheme: a b a b c d e f
Editions: Järnström and Långfors, 2: 142;
   Gennrich, no. 21
Contrafacta: R. 221; R. 227a; R. 530a; R. 1179

21 True love and high hopes

1 True love and high hopes cause me
   to sing a new song
   of her who advances all those who
      wish to love her
   with all their heart.
   Therefore I wish to praise the mother of
      God
   in this song which I begin:
   everyone ought to place their desires in
      serving and loving her.

2 Should not everyone place all power
   in honouring this lady
   who never ceases to beseech her dear
      son for us,
    without hesitation,
   and calls for mercy on all those who
      have firm belief in him?
   Never can anyone be so miserable
   that she will not advance him if he
      seeks mercy.

3 Lady, I know without a doubt
   that I cannot save myself without you,
   for I have not done enough penance to
      reassure myself,
   nor to reconcile myself with your dear
      son
   about my sins for which I am in peril:
   thus I have great fear of falling
   if I do not have your support.

4 Sweet virgin, pure and intact,
   who Jesus Christ so loved
   that he made you his dear mother
   without wounding you in any way;
   Virgin worthy of praise, make a prayer
      to your son
   that he cast us away from the bitter
      peril
   where Lucifer bears the light.

5 Gentle lady who was clean and refined
      in this conception,
   and intact in giving birth,
   if the Scriptures do not lie to us;
   sweet virgin,
   gently uproot from my heart the thorn
      of sin,
   which never ceases to prick me so
      painfully.

21 Fine amor et bone esperance

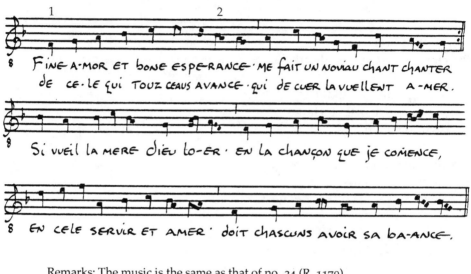

Fine a·mor et bone esperance · me fait un noviau chant chanter
de ce·le qui touz ceaus avance · qui de cuer la vuellent a·mer.

Si vueil la mere dieu lo·er · en la chançon que je comence,

En cele servir et amer · doit chascuns avoir sa ba·ance.

Remarks: The music is the same as that of no. 24 (R. 1179).
1 S. occ.: ■
2 S. occ.: ♪

Fine a - mor et bone e - spe - ran - ce me fait un no -
ce - le qui touz ceaus a - van - ce qui de cuer la

1.
viau chant chan - ter de

2.
vuel- lent a - mer. Si

vueil la me - re

Dieu lo - er en la chan- çon que je co - men - ce: en ce - le ser- vir

et a - mer doit chas - cuns a - voir sa ba - än - ce.

22 De penser a vilainie

1 De penser a vilainie
me devroie mes tenir,
et de toute felonie
car nus biens n'en puet venir.
Or mes me doit souvenir
de la tres douce Marie,
et servir sans tricherie.
Cil qui la sert de cuer verai,
cil avra amoretes au cuer qui le tendront gai.

2 C'est cele qui done au monde
joie et toute clarté,
c'est cele par qui habonde
au monde toute bonté,
c'est cele qui a geté
les gens d'enferté parfonde.
C'est cele qui n'a seconde,
et qui la sert sanz delai,
cil avra amoretes au cuer qui le tendront gai.

3 C'est cele qui tout nos done,
c'est cele qui nos retient,
et tant est bele et tant est bone,
que tout le monde maintient.
C'est cele qui nos i tient,
ce est la saintisme persone
par qui touz biens nos habonde.
Cil qui la sert sans esmai,
cil avra amoretes au cuer qui le tendront gai.

4 Ce est la sainte racine
qui toz nos a dressiés,
ce est la sainte pechine
qui nos osta de pechiés
dont li mont ert entechiés.
C'est la sainte medecine
...[1]
cil qui la sert de cuer gai,
cil avra amoretes au cuer qui le tendront gai.

5 C'est li formens, c'est la graine,
dont Dex nos a repeü,

ce est la sainte fontaine
dont nos avons tuit beü.
Par li somes nos meü
por aler en joie saine:
qui de li servir se paine
de loial cuer et de verai,
cil avra amoretes au cuer qui le tendront gai.

Sources: BN, Manuscript X, f. 267; R. 1239
Text category: La
Music category: Se
Rhyme scheme: 8a 7b 8a 7b 7b 8a 8a 7c:
   7+7c
Musical scheme: a b_x a b_x c d e e_x f e_x
Editions: Järnström and Långfors 2: 144;
   Gennrich, no. 22
Contrafactum: R. 1240

1 The line is missing in the manuscript.

22 From thinking of villainy

1 I ought to hold myself always from
    thinking of villainy
  and from all felony,
   for no good can come of them.
  I should always remember the most
    sweet Virgin Mary,
  and serve without treachery.
  He who serves her with a true heart,
  He shall have love in his heart to keep him
    happy.

2 It is she who gives to the world joy and
    all clarity,
  it is she through whom all goodness
    abounds in the world,
  it is she who has cast out the people
    from deepest hell,
  she who has no equal.
  He who serves her without delay,
  He shall have love in his heart to keep him
    happy.

3 It is she who gives us all things,
  she who maintains us,
  and she is so lovely and good that she
    sustains all the world.
  It is she who keeps us there,
  the most saintly person through whom
    all good comes to us.
  He who serves her without worry,
  He shall have love in his heart to keep him
    happy.

4 She is the holy root which has directed
    all of us,
  the holy pool which removes the sins
    with which the world was stained.
  She is the blessed medicine ...
  He who serves her with a joyous heart,
  He shall have love in his heart to keep him
    happy.

5 She is the wheat, she is the grain
  from which God nourished us,
  she is the most holy fountain from
    which we have all drunk,
  by her are we moved to go forth in
    complete joy.
  He who troubles himself to serve her
    with true and loyal heart,
  He shall have love in his heart to keep him
    happy.

22 De penser a vilainie

de penser a vilaini-e · me de-vroi-e mes te-nir
et de toute felo-ni-e , car nus biens n'en puet ve-nir.

Or mes me doit souvenir · de la tres douce Mari-e

Et servir sans tricheri-e ·

cil qui la sert de cuer ve-rai ,

Cil avra amo-re-tes · au cuer qui le tendront gai.

1 First occ.: ◆
2 First occ.: ◆

De pen - ser   a   vi - lai - ni - e   me   de - vroi - e   mes   te - nir,
et   de   tou - te   fe - lo - ni - e   car   nus   biens n'en   puet   ve - nir.

Or   mes   me   doit   sou - ve - nir   de   la   tres   dou - ce   Ma - ri - e,

et   ser - vir   sans   tri - che - ri - e.   Cil   qui   la   sert   de   cuer   verai,

cil   a - vra   a - mo - re - tes   au   cuer   qui   le   ten - dront   gai.

23 Et cler et lai

1 Et cler et lai
   tout sanz delai
   or escoutés m'entente:
   chançon ferai,
   si chanterai de la roïne gente
   en qui costéz Dex descendi,
   qui de dolor nos desfendi
   et de grant tormente.
   Chantons en sans atente,
   que je me puis mout bien chanter.
   De cele devons nos chanter
   qui touz nos rendi vie:
   Or nos aidiez
   et conseillés,
   douce virge Marie.

2 Dame de pris,
   tant ai apris
   de vostre grant hautece.
   Nus et depris
   et mort et pris
   fussiens, et sanz leëce.
   Par la bonté qui en vos maint
   sont sauvées maintes et maint
   et fors de grant tristesse.
   Dame de grant noblece,
   cil qui de cuer vos servira
   droit en paradis s'en ira
   en Dieu la compaignie:
   Or nos aidiez
   et conseillés,
   douce virge Marie.

3 Fons [de]¹ pitié,
   d'umelité,
   douce chose honorée,
   tu as quité
   par amisté
   voir, mainte ame esgarée.
   Tant a en toi pris et bonté
   que ta bonté a remonté
   mainte ame desmontée
   qui ores est remontée.

Por la vostre amor deservir
doit chascun noit et jor servir
qu'en vos a bone amie:
Or nos aidiez
et conseillés,
douce virge Marie.

4 Dame en qui cors
   toz bon acors
   est, et toute concorde:
   cors sans descors,
   misericors
   vostre misericorde.
   Nos a de corde descordés
   dont chascun estoit encordés:
   cil qui a vos s'acorde
   de lui ostés la corde
   dont Adans touz nos acorde.
   Vostre bonté nos racorda
   et mist en seignorie:
   Or nos aidiez
   et conseillés,
   douce virge Marie.

5 Cors qui rendis
   et estendis
   seur nos touz ta lumiere,
   chascuns mendis
   en fais, en dis,
   vos doit avoir mout chiere.
   Cil qui vos sert sanz escondis
   sera poséz en paradis
   et pris a lïe chiere
   ...²
   Ja nus n'iert si enmaladis
   que maintenant ne soit gueris,
   se de bon cuer vos prie:
   Or nos aidiez
   et conseillés,
   douce virge Marie.

Sources: BN, Manuscript X, ff. 267v–8v;
   R. 82
Text category: La
Music category: Se

23 Both cleric and laic

1 Both cleric and laic,
   without delay,
   listen now to my meaning:
   I will make a song,
   and sing of the noble queen
   into whose sides descended God,
   who defended us from pain and great
       torment.
   Let us sing of this without waiting, for I
       can sing well:
   we ought to sing of her who gave life to
       us all.
   Now aid and counsel us,
       sweet Virgin Mary.

2 Lady of worth,
   I have learned much of your high
       power.
   Naked and bare, we would have been
       put to death,
   and without joy,
   but through the goodness which abides
       in you
   many women and men are saved,
   and taken far from great sadness.
   Lady of great nobility,
   he who serves you from the heart
   will go straight to paradise in the
       company of God:
   Now aid and counsel us,
       sweet Virgin Mary.

3 Fountain of pity and humility,
   sweet honoured one,
   you have restored through true friend-
       ship many a lost soul.
   You have in you such worth and good-
       ness
   that your goodness has raised many a
       cast-down soul
   that now is restored.
   To deserve your love, everyone ought
       to serve you

night and day as a true friend:
Now aid and counsel us,
    sweet Virgin Mary.

4 Lady in whose body is all good accord,
   and all concord:
   body without discord,
   have mercy.
   Your mercy has untied from us
   the cord that tied everyone:
   when someone accords himself to you,
   you lift from him the cord with which
       Adam tied us all.
   Your goodness brings us together and
       puts us in noble state:
   Now aid and counsel us,
       sweet Virgin Mary.

5 Body which renders and extends your
       light to us,
   every mendicant should hold you dear
       in word and deed.
   He who serves you unconditionally
   will be placed in paradise
   and taken to blessed joy ...
   No one has ever been so ill
   that he will not be cured,
   if he prays to you with a good heart:
   Now aid and counsel us,
       sweet Virgin Mary.

Rhyme scheme: 4a 4a 7b 4a 4a 7b 8c 8c 7b 7b
   8d 8d 7e : 4f 4f 7e
Musical scheme: a b c a b c′ d d′ e f d d e : a
   b c
Editions: Järnström and Långfors 2: 146;
   Gennrich, no. 23
Contrafactum: R. 2005 (Jean Erart)
Remarks: The metric scheme and the extent
   of wordplay are unusual, and they may
   represent a more learned (e.g., clerical)
   authorship than is the norm for this
   collection.

1 The word is added to clarify the sense
   and rectify the metre.
2 The line is missing in the manuscript.

23 Et cler et lai

Et cler et lai · tout sanz delai · or escoutés m'entente;

Chançon ferai · si chanterai · de la ro-ï-ne gente

En qui costéz · dex descendi · qui de dolor nos desfendi

Et de grant tormente. Chantons en sans atente

que je me puis mout bien chanter,
de ce-le de-vons nos chanter ~ qui touz nos rendi vi-e:

Or nos aidiez · et conseillés · douce virge Mari-e.

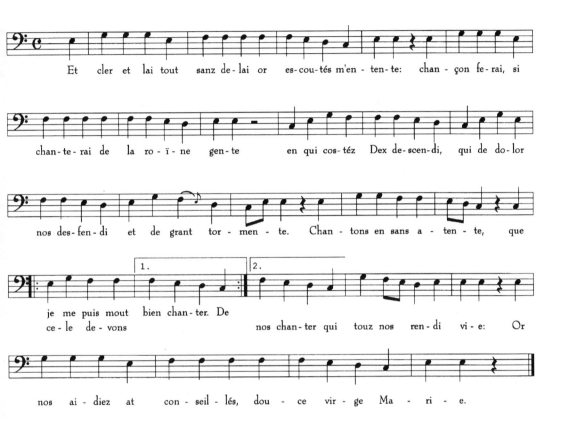

See appendix C for alternative notation.

24 Douce dame, virge Marie

1 Douce dame, virge Marie,
   la roïne de paradis,
   vostre conseil et vostre aïe
   requier et requerrai touz dis
   que vos prïez vostre chier filz
   baptesme ne me faille mie:
   trop en ai esté escondix,
   si le requier sanz vilainie.

2 Douce dame, j'ai grant fiance
   en cil qui en crois fu penés.
   Qui en celui n'a sa creance
   certes por droit noient est nez:
   son esperit ert dampnéz
   ens el puis d'enfer sanz faillence,
   et cil qui ert chrestiens claméz
   il n'a d'enfer nule doutance.

3 Hé las, je l'ai tant desirée
   et si ne la puis pas avoir:
   toute est m'entente et ma pensée
   en crestïenté recevoir.
   Feme, or et argent ne avoir
   ne nule riens tant ne m'agrée
   con fait crestïenté por avoir,
   si ne me peut estre donée.

4 A vos, douce virge honorée,
   proi et requier mout bonement
   que vostre fiz sanz demorée
   proiés por moi prochainement:
   que de ceus m'achat vengement
   qui crestïenté m'ont v[e]ée,
   ensi con je croi veraiement
   celui qui fist ciel et rosée.

Sources: BN, Manuscript X, f. 268v; R. 1179
Text category: Pr
Music category: Ch
Rhyme scheme: 9a 8b 9a 8b 8b 9a 8b 9a
Musical scheme: a b a b c d e f
Editions: Järnström and Långfors, 2: 149;
    Gennrich, no. 24
Contrafacta: R. 221 (Pierre de Molins,
    Chastelain de Couci, Gace Brulé); R. 222
Remarks: Järnström and Långfors ascribe
    this text to someone who has been
    refused baptism, possibly a Jew. Accord-
    ing to Father Leonard Boyle of the Vati-
    can Archives, with whom I discussed the
    text, it may refer instead to the author's
    fear of failing to be worthy of his baptism
    and his wish to receive faith on more
    than a nominal level.

24 Sweet lady, Virgin Mary

1 Sweet lady, Virgin Mary, the queen of
    paradise,
  I seek and always will request your aid
    and counsel
  that you pray your dear son that
    baptism will not be denied me:
  too long I have refused it,
  now I seek it without guile.

2 Gentle lady, I have great faith
  in him who was made to suffer on the
    cross.
  Anyone who does not put faith in him
    was certainly born in vain:
  his spirit will be damned in the pit of
    hell without a doubt,
  and anyone who calls himself a
    Christian has no doubt of hell.

3 Alas, I have so desired it,
  and thus am not able to have it:
  all my desire and thought is to be
    received into Christianity.
  Possession of women, silver, or gold,
  nor any other thing can satisfy me
  as does Christian faith for my fortune,
  yet it cannot be given to me.

4 To you, sweet honoured virgin,
  I pray and request with good intention
  that to your son without delay
  you pray for me immediately:
  that he grant vengeance to me
  on those who have denied me
    Christian faith,
  since I truly believe in him who made
    the sky and the dew.

24 Douce dame, virge Marie

dou-ce da-me, virge Mari-e, la ro-ï—ne de para-dis,
vostre conseil et vostre a-ï-e · requier et requerrai touz dis

que vos priez vo-stre chier filz

baptesme ne me faille mi-e;

Trop en ai esté escondix · si le requier sanz vilani-e .

Remark: The music is the same as that of no. 21 (R. 222).
1 S. occ.: ⌐
2 S. occ.: ⌐ (dc)

Dou-ce da-me, vir-ge ma-ri-e, la ro-ï-ne de pa-ra-dis,
vos-tre con-seil et vos-tre_a-ï-e re-quier et re - - - -

1.

2.
que vos prï-ez vo-stre chier filz bap -
quer-rai touz dis

tes-me ne me fail-le mi - e: trop en ai e-sté

es-con-dix, si le re-quier sanz vi-lai-ni - e.

25 Chançon ferai, puis que Diex m'a doné

1 Chançon ferai, puis que Diex m'a doné
grace, que j'ai laissié toute amor vaine:
si me repent que tant ai demoré
en folie, ou il n'a fors que paine.
Or me gart et voi trop bestorné
tout le siecle ceus que fole amor maine:
je le vos di por Gace le Brullé,
assez chanta dont Dex ne li set gré.

2 Trestuit si chant sont de la fleur d'esté
ou de vert bois, ou de ru de fontaine,
ou d'aucune a qui Dieus a presté
en cest siecle un pou de biauté vaine.
Bon sont si chant, por c'en ai
    g'enprunté,
mes sachiés bien c'une autre amor me
    maine:
c'est de la mere au roi de verité
qui tout cria, et yver et esté.

3 Bien sont cil fol et plain de vanité
qui font chançons ne d'Iseut ne
    d'Alaine,
et sage sont tuit cil qui ont chanté
de la dame qui porta Dieu sanz paine.
Onques feme n'ot tant d'umilité
que Dex la fist de toutes graces plaine:
seur toutes roïnes fu de pité,
et de tout sens, et de toute bonté.

4 Avugles est, et s'abat de son tour
qui en biauté de cest siecle se fie.
Regardés bien ces dames chascun jor:
beles sont hui, demain ne seront mie.
S'un pou de mau les prent ainz le quart
    jor,
seront eles plus jaune que sofie:
bien les poöns conparer a la flor
qu'en queut matin, au soir pert sa
    color.

5 Bien voi que nus ne porra eschaper
que de la mort ne paït le treuage,
et quant tel saut avons tuit a passer,
bien devroient a ce penser li sage:
car qui porroit de la mort eschaper
par richesses, par pleges ou par gaiges,
trop feroit melz li siecles a amer:
qui or fait mout a touz a redouter.

Sources: BN, Manuscript X, ff. 268v–9v;
    R. 425
Text category: Pr
Music category: Rn
Rhyme scheme: 10a 11b 10a 11b 10a 11b 10a
    10a
Musical scheme: a b_x c b'_x d_y e f_y e_x
Editions: Järnström and Långfors, 2: 151;
    Gennrich, no. 25
Contrafactum: R. 437 (Gace Brulé)

25 I will make a song, since God has given me grace

1 I will make a song, since God has given
  me grace,
  for I have left behind all vain love;
  yet I regret that I remained so long in
    folly,
  where there is nothing but pain.
  Now I take care, and see all those in
    this world
  who are led by foolish love turned
    upside down:
  I tell you this for Gace Brulé,
  he sang much of matters that did not
    please God.

2 All of his songs were of the flowers of
    summer,
  or the green wood, or the flow of the
    fountain,
  or of any woman in this world
  to whom God has lent a bit of vain
    beauty.
  His songs are good, for which reason I
    have borrowed from them,
  but now another love leads me:
  it is of the mother of the king of truth
  who created all things, both summer
    and winter.

3 They are foolish and full of vanity,
  those who make songs about Isolde or
    Helen,
  and they are wise who have sung about
    the lady
  who bore God without pain.
  No other woman had such humility
  that God made her full of all graces:
  above all others she was queen
  of mercy, wisdom, and goodness.

4 He is blind and falls down from his
    tower

who takes pride in the beauty of this
  world.
Take a good look at these ladies each
  day:
lovely today, and not at all tomorrow.
If a little quartan fever takes them,
they turn more yellow than sulphur:
we can well compare them to a flower
which one seeks in the morning,
and by evening it fades.

5 I see that no one can avoid paying
    death his tribute,
  and when we have all taken this leap,
  the wise ought to think of this:
  for he who would escape death
  through riches, pledges, or payments
  has too much love for this world;
  he will have much to fear.

25 Chançon ferai, puis que Diex m'a doné

Chançon ferai, puis que diex m'a do-né· grace que j'ai laissié toute amor vaine,

si me repent que tant ai demo-ré· en foli-e ou il n'a fors que pai-ne.

Or me gart et voi trop bestor-né

tout le siecle ceus que fole amor mai-ne;

je le vos di por Gace le brullé, assez chanta dont dex ne li set gré.

Chan - çon fe - rai, puis que Diex m'a do - né

gra - ce, que j'ai lais - sié tou - te_a - mor vai - ne:

si me re - pent que tant ai de - mo - ré

en fo - li - e, ou il n'a fors que pai - ne.

Or me gart et voi trop bes - tor - né

tout le sie - cle ceus que fo - le_a - mor mai - ne:

je le vos di por Ga - ce le Brul - lé,

a - sez chan - ta dont Dex ne li set gré.

26 Por ce que verité die

1 Por ce que verité die
  vueil ma chançon comencier
  por deduire et solacier
  ceus qui sont en bone vie;
  et ceus qui sont en folie,
  en guille et en tricherie,
  vueill blasmer et leidengier,
  et mostrer leur maladie.

2 Quant n'apert la maladie,
  nus mires n'en puet aidier
  ne bien a droit conseiller.
  Ensit est d'ypocresie:
  qui le cors a plain d'envie
  ne par dehors ne pert mie,
  ainz sont tel fois au mostier
  que leur cuers est en folie.

3 Dex nos a mostré par vie,
  par sarmons, par prëechier,
  coment nos devons laissier
  tout pechié, toute folie,
  tout mal, toute tricherie,
  tout orgueill, et toute envie,
  et nos prie d'esloingnier
  doublesse d'ypocresie.

4 Honi soit lor conpaignie
  qu'en n'en fait qu'enpirie:
  bien la devons esloignier,
  Saint Gregoires nos en prie.
  Bien puis conparer leur vie
  a fausse pome porrie
  qu'en met en tas estoier
  et ses conpaignes conchie.

5 É dame, sainte Marie,
  bien devés a ceus aidier
  qui de bon cuer et d'entier
  vos servent sanz tricherie:
  qui ne font par symonie
  ne par fausse ypocrissie

les biens, mes por gäaignier
joie qui ne faudra mie.

Sources: BN, Manuscript X, ff. 269v–70r;
  R. 1136
Text category: Pl
Music category: Th
Rhyme scheme: 8a 7b 7b 8a 8a 8a 7b 8a
Musical scheme: a b c d e f g h
Editions: Järnström and Långfors, 2: 152;
  Gennrich, no. 26
Contrafactum: R. 1216 (Moniot)

26 Because it speaks truth

1 I wish to begin my song because it
     speaks truth
   to delight and comfort those who live a
     good life;
   and I wish to blame and affront
   those who live in folly, guile, and
     treachery,
   and show their weakness.

2 When a malady is not apparent,
   no physician can give aid or proper
     counsel.
   Hypocrisy is like this:
   those who have a body full of greed
     and hatred
   that does not appear on the outside,
   no matter how many times they are in
     a church,
   their hearts remain in folly.

3 God has shown us
   through his life, sermons, and
     preaching,
   how we ought to leave all sinning,
    folly, evil, treachery, pride, and envy,
   and he entreats us to recoil
   from the doubleness of hypocrisy.

4 Shame be on the company of those
   who can do nothing but degrade;
   St Gregory asks us to avoid them.
   Their lives can be compared to a rotten
     apple
   that one leaves to rest on a heap,
   so that it spoils its companions.

5 Lady, holy Mary,
   you come to the aid of those
   who, with full and good heart,
   serve you without treachery:
   who do good not through simony

nor through false hypocrisy,
but to gain the joy which never ceases.

26　Por ce que verité die

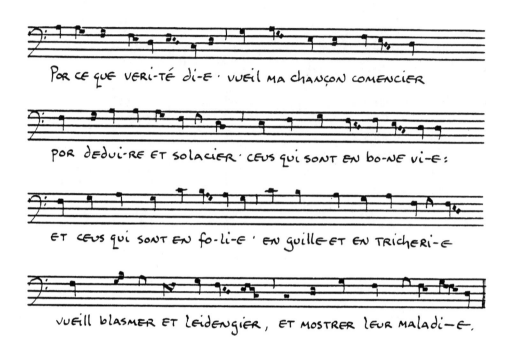

Por ce que veri-té di-e · vueil ma chançon comencier

por dedui-re et solacier · ceus qui sont en bo-ne vi-e:

et ceus qui sont en fo-li-e · en guille et en tricheri-e

vueill blasmer et leidengier, et mostrer leur maladi-e.

Por ce que ve - ri - té di - e vueil ma chan - çon co - men - cier

por de - dui - re et so - la - cier ceus qui sont en bo - ne vi - e;

et ceus qui sont en fo - li - e, en guille et en tri - che - ri - e,

vueill blas - mer et lei - den - gier, et mos - trer leur ma - la - di - e.

27 Au douz comencement d'esté

1 Au douz comencement d'esté
une chançon comencerai,
non pas por ce que de vert pré
me viegne la joie que j'ai.
Ançois me semble fausseté
et baras et desloiauté
trestout quant qu'en cest siecle voi.

2 Tres grant force ne biauté
ne me plest pas, bien sai por quoi:
por ce qu'en honte et en vilté
nest hom et muert hom, bien le voi.
Por c'a droit qui en charité
et en huevre d'umilité
est touz jors, et en veraie foi.

3 Je ne sai querre verité,
que chascuns l'acoile endroit soi:
en evesque n'en blanc abé
n'en truis je point, ce poise moi,
car gieus a si touz sousplanté
qu'en justifie fausseté
et qu'on dampne povre home verai.

4 Par flaterie sont guilé
toutes les gens, et clerc et lai,
et par grans dons sont honoré
li riche plain de povre foi:
mes li povre home degeté
desferment par humilité
paradis, et deviennent roi.

5 Nus hons n'a grant benëurté
fors cil qui ame de cuer verai
cele qui par humilité
devint roïne et mere au roi:
je li ai tout mon cuer doné,
ne jamés tant con je vivrai
de li servir ne recrerai.

Sources: BN, Manuscript X, f. 270r; R. 435
Text category: Pl
Music category: Rn
Rhyme scheme: 8a 8b 8a 8b 8a 8a 8b
Musical scheme: a b a b c c' b
Editions: Järnström and Långfors, 2: 154 ;
    Gennrich, no. 27
Contrafacta: R. 1465 (Gace Brulé); R. 1897a
    (Blondel); R. 430 (Cuens de Couci). See
    also *Rex et sacerdos prefuit* by Philip the
    Chancellor, in *Analecta hymnica* 21: 243.

27 At the sweet commencement of summer

1 At the sweet commencement of
     summer,
  I will begin a song,
  but not because the joy I feel
  comes from the green fields:
  for all that I see in this world seems to
     me
  falseness, fraud, and disloyalty.

2 Neither great power nor great beauty
     can please me,
  and I know why:
  because I see that humankind
  is born and dies in shame and vileness.
  Therefore he is right
  who keeps himself always in charity,
  works of humility, and true faith.

3 I do not know where to seek truth,
     for each one gathers it in his own place:
  I don't find it at all in bishops nor white
     abbots,
  which disappoints me,
  for mockery has so reversed them that
     they justify falsity
  and condemn the poor man who holds
     to the truth.

4 All are beguiled by flattery,
     both cleric and layman,
  and the rich, whose faith is poor,
     are honoured by grand gifts:
  but poor men, rejected,
  will open paradise by their humility,
  and become kings.

5 No man has great good fortune
     but the one who loves with a true heart
  her who, through humility,
     became a queen and the mother of a
        king:

I have given her my whole heart,
nor will I rest from her service as long
     as I live.

27 Au douz comencement d'esté

8 Au douz comence-ment d'esté · u-ne chançon comen-ce-rai,
Non pas por ce que de vert pré me viegne la joi-e que j'ai.

8 Ançois me semble faussëté · et baras et desloiauté

8 Trestout quant qu'en cest siecle voi.

Au douz co-men-ce - ment d'es-té   u - ne chan-çon co - mence - rai, non
pas por ce que   de vert pré   me   vie-gne la joi - - - -

An - çois me sem-ble   faus-se - té   et   ba-ras et des -
e   que   j'ai.

loi - au - té   tres - tout quant qu'en cest   sie - cle   voi.

28 Buer fu néz qui s'apareille

1 Buer fu néz qui s'apareille
a Dieu amer et servir,
et qui en oroisons veille
en ferveur et en desir:
car qui sert Dieu en sa vie
de loial cuer et d'entier,
il l'en rendra grant baillie
qu'en la soë conpaignie
vendra les mauvais jugier
et les justes essaucier.

2 Droite raison me conseille
que je doi dou tout servir
cele qui est sans pareille
et qu'a li doi obeïr.
C'est la rose espanie
qui Gabrïaus vint noncier
'Dex te saut, virge Marie':
lors devint parole vie,
quant la virge sans touchier
conçut le roi droiturier.

3 Ce li vint a grant merveille
quant li sains angres li dist
'Dex te saut, tendre vermeille,
tu porteras Jhesu Crist;
Dex t'a de sa grace emplie,
tu ne pues jamés pechier.'
Humblement respont Marie,
'Sur ce ne voi je mie,
que pucele sanz touchier
a home puist enchargier.'

4 'Douce dame droituriere,
je te vieng dire et noncier
qu'ausi con par la verriere
entre solaus en mostier,
ausi con ça en arieres
ardoit sanz amenusier
li buissons en la bruiere,
concevras nete et [en]tiere

par parole, sans touchier,
ne virginité brisier.'

5 Prions la virge Marie
que nos devons tui[t] amer,
que en ceste mortel vie
nos doint si bien confesser
que perdre ne puissons mie
ce qu'on ne puet recovrer:
ce est la soe conpaignie
de joie si bien garnie
que nus n'el puet recouvrer,
ne cuers ne porroit penser.

Sources: BN, Manuscript X, ff. 270r–1v;
    R. 563
Text category : Ca
Music category: Ch
Rhyme scheme: 8a 7b 8a 7b 8a 7b 8a 8a 7b
    7b
Musical scheme: a b a b' c d e f g h
Editions: Järnström and Långfors, 2: 156;
    Gennrich, no. 28
Contrafactum: R. 565 (Gace Brulé)

28 He who prepares himself

1 He who prepares himself
   to love and serve God was born fortu-
      nate,
   as was he who stays awake in prayer
      and fervour and desire:
   for the one who serves God in his life-
      time with full and loyal heart;
   God will give him great reward in his
      own presence
   when he comes to judge the wicked
      and exalt the just.

2 True wisdom counsels me that in all
      things
   I ought to serve her who is without
      equal,
   and that I must obey her.
   She is the full-blown rose to whom
      Gabriel came to announce
   'God save you, Virgin Mary,'
   then the word came alive, when the
      untouched virgin
   conceived the true king.

3 This came as a great astonishment,
   when the holy angel said to her
   'God save you, tender rose – you will
      bear Jesus Christ;
   God has filled you with his grace, you
      can never sin.'
   Mary responded humbly,
   'I have never seen such a thing,
   that a maiden could be impregnated by
      a man
   without being touched.'

4 'Gentle true lady, I am come
   to tell and announce to you
   that just as the sunlight enters a church
   through the glass window,
   just as God long ago caused a bush on
      the heath

to burn without being consumed,
you will conceive clean and intact,
   through a word,
untouched and without breaking your
   virginity.'

5 We pray the Virgin Mary, whom we all
      should love,
   that in this mortal life she guide us so
      well to confess
   that we are unable to lose what can
      never be recovered:
   that is her own company, so well
      adorned with joy
   that no one can obtain it, nor can any
      heart imagine it.

28 Buer fu néz

Buer fu nez qui s'apareille · a dieu a-mer et servir

et qui en o-roisons veille · en ferveur et en de-sir ;

car qui sert dieu en sa vi-e · de loi-al cuer et d'entier

il l'en rendra grant bailli-e · qu'en la so-é conpaigni-e

vendra les mauvais ju-gier · et les justes essau-cier .

Buer fu néz qui s'a - pa - reil - le a Dieu a - mer et ser - vir,

et qui en o - roi - sons veil - le en fer - veur et en de - sir:

car qui sert Dieu en sa vi - e de loi - al cuer et d'en - tier,

il l'en ren - dra grant bail - li - e qu'en la so - ë con - pai - gni - e

ven - dra les mau - vais ju - gier et les jus - tes es - sau - cier.

29 Qui de la prime florete

1 Qui de la prime florete
voudra doucement chanter,
il covient qu'il s'entremete
de ses meffais amender
et sa consciënce nete
tenir, et son cuer mender:
car ce devons nos de dete
sans autrement amender[1]
a Jhesu, qui est florete
des fleurs, et la plus doucete
c'on puist jamés recouvrer.

2 Ceste flors a tel semblance
qui ne fait pas a blasmer,
car ele est vermeille et blanche,
s'en fait mout melz a amer.
Li blans est senefiance
de virginité garder,
li vermeus est remembrance
dou sanc Jhesu, qui sauver
vint touz ceus qui ont fiance
en li, sanz desesperance:
tel flor doit chascuns porter.

3 Herbe dont la flor est née
ne doit l'en pas oublier,
car por noif ne por gelée
ne la vit nus hons muer;
toz tens est si bien gardée
que ele ne puet enpirer,
n'est riens en terre criée
c'on puist a li conparer.
C'est la tres douce Marie
qui pechié ne vilainie
n'ot onques en son penser.

4 Douce dame sainte et franche,
je vos pri que vos m'acordés
a Jhesu, dont par errance
me sui souvent descordéz;
et que me tiegne en soufrance
tant que touz aie amendéz

mes pechiés par penitence,
dont je sui si enconbrés:
et me doint telle aliance
que n'en soit prise venjance
en enfer o les dampnés.

5 Chançon, va t'en a la bele
car je t'i vueil envoier:
c'est a la virge pucele
de qui me vueill racointier.
Va t'en tost, soiés isnele
de ma besoigne noncier
de li, qu'ele me rapele,
car g'en ai mout grant mestier:
et m'envoit tele estancele
por ceste chançon novele
qui me garde de pechier.

Sources: BN, Manuscript X, f. 271; Metz,
  Stadtbibliothek, Manuscript 535, f. 171;
  R. 981
Text category: Co
Music category: Rn
Rhyme scheme: 8a 7b 8a 7b 8a 7b 8a 7b 8a
  8a 7b
Musical scheme: a b a c a b a' c d e c
Editions: Järnström and Långfors, 2: 157;
  Gennrich, no. 29
Contrafactum: R. 982

1 In manuscript 535 at Metz: 'conmander'

29 About the first budding flower

1 He who wishes to sing softly
about the first budding flower
must apply himself to amending his
misdeeds,
to keeping his conscience clean and
mending his heart:
for we ought to do this as a debt,
without taking on any other,
to Jesus, who is the new flower of
flowers,
and the sweetest that anyone can
discover.

2 This flower appears without blemish,
for it is red and white, which makes it
best beloved.
The white signifies that it keeps
virginity;
the red is remembrance of the blood of
Jesus,
who came to save all those who had
faith in him,
without despair:
this is a flower that everyone ought to
wear.

3 One must not forget the plant
from which this flower was born,
for no one saw it fade in snow or in ice:
it is so well kept at all times that it
cannot decline;
there is no other created on the earth
that can be compared with it.
It is the most sweet Mary,
who never had a thought of sin nor
villainy.

4 Sweet lady, holy and generous,
I pray that you put me in accord with
Jesus,
with whom, through error, I am often
in discord;

and that he hold me in sufferance
until I have amended all my sins,
which so encumber me, through
penance;
and that he give me such alliance
that I will not be taken for vengeance
into hell with the condemned.

5 Song, go along
to the beauty to whom I wish to send
you:
it is the virgin maid of whom I wish to
tell.
Go quickly, be swift to announce my
desire to her,
so that she will call me, for I have great
need;
and that she might grant me such
standing,
as reward for this new song,
that it will keep me from sinning.

29 Qui de la prime florete

Qui de la pri-me florete · voudra doucement chanter

il couvient qu'il s'entremete · de ses meffais amender

et sa consci-ence ne-te · tenir, et son cuer mender;

car ce devons nos de dete · sans autrement amender

a Jhesu qui est florete · des fleurs, et la plus doucete

c'on puist james recouvrer.

Qui de la pri - me flo - re - te   vou - dra dou - ce - ment chan - ter,

il cou - vient qu'il   s'en - tre - me - te   de ses mef - fais   a - men - der

et sa con - sci - ën - ce   ne - te   te - nir,   et son   cuer men - der:

car ce de - vons   nos de de - te   sans au - tre - ment   a - men - der   a Jhe - su, qui

est flo - re - te   des fleurs, et la   plus dou - ce - te   c'on puist ja - més   re - cou - vrer.

30 Une tres douce pensée

1 Une tres douce pensée
   que ja ne vueil oublier
   m'a si doucement navrée
   que souvent me fait penser
   ce que tant nos veut amer,
   cele biauté desirrée:
   Hélas, coment puet durer
   mes cuers qu'il ne muert d'amer?

2 Une douceur enmiellée
   ne me puis tenir d'amer,
   une biauté esmerée
   que Dex fist por soi loer:
   qu'en ciel n'en terre n'en mer
   n'est sa bonté si provée
   come en cele qui, sans per,
   fu digne de lui porter.

3 Quant j'ai d'amors remenbrance,
   bien doi de joie chanter
   et tout metre en oubliance,
   qu'amors me fait sospirer
   et doucement desirrer
   Jhesu, qui dou cors la lance
   vout ouvrir por li entrer
   et en s'amor reposer.

4 Quant j'ai de li remenbrance,
   lors me covient mercier
   Dex, qui en sa douce enfance
   si se vout a li doner.
   Nus cuers ne porroit penser
   la grant joie sans doutance
   qu'ele ot de lui enfanter:
   plus ne la pout honorer.

5 Quant je pens a sa naissance,
   lors covient l'amor doubler:
   a cele tres douce enfance
   Dex, qui soi nos vout doner
   le pain blanc et le vin cler
   que nos espandi la lance

qui aprent a bien amer
cuer qui s'en puet enyvrer.

Sources: BN, Manuscript X, ff. 271v–2r;
   R. 541
Text category: Pr
Music Category: Rn
Rhyme scheme: 8a 7b 8a 7b 7b 8a 7b 7b
Musical scheme: a b a b c d c' e
Editions: Järnström and Långfors, 2: 160;
   Gennrich, no. 30
Contrafactum: R. 244 (Robert de Mem-
   beroles or Mauvoisin).
Remarks: This text has a mystical tone reminiscent of contemporary Persian Sufi
   devotional poetry. Hafiz in particular
   uses the image of drunkenness as a metaphor for spiritual union; the state of
   enlightenment is seen as blinding the
   adept to worldly concerns and functions.
   Given the abundance of critical theories
   tracing influences from the Middle East
   on European poetry and music in the
   period of the Crusades, the possibility of
   influence is not entirely remote.

30 A sweet thought

1 A sweet thought, which I hope never to
      forget,
   has so gently wounded me
   that it often turns my thoughts to that
      desired beauty
   who wishes so much to love us:
   Alas, how can my heart endure,
   and not perish with love?

2 I cannot help loving a honeyed
      sweetness,
   a pure beauty
   which God made for his own
      glorification;
   for nowhere in heaven, earth, or sea
   is his goodness so proven
   as in her who, without equal,
   was worthy to bear him.

3 When I remember that love,
   I must sing with joy and forget all else,
   for love makes me sigh and sweetly
      desire
   Jesus, whose body the lance wished to
      open
   in order to enter and rest in his love.

4 When I remember this,
   I must thank God,
   who wished to give himself to her in
      his sweet infancy.
   No heart can imagine the great joy
   which she had in giving him birth:
   he could not have honoured her more.

5 When I think of his birth, love is
      doubled:
   God, from that most sweet childhood,
   wished to give himself to us
   in the white bread and the clear wine
   poured out for us by the lance
   which teaches the heart

that can become drunk with this wine
to love well.

30 Une tres douce pensée

U-NE TRES douce PENSÉ-E · que ja NE vueil oubli-ER
M'A si dou-CEMENT NAVRÉ-E · que souvent ME fait PENSER

CE que TANT NOS VEUT A-MER · CELE biauté desirRÉ-E;

hé las, coment puet du-RER · MES cuers qu'il NE muert d'A-MER ?

1 S. occ.:
2 S. occ.:
3 S. occ.:
4 S. occ.:
5 S. occ.:

U - ne tres dou - ce pen - sé - e   que ja ne vueil   ou - bli - er
m'a si dou - ce - ment nav - ré - e   que sou - vent me   fait pen - ser

ce que tant nos   veut   a - mer,   ce - le biau - té   de - sir - ré - e:

hé - las,   co - ment   puet   du - rer   mes cuers qu'il   ne   muert d'a - mer?

31 Chanter m'estuet de cele sans targier

1 Chanter m'estuet de cele sans targier
 qui de mer est luissans estoile clere:
 servir la doit chascuns de cuer entier,
 car fors nos mist de la tormente amere
 ou mis nos ot Adans, no premier pere.
 Le fruit manja par Evain sa moillier
 que Dex li ot desfendu a mangier;
 s'en cheïmes trestuit en grant misere,
 quant de li fist li douz Jhesus sa mere.

2 Mout l'ama Dex et grant honeur li fist
 quant il l'eslut seur toutes damoiseles,
 et char et sanc dedens ses costés prist
 et aleta le let de ses mameles
 qui tant par son[t] precieuses et beles.
 La virge mout forment s'espäori
 quan[t] Gabriel de par Jhesus li dit:
 'Ave Marie, la dame des puceles,
 de par Jhesu t'aport je ces novelles:

3 Li sains espirs en toi s'äonbrera
 come hons humains, de ce ne doutés
   mie.'
 La virge dit: 'Coment estre porra,
 quant onc ne fui de nul home
   atouchie?'
 L'angre respont: 'Ne t'esmaier, Marie,
 li sains espirs bien faire le porra.'
   ...[1]
 'S'ancele sui, si sui en sa baillie,
 faire en puet bien toute sa comandie.'

4 Benëois soit li fruis qu'ele porta,
 car pechëors remist de mort a vie:
 por pechëors tant s'umilia
 quant en crois fu sa douce char partie
 por nos geter fors de la punasie
 d'enfer le let, dont Dex qui tout cria
 gart trestouz ceus qu'a s'image forma,
 et si nos doint avoir la seignorie
 de paradis avec sa conpaignie.

Sources: BN, Manuscript X, f. 272; R. 1315
Text category: Ca
Music category: Ch
Rhyme scheme: 10a 11b 10a 11b 11b 10a 10a
   11b 11b
Musical scheme: a b a b c d c' f g
Editions: Järnström and Långfors, 2: 162;
   Gennrich, no. 31
Contrafactum: R. 1267 (Raoul de Soissons)

1 The line is missing in the manuscript.

31 I must not delay singing of her

1   I must not delay singing of her,
    who is the clear shining star of the sea:
    everyone ought to serve her with his
        whole heart,
    for she removed us far from the bitter
        torment
    where Adam, our first father, put us.
    He ate the fruit, which God had forbid-
        den him to eat,
    because of his wife Eve;
    thus we had all fallen into great
        misery
    when sweet Jesus Christ made her his
        mother.

2   God greatly loved her, and gave her
        great honour
    when he chose her over all other
        maidens,
    and took flesh and blood within her
        sides
    and nursed from the milk of her breasts
    which were so lovely and precious.
    The virgin was terribly frightened
    when Gabriel, from Jesus, said to her,
    'Hail, Mary, lady among maidens,
    I bring news to you from Jesus:

3   The Holy Spirit will shelter itself in you
    like a human man, do not doubt this.'
    The virgin said: 'How can this be,
    when I have been touched by no man?'
    The angel responded: 'Do not be dis-
        mayed, Mary,
    the holy spirit is well able to do this' ...
    [Mary]: 'If I am his handmaid, I am in
        his protection:
    he can well do all that he commands.'

4   Blessed be the fruit that she carried,
    for it restores sinners from death to life:
    for sinners he humbled himself

when his sweet flesh was parted on the
    cross
to cast us far from the stench of hid-
    eous hell,
from which the God who created all
    things
forever guards those formed in his
    image,
and thus may he grant us that we gain
the noble state of paradise in his
    company.

31 Chanter m'estuet de cele sans targier

Chanter m'estuet de cele sans targier
ser-vir la doit chascuns de cuer en-tier,

qui de mer est luissans estoile cle-re;
car fors nos mist de la tormente a-me-re

ou mis nos ot Adans, no premier pe-re.

Le fruit manja par Evain sa moillier

que dex li ot desfendu a mangier

s'en che-ï-mes trestuit en grant mise-re

quant de li fist li douz Jhesus sa mere.

1 S. occ.: ♩

Chan - ter   me - stuet   de   ce - le   sans   tar - gier
ser - vir   la   doit   chas - cuns   de   cuer   en - tier,

qui   de   mer   est   luis - sans   es - toi - le   cler - re:
car   fors   nos   mist   de   la   tor - men - te_a - me - re

ou   mis   nos   ot   A - dans,   no   pre - mier   pe - re.

Le   fruit   man - ja   par   E - vain   sa   moil - lier   que   Dex   li

ot   des - fen - du   a   man - gier;   s'en   che - ï - mes   tres - tuit

en   grant   mi - se - re,   quant   de   li   fist   li   douz   Jhe - sus   sa   me - re.

See appendix C for alternative notation.

32 Vivre touz temps

1 Vivre touz temps et chascun jour morir,
ce doit li hons saigement esperer:
au vivre doit penser por lui chevir,
et au morir por les maus eschivier.
Qu'ensi le fet, il ne puet meserrer,
ne perdre Dieu, ne povreté servir.[1]
A tel conseil se fet bon assentir,
car on en puet l'ame et le cors sauver.

2 Or vuil a touz plainement faire cler
comment on puet ces deus choses fornir.
Qui bien les veut ambedeus achever,
si li couvient saigement maintenir
que qu'il en doie en ceste siecle avenir,
qu'il n'ait le cuer outrageus ne aver,
et qui ensi le puet a mesurer
bone vie et glorious fenir.

3 Quant li hons naist, lors commence a
    morir,
et quant plus vit et mains a a durer,
et touz jorz veut la chart l'ame trahir.
Tel compaignon doit on bien redouter
qui vergoigne ce qu'il doit honorer:
car si tost com li cors est sanz l'espir,
cil l'eschivent qui le suelent cherir,
et tout couvient seur l'ame retourner.

4 Nus ne se puet contre la mort tenser,
n'estre certains quant ele doit venir.
Por ce doit si chascuns son cuer fermer
de toz biens faiz, que n'i puist avenir
cil qui ne quiert fors les ames ravir
et nos souduire, et le mal enorter.
Si n'i a tel que des ames armer
vers l'aversier qui tant set descremir.

5 Se bien nos veut de la mort souvenir
que Jhesu Crist soffri por nos sauver,
nos ne poöns a la joie faillir
qu'il donne a ceus qui le sevent amer.
Sa douce mere en devons reclamer,
qui si vuille noz ames garantir

au perillous besoing des cors partir,
qu'ele les face ovec li osteler.

6 Quant le filz Dieu nos vendra reprouver
la destrece qu'il vint por nos soffrir,[2]
que nos verrons ciel et terre crouler,
l'air corrompu et le monde bruïr,
cors relever et buisines tentir,
pierres partir, soloil descoulorer.
Les plus hardiz fera mult redouter
le jugemenz qu'il devront oïr.

7 Lors se devront li mauvais esbahir,
qui de nul bien ne se devront vanter,
quant Diex fera les bons o lui venir,
et les mauvés ou feu d'enfer aler
a touz jorz mes, sanz merci recouvrer.
Por ce doit on en sa vie servir
son creator, por avoir au fenir
saint paradis, qu'il nos vuille donner.

Envoi: Chançon, va t'en la dame saluer
en cui cil fest parole en char muer
qui en la croiz daigna por nos morir.

Sources: BN, Manuscript V, f. 148r; Bern,
    Stadtbibliotek, Manuscript C, f. 245;
    Oxford, Bodleian Library, Manuscript I,
    f. 40; R. 1431
Text category: Ca
Music category: Ch
Rhyme scheme: 10a 10b 10a 10b 10b 10a 10a
    10b
Musical scheme: a b a b c d e f
Edition: Järnström and Långfors, 1: 20
Contrafacta: R. 407 (Thibaut de Navarre);
    R. 307 (Andrieu Contredit)
Remarks: The two-line variant reading in
    stanza 6 in manuscript C is not men-
    tioned in the Järnström and Långfors
    edition. The envoi should be sung to the
    last three phrases of music, which has the
    effect of enhancing the final cadence by
    repetition.

1 As in manuscript V; in C: 'povreté sentir'
2 In C: 'Quant Deus vaurait la destrece
    moustreir / k'il volt por nos soffrir et
    endureir'

32 Living forever

1 One ought to aspire, wisely,
to living forever and dying each day:
one must think of living, in order to
reach one's goal,
and of dying, in order to avoid evil.
He who does so will not go astray, nor
lose God, nor be a slave to poverty.
It is wise to follow such advice, for one
can save both soul and body.

2 Now I wish to make clear to all,
plainly, how to accomplish these two
things.
Whoever wishes to achieve them both
must act wisely,
so that, whatever should befall him in
this world,
he has neither excess nor avarice in his
heart,
and by these means he will be able to
measure a good life and a glorious
end.

3 When a man is born, he begins to die,
and the longer he lives, the less time
remains to him:
each day the flesh seeks to betray the
soul.
Such a companion, who shames what
he should honour, must be feared:
for once the body leaves the spirit, and
men spurn what they were once
accustomed to hold dear,
everything must return to the soul.

4 No one can defend himself against
death,
or be certain when it will come.
Therefore, everyone must fortify their
hearts with good deeds,
to prevent the winning of him who
seeks only to snatch away our souls
and seduce us and instigate evil.
Thus there is no one to aim our souls
against the adversary who knows so
well how to degrade.

5 If we wish to think of the death which
Jesus Christ suffered in order to save
us,
we cannot be lacking in the joy which
he gave to those who know how to
love him.
We should call out to his gentle mother
so that she will protect our souls, and
take them to live with him
when they undergo the dangerous
necessity of leaving the body.

6 When the son of God comes to blame
us
for the anguish which he suffered for
us,
then we will see the sky and earth
tremble,
the air shatter and the world burn,
corpses rise and trumpets blare, stones
split and the sun darken.
He will make the hardiest fear the
judgement which they must hear.

7 Then the evildoers will be afraid, for
they can boast of no good deed
when God takes the good with him
and makes the evil go to the fires of hell
forever, with no rescue through pity.
For this reason, one must serve the
creator throughout one's life,
in order to have, at the end, the holy
paradise which he wishes to give us.

Envoi: Song, go forth and salute the
lady in whom the word was made
flesh
by him who deigned to die for us on
the cross.

32 Vivre touz temps

Vivre touz temps et chascun jour morir:
Au vi-vre doit pen-ser por lui chevir

ce doit li hons saigement esperer:
et au mo-rir por les maus eschivier,

qu'ensi le fet, il ne puet meserrer

ne perdre dieu, ne povreté servir.

a tel conseil se fet bon assentir,

car on en puet l'ame et le cors sauver.

1 S. occ.: ◆ ◆ ◆
2 S. occ.: ∧
3 S. occ.: ⁊

Vi - vre touz temps et chas - cun jour mo - rir:
au vi - vre doit pen - ser por lui che - vir,

ce doit li hons sai - ge - ment es - pe - rer:
et au mo - rir por les maus es - chi - vier.

Qu'en - si le fet, il ne puet mes - er - rer,

ne per - dre Dieu, ne po - vre - té ser - vir.

A tel con - seil se fet bon as - sen - tir,

car on en puet l'a - me_et le cors sau - ver.

33 Chanter m'estuet de la sainte pucelle

1 Chanter m'estuet de la sainte pucelle,
  plaine dou saint espir,
  en cui daigna pour nos mortel cotele
  le rois des rois vestir.
  N'est mervoille [s'il la]¹ couvint fremir
  quant Gabriel li conta la novele,
  merveillouse a oïr,
  qu'en li devoit venir
  la deité de char couvrir,
  Damediex et hons devenir.

2 Seur tote riens est avenant et bele,
  cele dont je desir
  a mon poöir faire chose novele
  qui li viegne a plaisir.
  Et ce tuit cil me voloient nuisir,
  qui sont ou mont a leur poöir, et ele
  me voloit garentir,
  ne porroient fornir,
  tant me seüssent assaillir,
  chose qui me peüst nuisir.

3 Toute biautéz qu'en lui s'amoncelle
  la fet si resplendir
  qu'envers li sont li [solauz]² et la bele
  tenebrous a vëoir.
  Tout l'estouvroit avugler ou guenchir,
  qui son douz vis, qui de joie estancelle,
  oseroit a loisir
  remirer et choisir:
  de ses biens retraire et oïr
  se devroit [uns mors resjoïr.]³

4 Tant a douçour, qui de bon cuer l'apele,
  qu'ele ne puet soffrir
  qu'a nul besoing trebusche ne chan-
    celle.
  Tout ce doit gehir
  Theofilus, qui pres iert de perir⁴
  a toz jourz mes par son meffet, quant
    cele

qu'au siens ne set faillir
quant le vit repentir,
le fist a l'enemi guerpir
et a l'amour Dieu revenir.

5 Dame dou mont, de bien secorre
    ysnele,
  ne vuilliez consentir,
  lors quant la mort pardesouz la
    mamele
  fera mon cuer partir,
  m'ame de vous desevrer et saisir
  a l'anemi qui nuit et jour oisele
  a toute gent trahir
  et as ames ravir;
  et se je onques vous seü cherir,⁵
  [adonc]⁶ le me vuilliez merir.

Sources: BN, Manuscript V, ff. 148v–9r;
  Bern, Stadtbibliothek, Manuscript C, f. 37;
  R. 610
Text category: Co
Music Scheme: Ch
Rhyme scheme: 11a 6b 11a 6b 10b 11a 6b 6b
  8b 8b
Musical scheme: a b a c d e f b f' g
Edition: Järnström and Långfors, 1: 23
Contrafactum: R. 590 (Gautier d'Espinau or
  de Couci); see also the Marian hymn *Ave
  maris stella*

1 Manuscript V reads 'sillat.'
2 The word is 'solaziz' in manuscript V.
3 As in manuscript C; in V it is 'se devroit
  resjoï.'
4 In manuscript C it is 'tout ceu doit bien
  Thiophilus jehir / ki pres iert de perir.'
  This version is metrically faulty.
5 Manuscript C reads: 'servir.'
6 As in manuscript C; in V it is: 'vos le
  adonc.'

33 I must sing of the holy maiden

1 I must sing of the holy maiden, full of
   the Holy Spirit,
   in whom the king of kings agreed, for
   us, to dress in mortal vesture.
   It is no wonder that she began to
   tremble
   when Gabriel told her the news,
   marvellous to hear,
   that in her the deity would come to
   cover himself in flesh,
   and the Lord God would become man.

2 She is pleasant and lovely above all
   things,
   she for whom I wish within my power
   to make something new, which will
   come to please her.
   And if she wishes to protect me,
   all those in this world who through
   their power would wish to do me
   harm
   cannot accomplish anything to hurt me,
   however often they try their assaults.

3 The many forms of beauty that reside
   in her
   make her shine so brightly
   that beside her the sun and moon are
   dark to behold.
   Anyone who dares to look at leisure
   upon her sweet face shining with joy
   must choose to flee or be blinded:
   for to hear or be told of her goodness
   would make a dead man rejoice.

4 She has such gentleness that if anyone
   calls on her from the heart,
   she cannot bear to let him stumble for
   any reason.
   So said Theophilus, who was close to
   perishing forever because of his
   misdeed,

when she who cannot fail those who
   belong to her,
seeing him repent,
caused him to be cast away by the
   enemy
and returned him to the love of God.

5 Lady of the world, who gives swift
   succour, consent
   that when death causes my heart to
   depart from beneath my breast,
   my soul will be taken by you,
   and severed from the enemy who
   seeks, night and day,
   to betray all people and seize their
   souls:
   and if I have ever known how to
   honour you,
   let me then deserve this.

33 Chanter m'estuet de la sainte pucelle

Chanter m'estuet de la sainte pucelle · plaine dou saint espir

en cui daigna pour nos mortel cote-le · le rois des rois vestir.

n'est mervoille s'il la convint fre-mir

quant Gabri-el li conta la novele

merveillouse a o-ir · qu'en li de-voit ve-nir

la deïté de char couvrir · damediex et hons de-ve-nir.

Chan- ter m'es - tuet de la sain - te pu - cel - le, plai - ne dou

saint es - pir, en cui dai - gna pour nos mor - tel co - te - le le

rois des rois ves - tir. N'est mer-voil - le s'il la con - vint fre - mir quant

Ga - bri - el li con - ta la no - ve - le, mer - veill - ouse

a o - ïr, qu'en li de - voit ve - nir la de - i - té de char couv - rir,

Da - me - diex et hons de - ve - nir.

34 **Quant Diex ot formé l'omme**

1 Quant Diex ot formé l'omme a sa
    semblance,
li maus soudoianz qui le vout traïr
le fist par envie[1] rompre obedience
et mengier dou fruit qui le fist perir.
Mes cil qui seur tout le monde a
    puissance
ne vout endurer ceste mesestance:
pour lui rachater vint naistre et morir.

2 Li sires qui n'a fin ne commençance
sout bien la meillour dou monde
    choisir:
en li demonstra estrange muance
quant parole en char i fist convertir.
Ensi le devons croire sanz doutance,
et si s'en depart de ceste creance,
on le devroit en flamme bruïr.

3 Ne plus que li rais qui dou soleil lance
de riens ne corrout ne fait obscurcir,
ne fist a nul fuer sa sainte naissance
la virginité sa mere amenrir.
Vraie deitéz humaine substance
prist en ses costéz, pour la delivrance
a ceus qui de cuer la sevent servir.

4 En cesti doit on metre sa fiance,
en cui Damediex vout hons devenir.
Mains jointes, li fais de mon cuer
    lijance,
ame et vie et cuer vuil de li tenir.
Et puis que dou tout i ai m'esperance,
bien me doit tenser de toute grevance
et encontre touz son fief garantir.

5 Roïne dou mont, dame de vaillance,
estans de pitié qui ne set tarir,
vrais alegemenz de toute grevance,
qui tout paradis feistes resplendir,
de prier pour moi aiés remenbrance

celui cui Longis feri de la lance,
qu'aprés mon decés praigne mon espir.

Sources: BN, Manuscript V, f. 149r; Bern,
    Stadtbibliothek, Manuscript C, f. 194;
    R. 249
Text category: Ca
Music category: Rn
Rhyme scheme: 11a 10b 11a 10b 11a 11a 10b
Musical scheme: a_x b a_x b c c' b c_{xy} c_x b
Edition: Järnström and Långfors, 1: no. 25
Contrafactum: R. 620 (Blondel)

1 As in manuscript V; in manuscript C: 'par
    Evain'

34 When God formed man

1 When God formed man in his image,
the evil seducer who seeks to betray
   him
caused him, through envy [through
   Eve],
to disobey and eat of the fruit which
   brought his downfall.
But he who has power over all the
   world did not permit such misfortune:
in order to save him, he was born and
   died.

2 The Lord who has neither beginning
      nor end
knew well how to choose the best
   woman in the world.
In her he showed a strange mutation
   when he caused speech to become
   flesh.
Thus we ought to believe this without a
   doubt,
and one who departs from such belief
   should burn in flames.

3 No more than does the ray that darts
      from the sun
corrupt or obscure anything at all,
did his holy birth diminish the virginity of his mother.
True deity took human substance from
   within her sides
for the deliverance of those who know
   how to serve from the heart.

4 One ought to put his trust in this lady,
in whom the lord God wished to
      become man.
With joined hands I give her my heart's
   allegiance,
and I will hold to her with my life and
   soul.

And since my hope is entirely there in
   her,
she should protect me well from
   torment,
and guard her vassal's domain against
   all.

5 Queen of the world, lady of valour,
fountain of mercy that never dries up,
true solace of all torment, who has
      made all of paradise resplendent,
remember to pray for me to him who
   Longinus struck with the lance,
so that after my death he will take my
   spirit.

34   Quant Diex ot formé l'omme

Quant diex ot formé l'omme a sa semblance,
le fist par envie rompre o-be—di—en-ce

li maus soudoi-anz qui le vout traïr
et men-gier dou fruit qui le fist perir;

Mes cil qui seur tout le monde a puissance

Ne vout endurer ceste mes-estance;

Pour lui rachazer vint naistre et mo-rir.

1 S. occ.: ▪
2 S. occ.: ▪ ▫ ▪▪▪ ▪▫ ▪
    o-bedi—en-ce
3 S. occ.: ▪
4 S. occ.: ▪
5 S. occ.: ▪▪▪

Quant Diex ot for-mé l'omme a sa sem - blan - ce, li maus sou-doi-anz
fist par en - vie rom-pre_o - be - di - en - ce et men-gier dou fruit

qui le vout tra - ïr le cil qui seur tout le mon-de_a - puis -
qui le fist pe - rir. Mes

san - - ce ne vout en - du - rer ces - te mes es -

tan - ce: pour lui ra - cha - ter vint nais-tre_et mo - rir.

35 L'autrier m'iere rendormiz

1 L'autrier m'iere rendormiz
par un matin en esté:
adonques[1] me fu aviz
que la douce mere Dé
m'avoit dit et commandé
que seur un chant qui jadis
soloit estre mout joïs
chantasse de sa bonté,
et je tantost l'ai enpris:
Diex doint qu'il viegne en gré.

2 'Quant li rossinoil jolis
chante seur la fleur d'esté,'
c'est li chans seur quoi j'ai mis
le dit que je ai trouvé
de celi qui recouvré
nos a le saint paradis,
de quoi nos fusmes jadis
par Evain desherité.
Ceste dame nos a mis
de tenebres en clarté.

3 A la chaste flour de lis
repris en humilité
fu li sains anges tramis
de Dieu, qui humanité
prist en sa virginité
pour rachater ses amis.
En li fu noz rachas pris
dou saint sanc de son costé:
mout doit estre de haut pris
li hons qui tant a costé.

4 Se roches et quaillous bis
erent frait et destrempé
dou ru Rosne[2] et dou Lis,
et d'arrement attempré
[et] en parchemin covrée
fussent [ciel][3] et terre mis,
et chascun fust ententis
d'escrire la verité,

ja si bien par ces escriz
ne seroient recordé.

5 Glorieuse empereriz,
chambre de la deité,
ja ne sera desconfiz
qui vos sert sanz fauseté.
Aiez dou monde pité,
qui s'en va de mal en pis,
et moi, qui vous aim et pris
d'enterine volenté,
en vostre riche païs
conduisiez a sauveté.

Sources: BN, Manuscript V, f. 149r; Bern, Stadtbibliothek, Manuscript C, f. 140; R. 1609
Text category: Co
Music category: Ch
Rhyme scheme: 7a 7b 7a 7b 7b 7a 7a 7b 7a 7b
Musical scheme: a b a c d e f a g g'
Edition: Järnström and Långfors, 1: no. 26
Contrafacta: R. 1559 (Chastelain de Couci); R. 1266
Remarks: The image in stanza 4 of endless parchment and ink is also found in song no. 36 (stanza 5) and others; see also chapter 3.

1 Manuscript C reads: 'adouves me fut.'
2 The line starts in C as: 'dou ru dou Rone.'
3 The line in manuscript C reads: 'fussent ciel et terre mis.'

**35 I was asleep one summer morning
lately**

1 I was asleep one summer morning
    lately,
  when it seemed that the gentle mother
    of God spoke to me,
  and commanded that I take a joyous
    old melody and sing of her good-
    ness.
  This I immediately set out to do:
  God grant that it be pleasing.

2 'When the pretty nightingale sings
    upon the summer flower,'
  that is the tune to which I've set the
    words I found to tell of her
  who recovered holy paradise for us,
    from which by Eve we were exiled.
  This lady has brought us from dark-
    ness into light.

3 To the chaste lily-flower, seized with
    humility,
  was the holy angel sent by God,
  who took on humanity from her virgin-
    ity to redeem his friends.
  Our ransom was paid by him with the
    holy blood from his side:
  humanity, which cost so much, must be
    of great worth.

4 If the rocks and hard blue pebbles in
    the rivers Rhone and Lis
  were broken and crushed and tem-
    pered to make ink,
  and all the earth were covered with
    parchment,
  and everyone assigned to write the
    truth,
  even by such efforts this matter would
    not be fully recorded.

5 Glorious empress, chamber of deity,
  he who serves you without falseness
    will never be discomfited.
  Have pity on this world which goes
    from bad to worse,
  and guide me, who loves and prizes
    you with all my will,
  to safety in your powerful domain.

35 L'autrier m'iere rendormiz

L'autrier m'iere rendormiz · par un matin en esté ;

Adonques me fu a·viz · que la douce mere dé

m'avoit dit et commandé · que seur un chant qui jadis

soloit estre mout jo-ïs · chantasse de sa bonté,

et je tantost l'ai enpris : diex doint qu'il li viegne en gré !

L'au- trier m'ie - re   ren - dor - miz   par un ma - tin en   e - sté:

a - don - ques me   fu a - viz   que   la dou - ce   me - re Dé

m'a- voit dit   et   com - man - dé   que seur un   chant   qui   ja - dis

so - loit e - stre   mout   jo   -   ïs   chan- tas - se de   sa bon - té,

et je tan- tost   l'ai en - pris: Diex   doint   qu'il   li   vieg - ne_en gré.

See appendix C for alternative notation.

36 Quant froidure trait a fin

1 Quant froidure trait a fin
   contre la saison d'esté
   que florissent cil jardin
   et reverdissent cil pré,
   oiseillon qui ont esté
   pour la froidure tapin
   se renvoisent au matin
   espris de joliveté.
   Lors sui raviz a mon gré
   en un desir de cuer fin
   de remirer la clarté
   qui est et sera sanz fin.

2 Tuit li deduit enterin
   sont en cel riche regné:
   autant prise on le vin
   comme l'eue dou fossé.
   Tuit sont riche et assazé,
   n'i a povre ne frerin,
   n'i a riot ne venin,
   dolour ne aversité:
   tel yver et tel esté,
   tel le soir com le matin,
   chascuns a sa volenté,
   nus n'i va a declin.

3 Pires est d'un Sarrazin
   et de nul autre homme né,
   qui ne se trait au chemin
   de cel païs honnoré,
   gloriousement ourné
   par artefice devin.
   Iluec voit on cherubin
   servir en sa majesté
   trinité en unité,
   et maint autre, chief enclin.
   Courons a cest bon ostel,[1]
   nos qui sommes pelerin.

4 Adans, le peres Kaïn,
   quant Damediex l'ot formé,
   fist tout le monde orfelin

des [biens][2] dont je ai parlé.
Adonc erent tuit dampné,
bon et mal, viel et meschin,
quant Diex s'enclot en l'escrin
de pure virginité,
devant et apres fermé:
puis fu coronnéz d'espin,
et l'ocistrent a vilté
li Juïf felon mastin.[3]

5 Qui tout savroit le latin
   quant qu'en sevent li lettré,
   françois et grec et ermin,
   et tout languaige a prouvé,
   terre et ciel fussent mué
   en encre et en parchemin,
   et eüst le sens Merlin,
   ja ne diroit la bonté
   de cele qui par *Ave*
   conçut le douz enfantin
   qui le monde a delivré
   dou laz au mal Ysengrin.[4]

Sources: BN, Manuscript V, f. 149; Bern,
   Stadtbibliothek, Manuscript C, f. 207;
   R. 1366
Text category: Ca
Music category: Ch
Rhyme scheme: 7a 7b 7a 7b 7b 7a 7a 7b 7b
   7a 7b 7a
Musical scheme: a b a b c d c e f g h b'
Edition: Järnström and Långfors, 1: no. 28
Contrafacta: R. 1364; Raynaud, *Recueil*, 1: 62,
   177

1 The word in manuscript C is: 'ostei.'
2 In manuscript V the line begins 'des
   dont je,' but in C it begins with 'des biens
   dont je.'
3 Anti-Semitism was endemic to medieval
   Christianity. It was based in part on the
   fear of an unfamiliar culture and in part on
   an interpretation of the Gospels that
   blamed the leaders of the Jewish community under the Roman Empire for the condemnation of Jesus. It was not until 1993
   that the papacy, in the document 'Nostra
   aetate,' officially repudiated anti-Semitism.

36 When cold weather comes to an end

1 When cold weather comes to an end in
     the face of the summer season,
   when gardens flower and the meadows
     go green again,
   the birds that were hidden silent
     through the cold
   reappear in the morning seized with
     ardent gaiety.
   Then am I ravished from my intent by
     a pure-hearted desire
   to see the light that is and will always
     be without end.

2 All complete delights of the flesh are in
     this rich kingdom;
   there one values wine as much as water
     that flows from the well.
   All are wealthy and satisfied,
   there is neither poor man nor
     mendicant,
   quarrel nor venom, pain nor adversity;
   summer and winter alike, the evening
     like the morning,
   each one following his will, nothing
     falls to ruin there.

3 He is worse than a Saracen, or any
     other man born,
   he who does not follow the road to this
     honoured country
   which is so gloriously ornamented by
     divine art.
   In this place one sees cherubim serving
     the majesty of the Three in One,
   and many others with heads bowed.
   Let us run to this good hostel, we who
     are pilgrims!

4 Adam, the father of Cain, when the
     lord God made him,
   made all the world an orphan, as I have
     told you.

Then were we all damned, good and
   evil, old man and youth,
when God enclosed himself in the
   coffer of pure virginity,
locked before and after;
then he was crowned with thorns,
and the wicked Jewish servile dogs
   vilely killed him.

5 If anyone knew all the Latin known by
     the learned,
   and could prove himself fluent in
     French and Greek and Armenian,
   and all other languages,
   and the earth and sky were turned to
     ink and parchment,
   and he had the wisdom of Merlin,
   he still could never tell the goodness of
     her who, through the *Ave*,
   conceived the tiny infant who
     delivered the world
   from the snare of the evil Isengrin.

―――――

4 This stanza may require a brief *explication
   de texte*. First, the image given in the first
   six lines occurs, with variations, in nine
   other songs. Its earliest source would
   appear to be the Koran (Ch. 31, 27), with
   reference to praise of God. Second,
   British Arthurian legends were popular
   in French literature of the time; see the
   massive prose cycles of Robert de Borron,
   as well as the earlier works of Chrétien
   de Troyes. Third, Ysengrin the wolf
   appears in the *Roman de Renart* as well as
   a host of earlier fables; see John Flinn, *Le
   Roman de Renart*. The wolf was a symbol
   of treachery, gluttony, and credulous-
   ness.

36 Quant froidure trait a fin

Quant froidu-re trait a fin · contre la saison d'esté
que flo-rissent cil jardin · et re-verd-i-ssent cil pré,

oiseillon qui ont esté · pour la froidu-re tapin

se renvoisent au matin · espris de jo-liveté.

Lors sui raviz a mon gré · en un desir de cuer fin

de remirer la clarté · qui est et sera sanz fin.

1 S. occ.: ⅂
2 S. occ.: ⅂
3 S. occ.: ⅂
4 S. occ.: ••
5 S. occ.: ▪
6 S. occ.: ▪

Quant froi - du - re   trait a   fin   con - tre   la sai - son d'e - sté
que flo - ris - sent   cil jar - din   et re - verd - i - ssent cil pré,

oi - seil - lon qui   ont   e - sté   pour la froi - du - re ta - pin

se ren - voi - sent   au ma - tin   es - pris de jo - li - ve - té.

Lors sui   ra - viz   a mon   gré   en un des - ir de cuer   fin

de re - mi - rer   la clar - té   qui est   et se - ra sanz fin.

37 De la gloriouse fenix

1 De la gloriouse fenix,
mere et fille au douz pellicant
qui por rachater ses amis
espandi son precious sanc,
m'estuet chanter d'ore en avant
ensi com je l'ai entrepris.
Ne ja tant com je soie vis
ne m'en trouvera recreant.
Ainz morrai, a mon escient,
en ceste volenté raviz
comme rousignol en chantant.

2 Ne plus que li hons endormiz
ne set se on le va esgardant,
ne set[1] la sainte empereriz
quant ele conçut son enfant.
Tant se mist gloriousement
en son cors li sainz esperis
que plantéz i fu et repris
Diex et hom tout en un moment,
et en nasqui si dignement
que de virginité floriz
fu ses cors apres et avant.

3 Ausi comme acate et rubiz
et esmeraude verdoiant
valent mieuz de quaillous bis,
seürmonte ele de valour grant
touz ceus qui or sont aparent
et seront, et furent jadis.
Tant est bele que paradis
de li enlumine et resplent,
et de douceur i a il tant
que ja n'en ira escondiz
qui l'aimme et prie coraument.

4 Ja nus n'avera tant mespris
envers le roi dou firmament
qu'a s'amour ne soi restabliz
par [li],[2] se de cuer s'en repent.
Theofilus, qui malement
estoit de l'a[ne]mi[3] soupris,

fu de sa chartre resaisis
par la dame dont je vous chant,
et li pardonna doucement
son meffait li douz Jhesu Criz,
quant [il][4] le vit vrai repentant.

5 Dame de qui [muet et] descent[5]
mes solaz, ma joie et mes ris,
deffendez m'ame de torment
et mes cors d'estre malbailliz.
Je croi que ja n'iert desconfiz
qui a vostre aide s'atent:
tres douce dame, a vous me rent.
Vostres cors de pitié garniz
ne fu onques las ne faintiz
de ceus aidier qui bonement
ont le vostre secours requis.

Sources: BN, Manuscript V, f. 149v; Bern,
    Stadtbibliothek, Manuscript C, f. 61;
    R. 1547
Text category: Co
Music category: Rn
Rhyme scheme: 8a 8b 8a 8b 8b 8a 8a 8b 8b
    8a 8b
Musical scheme: a_x b a_x b c d_x b' c d_x b' c'
Edition: Järnström and Långfors, 1: 30
Contrafactum: R. 1296

1 The word in manuscript C is 'sot la.'
2 Manuscript V reads: 'par se de cuer'; in C
   it is: 'par li se de cuer.'
3 In V: 'de l'ami'; in C: 'de l'anemi'
4 Manuscript V reads: 'quant le vit'; the
   phrase in C is: 'quant il le vit.'
5 The line in V reads: 'Dame de qui
   descent'; in C it is: 'Dame de cui muet et
   descent.'

37 Of the glorious phoenix

1 Of the glorious phoenix, mother and
    daughter of the gentle pelican
who, to ransom his friends, sheds his
    precious blood,
I must sing from now on, just as I have
    set out to do.
Nor ever, while I live, will I be found
    slacking:
thus will I die, as far as I know,
ravished by this desire like a
    nightingale glorying in song.

2 No more than does a sleeping man
    know when someone is looking at
    him
did the holy empress know when she
    conceived her son.
The Holy Spirit placed him in her body
    so gloriously
that he was put in and taken out as
    God and man all in one moment,
and was born so worthily that her body
    flowered in virginity before and
    after.

3 Just as the agate, the ruby, and the
    shining green emerald
are worth more than plain blue
    pebbles,
so she surpasses in valour all who are
    now present, and ever were, and will
    be.
She is so beautiful that paradise takes
    from her its luminescence and
    splendour;
there is such gentleness in her that
    anyone who loves and prays to her
    from the heart
will never be sent away with a refusal.

4 No one has ever erred so badly against
    the king of the firmament
that he was not re-established in his
    love, if he repented sincerely.
Theophilus, who was wickedly taken
    by the enemy,
was restored to his covenant by the
    lady of whom I sing,
and sweet Jesus Christ gently
    pardoned his misdeed
when he saw him truly repentant.

5 Lady from whom descends my solace,
    joy, and laughter,
defend my soul from torment and my
    body from being mistreated.
I believe that one who depends on your
    help will never be disappointed:
Sweet lady, I give myself to you!
Your heart, garnished with mercy, will
    never be weak nor faint
in aiding those who sincerely ask for
    your help.

37 De la gloriouse fenix

de la glo-ri-ou-se fenix, mere et fille au douz pellicant
qui por rachater ses a-mis es-pan-di son pre-ci-ous sanc,

m'estuet chanter d'ore en a-vant. en-si com je l'ai entrepris;
ne m'en trou-ve—ra re-cre-ant. Ainz morrai a mon esci-ent

ne ja tant com je soi-e vis.
en ce-ste vo-len-té ra-viz comme rousignol en chantant.

1 S. occ.: ♪
2 S. occ.: ♪♪ (c d-b)
 —TER SES
3 S. occ.: ♪♪
4 S. occ.: ♪
5 S. occ.: ♪
6 S. occ.: ♪
7 S. occ.: ♪♪
8 S. occ.: ♪
9 S. occ.: ♪
10 S. occ.: ♪♪ ♪ (d-b-a c-d)
 es—ci —
11 S. occ.: ♪
12 S. occ.: ♪♪
13 S. occ.: ♪♪
14 S. occ.: ♪

De la glo - ri - ou - se fe - nix, me - re_et fille_ au douz
por ra - cha - ter ses a - mis es - pan - di son pre -

pel - li - cant qui   m'e - stuet chan - ter d'ore en a - vant en -
                ci - ous sanc,   m'en trou - ve - ra re - cre - ant. Ainz

si com je l'ai en - tre - pris.   Ne   ja tant com   je
mor - rai a mon e - sci - ent   en   ce - ste vo - len -

soi - e vis ne   me rou - si - gnol   en chan - tant.
té - ra - viz com -

38 La volentéz dont mes cuers est raviz

1 La volentéz dont mes cuers est raviz
ou desierrier de la virge Marie,
me fet chanter, pour ce qu'il m'est a vis
que seur toutes est sa valour trïe.
Paradis a qui de bon cuer l'en prie,
se trestuit cil l'en voloient grever,
cui Diex a fet ovec lui osteler.

2 Mere de Dieu, saintesme empereriz,
mout seroit plains de grant forsenerie
qui oseroit jugier que vostre filz
ne vous aint seur toute humaine lignie:
et puis que vous estes sa mieudre amie,
ne die nus qu'il vous seüst veër
quant qu'il porroit as autres refuser.

3 Se trestuit cil qui sont en paradis
et enfer, et a naistre et en vie,
erent present, et fu chascuns garniz
com Salemons de sens et de clergie,
vostre valor ne retrairoient mie
qu'on puet des biens qu'afiert a vous
    loer
mil foiz les poinz de l'eschiquier
    doubler.

4 Comme li hons de maltalent espris,
vuil descochier seur cele gent Juïe
qui renient que li douz Jhesu Criz
nasquist de vous en ceste mortel vie.[1]
Trop maintienent longuement lor folie:
quant par souhait fist ciel et terre et
    mer,
bien peust ces moz en char
    transfigurer.

5 Vaspasien, quar fussiez or vis[2]
enz ou voloir et en la seignorie
ou vous estiez, quant vous trente de ces
    Juïs
donnastes a denier en Surie.[3]

Ne demorroit sabbas ne Juïerie,
se Damediex ne les voloit tenser:
a martire les feriez devier.

6 Chançon, va t'en a un de mes amis,
le seneschal, si ne le cele mie:
di li que on voit mout d'arbres bien
    floriz
dont la racine est forment entechie.
Por ce est li fox qui a son vivant s'afie:
qui saiges est si se doit atorner
com s'il devoit maintenant devier.

Sources: BN, Manuscript V, f. 150; Bern,
    Stadtbibliothek, Manuscript C, f. 140;
    R. 1607
Text category: Co
Music category: Ch
Rhyme scheme: 10a 11b 10a 11b 11a 10b 10b
Musical scheme: a b a b c d e
Edition: Järnström and Långfors, 1: 33
Contrafacta: R. 1789 (Robert du Chastel);
    R. 1248 (Guiot de Provins); R. 1262;
    R. 1648
Remarks: Järnström and Långfors, 1: 35,
    cite a medieval legend as the source of the
    fifth stanza. It was widely believed in
    thirteenth-century Europe that the
    Roman emperor Vespasian destroyed the
    city of Jerusalem as retribution for the
    involvement of Jews in the death of
    Christ. The text of the song is garbled,
    however, and may conflate more than
    one legend.

1 See remarks for song no. 36 on the
    endemic anti-Semitism of the period.
2 In manuscript C the text reads: 'fussiez
    vos or vis.'
3 The phrase in manuscript C reads: 'quant
    vos de ces Juïs / trente a denier donnas-
    tes en Surie.'

38 The willingness which transports my heart

1 The willingness which transports my
     heart
  in the desiring of the Virgin Mary,
  causes me to sing, for it is evident to me
  that her worthiness is chosen above all
     others.
  He who calls with open heart to her,
     whom God has taken to dwell with
     him,
  shall gain paradise
  even if all others are against him.

2 Mother of God, most holy empress,
  he who dares to state that your son did
     not love you above all human
     lineage
  would be full of great raging madness;
  and since you are his greatest love,
  none can say that he is able to refuse
     you, even when he denies others.

3 If all those who are in heaven and hell,
  both unborn and living, were present,
  and each one were adorned like
     Solomon with wisdom and learning,
  your worth is such that they could not
     describe it
  any more than one can praise you
     sufficiently
  by doubling the squares of the chequer-
     board a thousand times.

4 Like a man seized with anger I wish to
     lash out against the nation of Jews
  who deny that sweet Jesus Christ was
     born of you into this mortal life.
  They have maintained their error too
     long:
  since he could make the sky and earth
     and sea by his intention,

he could certainly transform his words
   to flesh.

5 Vespasian, would that you were still
     living
  and were in the frame of mind and
     authority
  when you sold thirty of these Jews to
     ransom in Syria.
  Neither sabbath nor Jewry would
     remain if the Lord God did not wish
     to preserve them:
  otherwise you would put them to a
     martyr's death.

6 Song, go to one of my friends, the
     seneschal, and do not hide from him:
  tell him that one can see many trees in
     flower whose roots are spoiled.
  Therefore he is a fool who vows by his
     life:
  the wise man ought to be prepared as if
     he must die at this moment.

38 La volentéz dont mes cuers est raviz

LA VO-LEN-TEZ DONT MES CUERS EST RAVIZ
ME FET CHANTER POUR CE QU'IL M'EST A-VIS
OU DESIERRIER DE LA VIRGE MARI-E
QUE SEUR TOU-TES EST SA VALOUR TRI-I-E.
PARADIS A QUI DE BON CUER L'EN PRI-E
SE TRESTUIT CIL L'EN VOLOIENT GREVER
CUI DIEX A FET OVEC LUI O-STELER.

1 S. occ.: ♦ (a)
2 S. occ.: ⌐
3 S. occ.: ⌐
4 S. occ.: ⌐
5 S. occ.: ⌐
6 S. occ.: ⌐
7 S. occ.: ▪
8 S. occ.: ▪
9 S. occ.: ⌐

La vo - len - téz dont mes cuers est ra - viz
me fet chan - ter, pour ce qu'il m'est a - vis

ou des - ier - rier de la vir - ge Ma - ri - e,
que seur tou - tes est sa va - lour tri - ï - e.

Pa - ra - dis a qui de bon cuer l'en pri - e,

se tres - tuit cil l'en vo - loi - ent gre - ver,

cui Diex a fet o - vec lui o - ste - ler

39 Cuers qui son entendement

1 Cuers qui son entendement
met en grant chose traitier
ce doit a ce travailler:
qu'il ait bon commencement.
Car, si com dient li saige,
des que[1] nos somes apris,
commencemenz de haut pris
est la moitiéz de l'ouvraige.
Pour ce me vuil travaillier:
a hautement commencier.

2 Pardesus le firmament,
plus haut c'on ne puet cuidier,
pour paradis esclairier,
se siet honnoréement
e'l plus glorious estage
la saintiesme empereriz
de qui nasqui Jhesu Criz
sans quasser son pucelage:
porte close et cors entier,
[se vint en li herbergier].[2]

3 Ciel et terre et mer et vent,
pensés de glorifier
cele qui si grant mestier
ot a nostre sauvement
quant, par le conseil volage
d'Evain ou li anemis
s'estoit par envie mis
dedenz la prison ombraige
ou soudoiant avresier
couvenoit chascun plungier.

4 Solaus, lune, et element,
anges et arcanges efforcier,
vous devez de li prisier,
quar quant qu'on voit et entent,
tout [ait] en son[3] signoraige.
Bon fu néz, ce m'est a vis,
qui en s'amour est raviz:
conquis a [en] heritaige[4]

saint paradis de louier,
qui l'aimme de cuer entier.

5 Dame, or vos viegne en talent
de vostre chier filz proier
qu'il nos destourt d'encombrier,
et doint tel entendement
a ceus qu'il fist a s'ymaige,
qu'il ne lor soit contrediz
li regné de paradis
au triste pelerinage
quant l'ame estouvra lessier
le cors qui la fist pechier.

Sources: BN, Manuscript V, f. 150; Bern,
Stadtbibliothek, Manuscript C, f. 37;
R. 670
Text category: Co
Music category: Th
Rhyme scheme: 7a 7b 7b 7a 8c 7d 7d 8c 7b
7b
Musical scheme: a b c d e f g h i j
Edition: Järnström and Långfors, 1: 35
Contrafacta: none

1 In manuscript C the text reads: 'de cui
nos.'
2 The line is missing in manuscript V and is
supplied from C.
3 In manuscript C the text reads: 'tout ait
en son'; V reads only: 'tout en son.'
4 In V: 'conquis a heritaige'; in C: 'conquis
ait en eritaige'

39 The heart that wishes

1 The heart that wishes to give its
    attention to important matters
ought to make this effort: that it have a
    good beginning,
for, as the wise say – from whom we
    have learned –
a worthy beginning is half the work.
For this I wish to strive: to begin high.

2 Above the firmament, higher than
    anyone can imagine,
in the most glorious place she sits in
    honour in order to illumine paradise;
this most holy empress from whom
    was born Jesus Christ
without destroying her maidenhood:
[he sheltered in her], a closed door and
    intact body.

3 Sky and earth and sea and wind,
    consider how to glorify
her who did such great service for our
    salvation;
when, by the inconstant counsel of Eve,
in whom the enemy was placed by
    envy
within the shadowed prison
into which the seductive adversary
    wishes to plunge everyone.

4 Sun, moon, and elements, mighty
    angels and archangels,
you should strive to honour her,
for however much one sees and hears,
    she has it all in her realm.
He who is lost in her love is fortunate;
    this is evident:
he who loves her with his entire heart
    has won forever
the holy paradise as his reward.

5 Lady, I come before you, desiring to
    pray your dear son
that he turn us from suffering,
and may he give such understanding to
    those he made according to his
    image
that the reign of paradise will not be
    forbidden to them
at the sad pilgrimage when the soul
    must leave the body which made it
    sin.

39 Cuers qui son entendement

Cuers qui son entendement · met en grant chose traitier

se doit a ce tra-vai-ller, qu'il ait bon commencement.

car si com di-ent li sai-ge · des quenos so-mes a-pris,

commencemenz de haut pris · est la moitiez de l'ouvrai-ge.

Pour ce me vuil travaillier · a hautement commencier.

Cuers qui son en - ten - de - ment   met en grant cho - se trai - tier

se doit a ce tra - vai - ller: qu'il ait bon com - men - ce - ment.

Car, si com di - ent li sai - ge, des que nos so - mes a - pris,

com - men - ce - menz de haut pris   est la moi - tiéz de l'ou - vrai - ge.

Pour ce me vuil tra - vail - lier: a hau - te - ment com - men - cier.

40 Tout ensement con retraient a l'aire

1 Tout ensement con retraient a l'aire
li oiseillon por nature assevir,
se doit chascuns vers la monjoie traire
dont il voie paradis resclarcir.
Li hons qui n'est certains de son aäge
face son preu et fuie son domaige
et mete en la mere Dieu son espoir,
si ne porra anemis decevoir.

2 Sa grant valour ne porroie retraire
se Salemons pöoie devenir:
quant que Diex fist et quant que il
   voudra faire,
dou temps Adan desqu'au siecle fenir,
ele deffent les siens de tout domaige,
et quant ce vient au perillous passaige
ou l'ame atent ce qu'ele doit avoir,
a seürté les maine en son manoir.

3 Mout a en li tres glorious aumaire
qui toute fu plainne dou saint espir:
por hebergier son saint cors la fist faire
Diex, qui en li voloit on devenir.
En li s'asist sanz violer la cage
li rossignos qui touz maus assouvaige:
entiere au naistre et virge au concevoir,
enlumina le monde de son hoir.

4 Dame de qui tout paradis esclaire,
ja recreanz n'iere de vos servir
si n'en demant fermail ne robe vaire,
emeraude, çainture, ne saphir.
Un don vos quier ou il n'a point
   d'outraige:
tout mon vivant me tensez de hontaige,
et quant de ci me couvendra mouvoir,
si me faites saint paradis avoir.

5 Chançon, faite de si haut saintuaire
qu'a li loer ne puet avenir,[1]
va a celui dont je tieng l'essemplaire

et la forme de cest chant retenir,
la vidame qui maint ou marescaige,
et si le di que par nul vasselaige
que li hons ne[2] puet il tant valoir,
comme de li servir a son voloir.[3]

Sources: BN, Manuscript V, f. 150v; Bern, Stadtbibliothek, Manuscript C, f. 243; R. 156
Text category: Co
Music category: Ch
Rhyme scheme: 11a 10b 11a 10b 11c 11c 10d 10d
Musical scheme: a b a b c d e f
Edition: Järnström and Långfors, 1: 37
Contrafacta: R. 496 (Jehan Bretel); R. 750 (Gace Brulé)

1 In manuscript C the phrase reads: 'ne puet nuls avenir.'
2 The line in C begins: 'que li hons ait ne.'
3 the last word in C is: 'pooir.'

40 Just as birds take to the air

1 Just as birds take to the air in order to
   follow their nature,
   so everyone ought to move toward the
   heights
   from which he might see paradise
   shining.
   The man who is not sure of his state,
   may he take what advances him and
   flee what will harm him,
   and may he place his hopes with the
   mother of God,
   so that the enemy cannot deceive him.

2 One could not describe her great
   worthiness,
   even if he could become Solomon:
   through all that God has done and all
   he will wish to do,
   from the time of Adam to the end of the
   world,
   she defends her own from all harm;
   and when they come to the perilous
   place
   where the soul waits to receive its due,
   she guides them to safety in her
   manor-house.

3 She has within her a most glorious
   reliquary
   which was filled with the holy spirit:
   God made her in order to shelter his
   holy body,
   for within her he wished to become a
   man.
   The nightingale that soothes all
   sorrows dwelt in her,
   without violating the cage:
   intact through the birth and virgin in
   conceiving,
   she enlightened the world with her
   heir.

4 Lady from whom all paradise takes its
   light,
   no supplicant can serve you if he
   demands brooch or robe of fur,
   emerald, belt, or sapphire.
   I ask one gift that is not excessive:
   keep me all my life from dishonour,
   and when I must move from here,
   bring me to holy paradise.

5 Song, composed from such a high
   sanctuary
   that it cannot fail in her praise,
   go to the one I hold as an example, the
   vidame who holds the marsh,
   and, retaining the form of this song, tell
   him
   that there is no vassalage a man can
   accomplish worthily
   save that of serving her with all his
   will.

40 Tout ensement con retraient a l'aire

Tout ensement con retrai-ent a l'aire
se doit chascuns vers la monjoi-e traire [1]

li oiseillon por nature assevir,
dont il voi-e pa-ra—dis resclarcir:

li hons qui n'est certains de son a-ä—ge

face son preu et fui-e son domai-ge

et mete en la mere dieu son espoir,

si ne porra a-nemis decevoir .

1 No music appears on the staff for this line until the final syllable (♩).
Since the ligature is placed on the same pitches as that at the end of
the first line, I have assumed that the melodic phrases are identical.

2 S. occ.: ♩ (e-g)

3 S. occ.: ♩

4 S. occ.: ▪

5 First occurrence: ♩▪ (d-b-b). The second b may be regarded as a
prolongation of the note, as an error, or as a cancellation of the
elision which would normally occur at 'nature‿assevir.'

Tout en - se - ment con re - trai - ent a l'ai - re
se doit chas - cuns vers la mon - joi - e trai - re

li oi - seil - lon por na - ture as - se - vir,
dont il voi - e pa - ra - dis re - sclar - cir.

Li hons qui n'est cer - tains de son a - ä - ge

fa - ce son preu et fui - e son do - mai - ge

et me - te_en la me - re Dieu son e - spoir,

si ne por - ra a - ne - mis de - ce - voir.

41 De fin cuer et d'aigre talent

1 De fin cuer[1] et d'aigre talent
vuil un sirventois commencier,
pour loer et pour regracier
la roïne dou firmament:
en sa loenge et de son non
vivent[2] tuit mi lai et mi son.
Ensi vuil user mon jouvent
en li servir en bon espoir
a quant que je porrai mouvoir.[3]

2 Gabriel gloriousement
a la ceste dame noncier
qu'en li se devoit herbergier
et prendre charnel vestement
cil qui fist Adan dou limon.
La virge qui fu en friçon
le crei, et fu erranment
parole chars, et conçut l'oir
qui puissance a [a] son voloir.

3 Nes que salemandre n'esprent
quand ele se gist ou brasier,[4]
ne mua ele a l'enchargier
ne au naistre de son enfant.
Virge porta son enfançon,
virge le tint en son geron,
...[5]
virge le vit mort recevoir,
et virge en paradis sëoir.

4 Se en ceste dame eüst noient
qui ne[6] feïst a proisier,
ja cil qui tout puet jouticier
n'i fust enclos si longuement.
Mes se tuit ierent Salemon,
homme et oisel, beste et poisson,
et [la loassent][7] bonnement,
ne porroient dire le voir
de s'onnour et de son pöoir.

5 Tres douce dame, a vous me rens:
se vous me volez conseiller,

je n'ai garde de perillier
d'aversité ne de torment.
Mere a l'aignel, mere au lyon,
mere et fille au vrai Salemon,
mere si que nule ensement,
menez nos a vostre manoir
ou nus mauvais ne puet manoir.

Sources: BN, Manuscript V, ff. 150v–1r;
    Bern, Stadtbibliothek, Manuscript C, f. 76;
    R. 734
Text category: Co
Music category: Th
Rhyme scheme: 8a 8b 8b 8a 8c 8c 8a 8d 8d
Musical scheme: a b c d e f g h i
Edition: Järnström and Långfors, 1: 39
Contrafactum: R. 2075 (Thibaut de Navarre)

1 In manuscript C the phrase reads: 'Fins de cuer.'
2 The word in C is 'muevent.'
3 In manuscript C the line reads: 'de tant com j'avrai de savoir.'
4 The two lines in C are: 'Nes plux ke li aire se mue / quant on i giete un esprevier.'
5 A line is missing in both sources.
6 In manuscript C the line begins: 'qui trop ne.'
7 In V the words are: 'le laissent'; in C: 'la loassent.'

41 From tender heart and active desire

1 From tender heart and active desire I
     wish to begin a *sierventois*
  in order to praise and to thank the
     queen of the firmament:
  in her praise and from her name my
     sounds, my lays, take life.
  Therefore will I spend my youth in
     serving her with good faith
  as long as I am able to move.

2 Gabriel gloriously announced to this
     lady
  that in her would take shelter and put
     on vestment of flesh
  the one who made Adam from the
     mud.
  The virgin, who was trembling,
     believed him,
  and right away the word became flesh,
  and she conceived the heir who has
     power at his will.

3 No more than the salamander is burnt
     when she lies in the brazier
  was *she* changed in the conception and
     birth of her child.
  Virgin she carried her tiny babe, virgin
     she put him in swaddling cloth ...
  virgin she saw him receive death, and
     virgin saw him seated in paradise.

4 If in this lady there had been anything
     not admirable,
  then he who is able to judge all would
     not have stayed so long enclosed
     there.
  But if all were like Solomon, man and
     bird, beast and fish,
  and praised him well, they could not
     tell the full truth of his honour and
     power.

5 Most sweet lady, I give myself to you:
  If you wish to advise me, I will fear no
     peril, adversity, nor torment.
  Mother of the lamb, mother of the lion,
  mother and daughter of the true
     Solomon,
  mother unlike any other,
  lead us to your realm where nothing
     evil can dwell.

41 De fin cuer et d'aigre talent

De fin cuer et d'aigre talent · vuil un serventois commencier

pour lo-er et pour regracier· la Ro-ï-ne dou firmament.

En sa lo-enge et de son non ·   vivent tuit mi lai et mi son;

Ensi vuil user mon jouvent · en li servir en bon espoir

a quant que je porrai mouvoir .

De fin cuer et d'ai - gre ta - lent vuil un ser - ven - tois com - men - cier, pour

lo - er et pour re - gra - cier la ro - ï - ne dou fir - ma - ment: en

sa lo - en - ge_et de son non vi - vent tuit mi lai et mi son. En - si vuil u - ser

mon jou - vent en li ser - vir en bon e - spoir a quant que je por - rai mou - voir.

See appendix C for alternative notation.

42 Quant glace et nois et froidure s'esloigne

1 Quant glace et nois et froidure
    s'esloigne
  que cil oisel ne finent de chanter,
  lors est raison que toute riens s'adoigne
  a la dame des anges honnorer,
  en cui s'enclost pour le monde sauver
  li rois des rois, qui les maus nos
    pardoigne
  dont nos devons les painnes redouter.

2 Ja n'avera grevance ne besoigne
  ne mors ne vis, cui ele veut tenser.
  Nus ne la sert qu'ele ne guerredonne
  plus gentement qu'il ne savroit penser,
  et por ce vuil en lui servir user
  et cuer et cors et vie sanz essoine,
  car trop m'est douz cis faissiaus a
    porter.

3 Mere a celui qui onc ne dit mençonge,[1]
  mieudre que nus ne savroit deviser,
  deffendez nos de mal et de vergoigne,
  et nos donnez tel cuer de vos amer
  qu'en nos ne prendre n'atraper[2]
  li soudoianz cui toz li mont resoigne,
  et nos menez en vostre regné cler.

Sources: BN, Manuscript V, f. 151; Bern, Stadtbibliothek, Manuscript C, ff. 207v–8r; R. 1778
Text category: Co
Music category: Ch
Rhyme scheme: 11a 10b 11a 10b 10b 11a 10b
Musical scheme: a b a b c d e
Edition: Järnström and Långfors, 1: 41
Contrafactum: R. 1779 (Gace Brulé)

1 The line in manuscript C reads: 'Mere a celui ki ains ne dist mensonge.' Thus, both sources alter the rhyme word at this line.
2 In C the line reads: 'ki ne nos puist soduire n'atraper.' It is emended in the edition of Järnström and Långfors to: 'que ne nos puist ne prendre n'atraper.'

42 **When ice and snow and cold
retreat**

1 When ice and snow and cold retreat,
      and the birds never stop singing,
   then there is reason why all things
      should give themselves to honouring
      the lady of the angels
   in whom the king of kings, in order to
      save the world, enclosed himself;
   he who pardons the sins whose pains
      we ought to fear.

2 He who holds to her will never feel
      misfortune nor need,
   while dead or while living.
   No one serves her who is not rewarded
      more nobly than he can imagine,
   and therefore I wish to use in her ser-
      vice my heart, my body, and my life,
   without reservation, for it is most
      sweet to carry this vessel.

3 Mother of the one who never told a lie,
      more worthy than anyone could ever
         devise,
   defend us from evil and shame, and
      give us such heart to love you
   that the seducer feared by all cannot
      capture or trap us;
   and lead us to your luminous realm.

42 Quant glace et nois et froidure s'esloigne

Quant glace et nois et froidure s'esloi-gne
Lors est rai-son que toute riens s'a-doi-gne

que cil oi-sel ne finent de chanter,
a la da-me des anges hon-no-rer,

en cui s'enclost pour le monde sau-ver

li rois des rois qui les maus nos pardoigne

dont nos devons les painnes redou-ter.

1 S. occ.: ♩
2 S. occ.: ▪ ♪ (e e-f-g)
3 S. occ.: ♩ (f)
4 S. occ.: ♩•♩
5 S. occ.: ▪♪
6 S. occ.: ••▪
7 S. occ.: c-d

Quant glace et nois et froi - du - re s'es - loi - gne
lors est rai - son que tou - te riens s'a - doi - gne

que cil oi - sel ne fin - ent de chan - ter,
a la da - me des an - ges hon - no - rer,

en cui s'en - clost pour le mon - de sau - ver

li rois des rois, qui les maus nos par - doi - gne

dont nos de - vons les pain - nes re - dou - ter.

43 Loée tant que loer

1 Loée tant que loer
  ne vous porroit autrement
  qui n'i feroit que penser
  jusqu'au jour dou jugement,
  mes qu'il eüst l'escient
  de Salemon et d'Omer:
  donnez moi de vous amer
  science et entendement.

2 Mere merveillousement
  sanz virginité quasser,
  meillours grains que de froment,
  terre portanz sanz pener,
  estandarz por recepter
  contre le voiseus serpent:
  celui qui de cuer entent
  a vos servir et amer.

3 Nes qu'il apert en la mer
  sente de poisson noiant,
  ne trace en l'air dou voler
  a un faucon descendant,
  n'out en son concevement
  ne en son chaste enfanter
  chose qui desvirginer
  la feïst en son vivant.

4 Qui la sert en son jouvent,
  ses merites doit doubler
  car plus vertuousement
  i puet entendre et ouvrer;
  et qui tant vuet sejorner
  que viellesce le sourprent,
  il trait son viel vestement
  por la mere Dieu donner.

5 Dame en qui on puet trover
  de touz maus aligement,
  en vous se doit on fier,
  car, se nature ne ment,
  li sires qui dignement
  se vint en vous osteler
  ne doit sa mere vëer
  riens qui li viegne a talent.

Sources: BN, Manuscript V, f. 151; Bern, Stadtbibliothek, Manuscript C, f. 141; R. 869
Text category: Co
Music category: Rn
Rhyme scheme: 7a 7b 7a 7b 7b 7a 7a 7b
Musical scheme: a_x b a'_x b' c d e_x b
Edition: Järnström and Långfors, 1: 43
Contrafacta: R. 393 (Jehan de Nuevile); R. 665 (Simon d'Autie); R. 831 (Audefroi le Bastart); R. 923 (Thomas Erier); R. 1870; R. 1942

43 You who are praised so much

1 You who are praised so much
   that even he who thinks only of your
      praise until the day of judgment
   could do no more,
   even if he had the wisdom of Solomon
      and of Homer:
   Give me wisdom and understanding to
      love you.

2 You, made mother marvellously, with-
      out breaking virginity,
   earth bearing better grain than that of
      wheat, without suffering,
   firm standard, giving asylum against
      the deceiving serpent:
   this one intends to serve and love you
      from the heart.

3 No more than the swimming fish
      opens a track in the sea,
   nor the descending falcon leaves a trace
      of flight in the air,
   no more than this was there anything
      in her life,
   neither her conception nor her chaste
      birthing,
   that altered her virginity.

4 He who serves her in his youth should
      double his merits,
   for he can put forth an effort and
      labour with more virtue.
   He who wishes to wait until old age
      surprises him
   brings only old clothing to give to the
      mother of God.

5 Lady, in whom one can find solace
      from all harm,
   one should confide in you,
   for, if nature does not lie,

the Lord who came with dignity to
   lodge within you
should not refuse his mother anything
   which pleases her desire.

43 Loée tant que loer

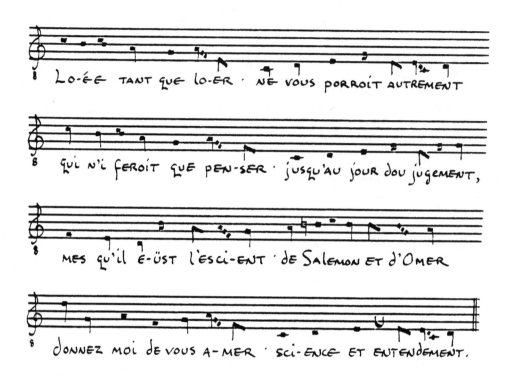

Lo-ée tant que lo-er · Ne vous porroit autrement

qui n'i feroit que pen-ser · jusqu'au jour dou jugement,

mes qu'il e-üst l'esci-ent · de Salemon et d'Omer

donnez moi de vous a-mer · sci-ence et entendement.

Lo - é - e tant que lo - er   ne vous por - roit   au - tre - ment

qui n'i fe - roit   que pen - ser   jus - qu'au jour dou   ju - ge - ment,

mes qu'il e - üst   l'e - sci - ent   de Sa - le - mon et   d'O - mer:

don - nez moi de   vous a - mer   sci - ence et en - ten - de - ment.

44 Rose cui nois ne gelée

1 Rose cui nois ne gelée
 ne fraint ne mue colour,
 dedenz haute mer salée
 fontenele de douçour,
 clere en tenebrour,
 joiouse en tristour,
 en flamme rousée.

2 Flour de bonté[1] esmerée
 et de triaie colour,
 chastiaus dont onc deffermée
 ne fu la porte nul jour,
 santéz en languor,
 repos en labour,
 et païs en meslée.

3 Fine esmeraude esprouvée
 de graciouse vigour,
 diamanz, jaspe alosée,
 saphirs d'Ynde la majour,
 rubiz de valour,
 panthere d'odour
 plus qu'embausemmée.

4 Ne seroit assez loée
 ceste monjoie d'onnour
 se toute humaine pensée
 ne servoit d'autre labor:
 tigre en mirëour,
 en ire et en plour
 solaz et risée.

5 Empereriz coronnée
 de la main au creatour,
 a la crueuse jornée
 quant li ange avront päour,
 prie au sauvëour
 que ton chantëour
 maint en sa contrée.

Sources: BN, Manuscript V, ff. 151–v; Bern,
 Stadtbibliothek, Manuscript C, f. 216;
 R. 519
Text category: La
Music category: Chanson
Rhyme scheme: 8a 7b 8a 7b 5b 5b 6a
Musical scheme: a b a b c d e
Edition: Järnström and Långfors, 1: 44
Contrafacta: none
Remarks: For the symbolism of animals and
 gemstones, see chapter 3.

1 In manuscript C the word is 'biaulteit.'

44 Rose which neither snow nor ice can destroy

1 Rose which neither snow nor ice can
      destroy, nor fade its colour,
   little fountain of sweetness within the
      high salt sea,
   light in darkness, joy in sadness, dew
      amid fire.

2 Flower of goodness purified, and of
      choice colour,
   castle whose door is never closed,
   health in languor, rest in labour, peace
      amid tumult.

3 Fine emerald of proven grace and
      vigour,
   diamond, esteemed jasper, greatest
      sapphire of India [or: of violet hue],
   ruby of valour, panther of odour
      sweeter than balsam.

4 This summit of honour would not be
      sufficiently praised
   even if all human thought were set to
      serve no other task:
   tiger in the mirror;
   in anger and weeping, solace and
      laughter.

5 Empress crowned by the Creator's
      hand,
   on the cruel day when the angels are in
      fear,
   pray to the Saviour that your singer
      may dwell in his country.

44 Rose cui nois ne gelée

Rose cui nois ne gelé-e · ne fraint ne mu-e colour,
dedenz hau-te mer salé-e · fonte —ne-le de douçour,

clere en te-nebrour, joiouse en tristour, en flamme rou-sé-e .

1 S. occ.: ▪
2 S. occ.: ¶
3 S. occ.: ▪
4 There is an additional note f in the manuscript, perhaps inserted at the change
  of clefs as a custos. I have taken the liberty of omitting it.

Ro - se cui nois ne ge-lé - e ne fraint ne mu - e co - lour, cle-re en te - ne -
de-denz hau - te mer sa-lé - e fon - te - ne-le de dou-çour,

brour, joi - ous-e en tris - tour, en flam-me rou - sé - e.

45 Per vous m'esjau

1 Per vous m'esjau, done [del firma-
        ment][1]
tres coralment.
Alumas et engrés
de vostre preis
laudar tant com podrie:
s'agrade a vous et Dé, mes non voldrie.

2 Quant Gabriel vous fist l'anonçalment,
tout erraument
se fu Diex en vous mes.
Car a con gres
qui bien ne le credrie,
et sap que Dex en s'arme part n'aurie.

3 Done de qui tout paravis resplent,
per vous se sent
a li grant de greu feis,
et rege en peis
toute humaine lignie:
vide per mort vostre fius nous rendrie.

4 Douce done, de vous mot et descent
lou jauziment
per que de vous chant[és].[2]
Done, marces:
preias Dé que non vie
sobre poder de quel que dampnans sie.

5 Mare au signar qui n'a començalment,
ne finalment non avra il ja mes,
coraus vous[3] pres
en iste mortel vie,
et o ton fil, en son regné nous guie.

Sources: BN, Manuscript V, f. 151v
Text category: Co
Music category: Th
Rhyme scheme: 10a 4a 6b 4b 7c 11c
Musical scheme: a b c d e f
Edition: Aubry and Jeanroy, 'Une chanson
    provençale(?) à la vierge,' *Annales du
    Midi*, 12 (1900): 67–71
Contrafacta: none
Remarks: The text is problematic and
    appears to be a polyglot of Provençal and
    French. Special thanks are due to Profes-
    sor Robert A. Taylor of the University of
    Toronto for his assistance in establishing
    this version of the text. An analogous
    case of a bilingual text which is not a
    descort appears in BN, fonds français 844
    (Manuscrit du Roi). Special thanks are
    also due to Professor Gary Donovan of
    the University of Calgary for his help in
    establishing the translation.

1 The original manuscript reads: 'done dis
    firmantet.'
2 In V this is: 'vous chanter.'
3 The manuscript is unclear here. Aubry
    and Jeanroy read it as 'grans vous pres,'
    of which they make little sense.

45 In you I rejoice

1 In you I rejoice, lady [of heaven], most
      heartfully.
    To praise your worth as best I can illu-
      mines and enflames me:
    I wish nothing more than to please you
      and God.

2 When Gabriel made the announcement
      to you,
    God was put within you immediately.
    What pain has he who does not believe
      this:
    knowing that God will have no part of
      his soul.

3 Lady whose brightness lights all
      paradise,
    through you the great one took sen-
      tience through suffering,
    and he rules in peace all the human
      race:
    life for death your son will give us.

4 Sweet lady, from you joy comes forth
      and descends,
    for which I sing of you.
    Lady, have mercy:
    pray God that I come not under the
      power
    of the one that is damned.

5 Mother of the Lord who has no
      beginning,
    nor will he ever have an end,
    from the heart I pray
    that you guide us in this mortal life
    and take us to your son in his kingdom.

45 Per vous m'esjau

Per vous m'esjau do-ne del firmament

tres co-ral-ment 'alumas et engrés

de vo-stre preis. laudar tant com podri-e

s'agrade a vous et dé, mes non voldri-e.

Per vous m'es-jau, do - ne del fir - ma - ment tres co - ral - ment. A - lu - mas et en - grés de vo - stre preis lau - dar tant com po - dri - e: s'a - gra - de_a vous et Dé, mes non vol - dri - e.

46 Talent me rest pris de chanter

1 Talent me rest pris de chanter
de la flour qui ne set vertir,[1]
c'est cele qui ains le florir
ne lessa por son fruit porter.
Tant la vout ses fruiz honorer
qu'a li enchargier et moustrer
en couvint nature esbahir.

2 Ceste flour doit on honorer
et seur toutes autres cherir,
en cui daigna hons devenir
Damediex, por le mont sauver.
Ceste n'a n'onques n'ot sa per,
car por son paradis parer
la fist Damediex espanir.

3 A sa grant valour recorder
ne porroit nus hon avenir,
car sens ne s'en porroit chevir,[2]
bouche dire, ne cuers penser.
N'a tant de goute d'eue en mer
quant bien ou il n'a qu'amender
la font en gloire resplendir.

4 Nus ne se puet tant honorer
n'avancier com de li servir,
[ne nuls ne puet tant deservir][3]
que plus ne puist guerredoner:
et por ce me veil atorner
a touz jourz, et abandonner
a son servise maintenir.

5 Mieudre que on ne porroit penser
d'ore jusqu'au siecle fenir,
veilliez nos ames de perir
et noz cors de touz maus tenser;
et quant vendra au trepasser
si nos menez ou regne cler,
la ou chascuns a son desir.

Sources: BN, Manuscript V, f. 151v; Bern,
   Stadtbibliothek, Manuscript C, f. 229;
   R. 793
Text category: Co
Music category: Th
Rhyme scheme: 8a 8b 8b 8a 8a 8a 8b
Musical scheme: a b c d a' e f
Edition: Järnström and Långfors, 1: 47
Contrafactum: R. 1285 (Moniot d'Arras)

1 In manuscript C the last word is: 'mercir.'
2 The line in C reads: 'car sens li ne porroit
   chevir.'
3 The line is missing in V and is supplied
   from C.

46 Desire compels me to sing

lead us to the shining realm
where each one has his desire.

1 Desire compels me to sing of the flower
    that knows no changing;
it is she who produced fruit before
    flowering.
So much did her fruit wish to honour
    her
that he astonished nature in the con-
    ception and the result.

2 One should honour this flower and
    cherish it above all others,
in whom the Lord God deigned to
    become a man, to save the world.
There is not and has never been an
    equal to her,
for in order to prepare his paradise, the
    Lord God caused her to blossom.

3 No one can ever arrive at being able to
    record her great valour,
for wisdom has not been able to
    achieve it,
mouth to speak it, nor heart to think it.
There are not sufficient drops of water
    in the sea
to spoil the purity of this fountain shin-
    ing with glory.

4 No one can be so honoured or so
    advanced as in her service,
nor can anyone deserve any more than
    her reward:
to this I wish to turn myself for all time,
and abandon myself to remaining in
    her service.

5 You who are better than anyone can
    imagine,
from now to the world's end,
protect our souls from perishing and
    our bodies from holding to evil;
and when it comes time to cross over,

46 Talent me rest pris de chanter

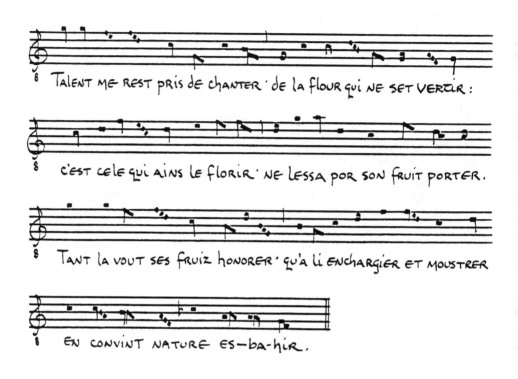

Talent me rest pris de chanter · de la flour qui ne set vertir :

c'est cele qui ains le florir · ne lessa por son fruit porter.

Tant la vout ses fruiz honorer · qu'a li enchargier et moustrer

en convint nature es—ba-hir.

Ta - lent me rest   pris de chan - ter   de   la flour   qui   ne set ver - tir,

c'est ce - le qui   ains le flo - rir   ne les - sa por son fruit por - ter.   Tant la vout ses

fruiz ho - no - rer   qu'a li en - char - gier et mous trer en con - vint na - tu re_es - ba - hir.

47 A la mere Dieu servir

1 A la mere Dieu servir
 doit chascuns entierement
 metre son entendement
 tant que son gré ait conquiz.
 C'est cele qui ses amis
 tense et retrait de torment
 et deffent
 d'estre malbailliz:
 pluseurs en a garantiz.

2 De fin cuer sanz repentir
 la servirai ligement:
 ne changerai cest talent
 tant jor com je soie vis.
 Plantéz i suis et repris,
 m'ame et ma vie li rens
 doucement,
 bien seroit gariz
 se de li sois conjoïs.

3 Cil n'a garde de perir
 qui a s'aïde s'atent,
 et qui la sert loiaument
 ja ne sera entrepris.
 Ele restraint les espris
 et as mors la vie rent
 soultiment,
 tout as anemis
 les cuers de pechié soupris.

4 Comment porroit nus venir
 si tost a son sauvement
 ne au haut avancement
 d'onnour, de cens, et de pris,
 com par honorer touz dis
 la dame dou firmament
 qui resplent
 de cors et de vis
 plus que trestout paradis?

5 Dame, or vos viegne a plaisir
 ce qui si tres coralment

ai dit a mon escïent
ce que de vos m'est a vis:
et quant li douz Jhesu Criz
sera en son jugement,
menez m'en
[en] vostre païs,
ou il n'a fors joie et ris.

Sources: BN, Manuscript V, ff. 151v–2; Bern,
    Stadtbibliothek, Manuscript C, f. 1;
    R. 1459
Text category: Co
Music category: Ch
Rhyme scheme: 7a 7b 7b 7c 7c 7b 3b 5c 7c
Musical scheme: a b a b′ c d e f
Edition: Järnström and Långfors, 1: 49
Contrafactum: R. 333 (Thibaut de Navarre)

47 Serving the mother of God

1 Everyone ought to put their efforts
   entirely into serving the mother of
      God,
   until her will is achieved.
   It is she who holds and pulls back her
      friends from torment,
   and defends them from being mis-
      treated:
   she has protected many from this.

2 With a pure heart, and without regret,
   I will serve her loyally;
   I will not change this intention, how-
      ever long I live.
   I am planted there and renewed,
   I render my soul and life to her;
   gently I will be well healed if I can be
      welcomed into her embrace.

3 He who seeks her help has no risk of
      perishing;
   and he who serves her loyally will
      never be taken by surprise.
   She prevents such attacks, and cleverly
      restores life to the dead,
   as she wrests from the enemy all souls
      tricked into sin.

4 How can anyone come so close to
      salvation,
   or to high advancement in honour,
      wisdom, and worthiness,
   except by hounouring all his days
   the lady of heaven, who shines in body
      and face
   brighter than all of paradise?

5 Lady, may that which I have promised
   so heartfully according to my under-
      standing,
   and that which is clear to me about
      you,

come to please you:
and when sweet Jesus Christ gives his
   judgment,
lead me into your country, where there
   is nothing but joy and laughter.

47 A la mere Dieu servir

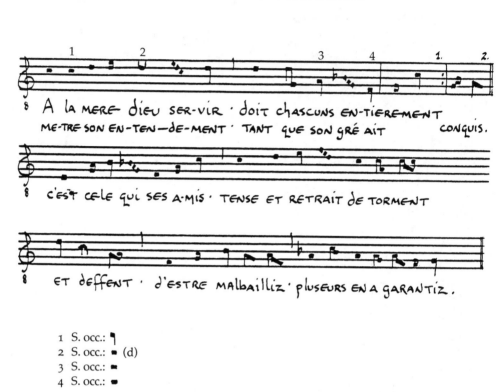

A la mere dieu ser-vir · doit chascuns en-tierement
me-tre son en-ten—de-ment · tant que son gré ait   conquis.

c'est cele qui ses a-mis · tense et retrait de torment

et deffent · d'estre malbailliz · pluseurs en a garantiz.

1 S. occ.: ╕
2 S. occ.: ▪ (d)
3 S. occ.: ▬
4 S. occ.: ➡

A   la   me - re   Dieu   ser -   vir   doit   chas - cuns   en -   tie - re - ment
me - tre   son   en -   ten - de -   ment   tant   que   son   gré

C'est   ce - le   qui   ses   a - mis   ten-se_et   re-trait   de   tor - ment
ait   con - quiz.

et   def - fent   d'e- stre   mal- bail - liz: plu - seurs   en   a   ga -   ran - tiz.

48 Avuegles, muëz et sourz

1 Avuegles, muëz et sourz
  ai esté tout mon vivant:
  or suis gariz et resours
  de ces maus, en escrivant
  a l'usage que fole norreture
  m'avoit torné aussis com de nature;
  quar mes cuers est d'une clarté espris
  dont je remir en quoi [je ai]¹ mespris.

2 Ma vie va en decors
  touz les jors d'ore en avant:
  si me convient tot le cours,
  par secours traire a garant
  a la dame qui tant est fine et pure,
  qu'envers li est toute clartéz obscure,
  et qui tant puet que ja n'iert entrepris
  qui son servise a loialment empris.

3 Dame, vous estes la tour
  qu'assauz n'enpire ne prent,
  refuges as pechëors
  contre le voiseus serpent.
  Qui touz maus chace et de nul bien n'a
    cure
  si qu'il ne puet embatre en mespresure
  ne periller, comment qu'il ait mespris
  le cuer que vos avez en garde pris.

4 Dame a cui toute l'onour
  dou ciel et de terre apent,
  essemples et mirëours
  de tout bon enseignement,
  bele et bone seur toute creature,
  estrangement se merveilla nature
  quant d'un salu en vostre cors repris
  nasqui de vous li filz Dieu Jhesu Criz.

5 Dame, en larmes et en pleurs
  ceste chançon vous present,
  et se la vostre douçours
  en gré la reçoit et prent,

joie en ai grant, et m'ame rest seüre
de la grant joie avoir qui touz temps
  dure.
Droiz est, se vous avez mon jovel prist
qu'aie de vous autre de grignor pris.

Sources: BN, Manuscript V, f. 152; Bern,
  Stadtbibliothek, Manuscript C, f. 1;
  R. 2040
Text category: Co
Music category: Th
Rhyme scheme: 7a 7b 7a 7b 11c 11c 10d 10d
Musical scheme: a b c d e f g h
Edition: Järnström and Långfors, 1: 52
Contrafactum: R. 958; 697 (Jehan de
  Grieviler)

1 As in manuscript C; in V: 'j'ai'

48 Blind, mute, and deaf

1 I was blind, mute, and deaf throughout
    my life:
  now am I healed and restored from
    these misfortunes,
  struggling against the ways to which
    foolish nourishments had turned me,
  just as is their nature;
  for my heart has been seized by a
    clarity,
  that lets me see how I was mistaken.

2 My life flows along all of its days from
    now on:
  when the full course of it is done, I will
    go for protection
  to the lady who is so fine and pure that
    next to her all light is dark,
  and who makes sure that one who has
    loyally undertaken her service
  will never be taken by surprise.

3 Lady, you are the tower that no assault
    nor empire can capture,
  a refuge for sinners against the
    malicious serpent.
  He who chases misfortune and has no
    care for goodness,
  so that he can fend off neither error nor
    danger,
  has greatly mistaken the heart that you
    protect.

4 Lady on whom all honour of sky and
    earth depends,
  example and mirror of all good
    teachings,
  lovely and good above all creatures,
  nature strangely marvelled when the
    son of God, Jesus Christ,
  placed in your body by a salutation,
    was born.

5 Lady, in tears and weeping I present
    this song to you,
  and if your gentleness willingly
    receives and takes it up,
  I will have great joy in this;
  and as for my soul, it will be certain of
    having the joy that lasts for all time.
  It is right, since you have taken my
    youth,
  that I should have from you another
    life of greater worth.

48 Avuegles, muëz et sourz

Avuegles, mu-ëz et sourz · ai esté tout mon vivant;

or suis gariz et re-sours · de ces maus en escrivant

A l'usage que fole norretu-re · m'a-voit torné aussis com de nature;

quar mes cuers est d'une clarté espris

dont je remir en quoi je ai mespris.

A - vue - gles, mu - ëz   et   sourz   ai e - sté tout   mon vi - vant:

or suis   ga - riz   et re - sours   de ces maus, en   e - scri - vant

a l'u - sa - ge que fo - le nor - re - tu - re   m'a - voit tor - né aus - sis

com de na - tu - re;   quar mes cuers est d'u - ne clar - té es - pris   dont

je re - mir en   quoi   je   ai   mes - pris.

49 Emplorant me couvient chanter

1 Emplorant me couvient chanter,
et si le doi faire ensement[1]
d'ire deüsse deschanter[2]
quant la voiz au cuer ne s'asent.
Mes se je chantoie autrement
que vos ci m'oëz deviser,
nus ne me devroit escouter
qu'en ces jours doivent toutes gent
de la mort Jhesu Crist plorer.

2 Chantepleure, a mon escient,
doit on ma chançon apeler:
se la voiz au chanter entent
et li cuers bée a dolourer,
comment porroit nus acorder
ces deus choses en un moment?[3]
Tes est la raison que j'en sent:
qu'il plaïst au cuer esconter[4]
de[5] cas de son dolosement.

3 En partie veil recorder
les dolors et l'aigre torment
que cel soffri por nos sauver
qui sires est dou firmament.
Il fu vendus premierement:
mes Judas ne sot marchander,
qui le seigneur qui n'a son per
osa por si petit d'argent
traïr et a la mort livrer.

4 Puis fu traitiéz vilainement:
pris et loiéz a un piler,
batuz et fustéz malement,
et sa croiz li fist on porter,
et por lui plus deshonorer
d'espines out coronnement,
derachiés despiteusement;
a boivre li firent doner
fiel et aisil communement.

5 En la croiz li firent pener:
sort mistrent en son vestement,

mains et piez li firent ferrer
de granz clous dolereusement.
Longis, se l'escripture ne ment,
li fist la lance ou cors croler:[6]
eue en issi o le sanc cler.
Terre en fu mute, et element
obscur, qui avant erent cler.

6 Mort, or te veil je demander
ou tu preis le hardement
de si sante chose adeser
qui seur tout a commandement.
On te devroit par jugement
essillier sanz mes rapeler
qui ton seignor osas tuer:
or di qu'il le vout ensement,
se tu t'en veuz bien escuser.

7 Douce dame por qui je chant,
comment peüstes vos durer
quant vos veïstes vostre enfant
si cruel martire endurer?
Bien fist parmi vo cuer passer
sa mort, se l'espée[7] trenchant
dont on avoit lonc tens avant
oï le profete parler:
l'escriture en trai a garant.

Sources: BN, Manuscript V, f. 152; Bern,
   Stadtbibliothek, Manuscript C, f. 64;
   R. 783
Text category: Ca
Music category: Th
Rhyme scheme: 8a 8b 8a 8b 8b 8a 8a 8b 8a
Musical scheme: a b c b' d e f g h
Edition: Järnström and Långfors, 1: 53
Contrafacta: R. 465; R. 818; R. 1535; R. 1664
   (Chrestien de Troyes); R. 1882

1 In manuscript C the last word is: 'ausi-
   ment.'
2 The line in manuscript C is: 'laissier
   deüsse lou chanteir.'
3 The word in C is: 'couvent.'
4 The phrase in C is: 'cuer a esconteir.'
5 In manuscript C the word is: 'lou.'
6 The word in C is: 'couleir.'

49 I am moved to sing while weeping

1 I am moved to sing while weeping,
   and if I must do it in this way,
   I shall have to sing discordantly,
   since the voice does not agree with the
      heart.
   But if I were to sing otherwise than in
      the manner which you will hear,
   no one would be able to hear me
      lament the death of Jesus Christ.

2 Indeed, one ought to call my song a
      lament:
   when the voice wishes to sing, and the
      heart desires to grieve,
   how can anyone combine the two at
      one time?
   Here is how I feel about it:
   that it would please the heart to tell the
      cause of its grieving.

3 I wish to record, in part, the pains and
      the sharp torment
   that he who is Lord of the firmament
      suffered to save us.
   First he was sold; but Judas was a
      foolish merchant,
   who for so little silver dared betray and
      deliver to death the Lord who has no
      equal.

4 Then he was treated villainously:
   taken and placed by a pillar, beaten
      and struck cruelly,
   and they made him carry his cross.
   To further dishonour him
   he was outrageously crowned with
      uprooted thorns,
   and they gave him gall and vinegar to
      drink.

5 They caused him to suffer on the cross:
   they cast lots over his clothing,

and painfully nailed his hands and feet
   with large nails.
Longinus, if the Scriptures do not lie,
made his lance tremble in the body:
water came out with the shining blood;
the earth quaked at this, and the skies,
   which had been clear, went dark.

6 Death, I wish now to ask you where
      you got the audacity
   to touch this holy one who has com-
      mand over all things!
   For judgment, one ought to exile you,
      who dared to kill your Lord, with no
      recall:
   Now I tell you that this is exactly what
      he wishes,
   so you must excuse yourself and leave.

7 Sweet lady for whom I sing, how could
      you bear it
   when you saw your son endure such
      cruel martyrdom?
   The trenchant sword must have passed
      through your heart at his death,
   as the prophet was heard to say a long
      time before:
   the Scriptures attest to it.

---

7 The line in manuscript C is: 'sa mort celle
   espée trenchant.' Variants of this sort are
   indicative of aural transmission; see the
   discussion in chapter 1.

49 Emplorant me couvient chanter

Emplorant me couvient chanter · et si le doi faire ensement

d'ire deü-sse deschanter · quant la voiz au cuer ne s'asent

mes se je chantoie autrement · que vos ci m'oëz · de vi-ser

nus ne me devroit escouter · qu'en ces jours doivent toute gent

de la mort Jhesu Crist plo-rer.

Em - plo - rant me cou - vient chan - ter, et si le doi fai -

re_en - se-ment d'i - re de - üs - se des - chan - ter quant la voiz au cuer

ne s'a - sent. Mes se je chan - toi - e_au - tre - ment que vos ci m'o - ëz

de - vi - ser, nus ne me de - vroit es - cou - ter qu'en

ces jours doi- vent tou - te gent de la mort Jhe - su Crist plo - rer.

50 De la mere Dieu doit chanter

1 De la mere Dieu doit chanter
chascuns qui set faire chançon,
qu'anemis ne puet enchanter
celui qui par devocion
la sert en bone entencion.
Qui de cuer la proie
ja ne sera proie
de doleur
a l'enchanteür
qui le mont guerroie.

2 Assez puet nature muser
ne savra comment Diex et hons
nasqui de la virge sanz per
par divine inspiracion,
por la nostre redempcion.
Qui de ce pourroie[1]
malement foloie:
son labour
pert, et en errour
s'embat et desvoie.

3 Cil qui fist ciel et terre et mer
et forma Adan dou limon
out bien puissance dou muer
parole en humainne façon.
Ensi fermement le creon,
quar qui se renoie,
s'il ne se ravoie,
ja nul jor
de son creatour
ne verra la joie.

4 Bele et bonne plus que penser
ne porroient mil Salemon,
rose, lis, estoile de mer,
virge de roial nacion,
columbe de relegion
qui ne faut ne ploie,
de bonté montjoie
et d'onour,

rubiz de valour,
de verité voie.

5 Dame, merci vos veil crier[2]
de cuer plain de contriccion,
de mon cors de meschiés sauver
et m'ame de dampnacion.
Repentance et confession
et pais nos avoie:
et ton chier fil proie,
par douçour,
qu'il nos doint s'amour
et otroit sa joie.

Sources: BN, Manuscript V, f. 152v; Bern,
    Stadtbibliothek, Manuscript C f. 62v;
    R. 804
Text category: Co
No music extant.
Rhyme scheme: 8a 8b 8a 8b 8b 6c 6c 3d 5d
    6c
Edition: Järnström and Långfors, 1: 56
Contrafactum: R. 879

1 The line in manuscript C is: 'Qui de ceu
    poentoie'
2 The last word in manuscript C: is 'proier.'

50 Sing of the mother of God

1 Everyone who can make songs should
     sing of the mother of God,
   for the enemy cannot cast a spell on the
     one who serves her
   with devotion and good understanding.
   One who prays to her heartfully will
     never be prey
   to misery from the enchanter who
   makes war on the world.

2 No matter how long nature ponders,
   it will never know how God and man
     was born to the peerless virgin
   by divine inspiration, for our redemp-
     tion.
   He who strays from this belief commits
     terrible folly:
   he loses the benefits of his labour,
   and is embattled and lost in error.

3 He who made the sky and earth and
     sea
   and formed Adam from the mud
   had plenty of power to change a word
     to human semblance.
   This we firmly believe, for he who
     denies it
   will never have the joy of seeing his
     creator.

4 Lovely and good,
   more so than a thousand Solomons
     could imagine;
   rose, lily, star of the sea, virgin of royal
     birth,
   dove of the faith which neither falters
     nor yields,
   summit of goodness and honour,
   ruby of valour, path of truth.

5 Lady, I wish to call upon your mercy
     with a heart full of contrition,

that you save my body from misdeeds
   and my soul from damnation.
Lead on the path to repentance and
   confession and peace,
and pray to your dear son sweetly
that he give us his love and grant us his
   joy.

51 Dame, s'entiere entencions

1 Dame, s'entiere[1] entencions
  et deserriers demesuréz
  doivent donner genz guerredons,
  donc suis je assez asseuréz
  que gentement guerredonez
  m'iert li servises[2] loiaus et lons
  donc ains ne fu mes cuers matéz.

2 Dame par qui li biaus, li bons,
  li sains, li sires, li senéz,
  li forz, li larges, li lions
  racheta ses amis dampnéz,
  a touz besoingz me secourez
  selonc ce que vo dignes nons
  est de moi aigrement améz.

3 Dame, deffensables donjons
  contre les deables dampnéz,
  vos estes la planche et li ponz
  ou mains pechierres est passéz,
  et des grans tenebres tensez
  qui, la ou il n'a fin ne fonz,
  se fust sans resort reverséz.

4 La douce anonciacion
  dont vostre cors fu honoréz,
  et la pure concepcion
  dont li filz Dieu fu de vos néz,
  et ce qu'il fu en croiz penéz,
  sa mort, sa resureccion,
  ont touz les bien créanz sauvéz.

5 Se chascuns estoit Salemons,
  néz et a naistre et trespasséz,
  et ne feïst de leur sermons
  mes que retraire vos bontéz,
  en bon estaz fust leur aëz
  tantdis com[3] durra li mont,
  n'en diroient le quart assez.

Sources: BN, Manuscript V, ff. 152v–3r;
  Bern, Stadtbibliothek, Manuscript C,
  f. 218; R. 1863
Text category: Co
No music extant
Rhyme scheme: 8a 8b 8a 8b 8b 8a 8b
Edition: Järnström and Långfors, 1: 57
Contrafactum: R. 954 (Gautier d'Espinau)

1 Manuscript C begins with: 'Sainte
  s'entiere.'
2 The word in C is: 'bons.'
3 In C the line begins: 'touz dis tant com.'

51 Lady, if wholehearted intentions

1 Lady, if wholehearted intentions and
     immeasurable longing
  should result in rewards,
  I am amply assured that you will nobly
     reward
  the long and loyal service
  in which my heart was never defeated.

2 Lady through whom the lovely, the
     good,
  the holy, the Lord, the wise, the strong,
     the generous,
  the lion redeemed his condemned
     friends;
  rescue me from all desires,
  for to me your worthy name is vehe-
     mently beloved.

3 Lady, defensible dungeon against the
     damned devils,
  you are the planking and the bridge
     where many a sinner has passed,
  and you have held him safe from great
     darkness
  in the bottomless place without end,
  he who was cast down without hope of
     return.

4 The sweet Annunciation which
     honoured your body,
  and the pure conception through
     which the son of God was born of
     you,
  and that which he suffered on the cross,
  his death, his Resurrection, have saved
     all believers.

5 If each one were a Solomon,
  those born, to be born, and passed
     away,
  and all did nothing with their speech
     but recount your goodness,

and they lived in good health until the
     end of the world,
they still could not tell one quarter of it.

52 De la mere Dieu chanterai

1 De la mere Dieu chanterai,
  et en chantant li prierai
  qu'ele me soit, quant je morrai,
  procheinne:
  La douce pucelle de tous biens plainne.

2 S'ele m'est pris, seürs serai
  quant de cest siecle partirai,
  quant je de m'ame a Dieu ferai
  estrainne,
  La douce pucelle de tous biens plainne.

3 Dame d'onnour et de valour,
  et la mieudre de la meillour,
  fluns de pitié, et de douçour
  fontainne,
  La douce pucelle de tous biens plainne.

4 Mieudre qu'on ne porroit penser,
  souviegne [vos] de nos tenser[1]
  quant vostre filz fera sonner
  s'erainne,
  La douce pucelle de tous biens plainne.

5 Or te pri je, Polidamas,
  si chier com ceste dame as,
  que dou chanter ne te soit gas
  ne painne,
  La douce pucelle de tous biens plainne.

Sources: BN, Manuscript V, f. 153; Bern,
  Stadtbibliothek, Manuscript C, f. 51; R. 67
Text category: Co
No music extant
Rhyme scheme: 8a 8a 8a 3b : 11b
Edition: Järnström and Långfors, 1: 59
Contrafacta: none
Remarks: Polidamas, in stanza 5, seems to
  be the name of a *jongleur*. The name also
  appears in two prose works of the same
  period, the *Roman de Trois* and the *Livre
  d'Artur;* see Louis-Fernand Flutre, *Table
  des noms propres*, 158. Järnström and
  Långfors edited the line as 'or te pri, je,
  poli damas,' explaining the term as a metaphor for Christ. Given the content of the
  stanza and its function as an *envoi*, this is
  unlikely.

1 As given in manuscript C; in V it is:
  'souviegne de nos tenser.'

52 I will sing of the mother of God

1 I will sing of the mother of God,
   and in singing I will pray her
   that she be close to me when I die,
   The gentle maiden full of all goodness.

2 If she esteems me, I will be secure
   when I depart from this world,
   when I make of my soul a gift to God;
   The gentle maiden full of all goodness.

3 Lady of honour and of valour,
   and best among the good,
   river of pity, fountain of sweetness,
   The gentle maiden full of all goodness.

4 You who are better than one can
         imagine,
   remember to protect us
   when your son makes the siren call to
         sound;
   The gentle maiden full of all goodness.

5 Now I pray you, Polidamas,
   as dear as you hold this lady,
   that in your singing you give no boast
         nor annoyance [to]
   The gentle maiden full of all goodness.

53   Bien est raison puis que Diex m'a donné

1   Bien est raison puis que Diex m'a
        donné
    l'entendement de sa mere servir,
    que je i aie le cuer abandonné
    quar nus ne si porroit tant aservir.
    Or ai mespris mes entendre au 'servir'
    qu'ele tantost n'eüst guerredonné
    plusqu'en mil anz n'en porroit
        deservir.

2   Qui son cler vis doucement façonné
    dont la biautéz n'a garde de marcir,
    et comment Diex a son chief coronné,
    porroit lassus ou firmament choisir
    nesqu'on ne puet la tigre departir
    dou mirëour quant l'ueil i a geté
    ne l'en porroit nus faire resortir.[1]

3   Nuit et jour a devant sa majesté
    trois puceles por faire son plaisir:
    Chiastéz i est ovec Humilitéz,
    si rest Pitiéz qui le cuers fet fremir.
    C'est cele qui fait a sa dame oïr
    ceus qui plus sont en grant aversité,
    et qui greignour doutance ont de perir.

4   Or pri Pitié qu'ele aït de moi pité,
    et prit celi qui tant veil obeir
    que mes chançons ele reçoive en gré,
    et de touz maus nos veille garantir:
    et li die que plus assez desir
    que je puisse faire sa volenté,
    dou tout en tout, que estre rois de Tyr.

5   Biau sire Diex, com glorieus *Ave*
    qui deité fist homme devenir,
    par cest *Ave* sont trestuit cil sauvé
    qu'Eve et Adans avoient fet perir.[2]
    Par cest *Ave* fist de son cors martir
    li filz Dieu, qui le monde a rachaté
    par son douz naistre et son aigre morir.

Sources: BN, Manuscript V, f. 153; Bern,
    Stadtbibliothek, Manuscript C, f. 36;
    R. 426
Text category: Co
No music extant
Rhyme scheme: 10a 10b 10a 10b 10b 10a 10b
Edition: Järnström and Långfors, 1: 60
Contrafactum: R. 261
Remarks: The use of allegory is unusual in
    the trouvère devotional works. See also
    song no. 54.

1   For a discussion of the image of the tiger
    at the mirror, see chapter 3.
2   The fifth stanza contains a play on words
    taken from Latin devotional literature:
    the 'Ave' of the angel's greeting to Mary
    is a reversal of 'Eva,' the Latin form of
    Eve, and thus regarded as a symbol for
    Mary's redemption of Eve's original sin.
    An occurrence of the same wordplay is
    found in the Latin hymn to Mary *Ave
    maris stella*, which was undoubtedly a
    model for vernacular examples.

53 It is a good thing since God has given me

1 It is a good thing,
 since God has given me the understanding to serve his mother;
 that I have abandoned my heart to her,
 for no one could serve her sufficiently.
 Now I am mistaken in calling 'service'
 that which she would so quickly
  reward
 even if it could not be deserved in more
  than a thousand years.

2 He who could discern above in the
  firmament
 her clear face so sweetly fashioned
 whose beauty need take no care of
  fading,
 and how God crowned her head,
 would be no more able to turn away
 than the tiger can leave a mirror when
  its eye has glanced there.

3 Night and day there stand before her
  majesty
 three maidens to do her pleasure:
 Chastity is there with Humility,
 and also Pity who makes the heart
  tremble.
 It is she who makes her lady hear those
  who are most in adversity
 and who have greatest fear of
  perishing.

4 Now I pray Pity that she have pity on
  me,
 and request of her, who so wishes to
  obey,
 that she receive my song willingly and
  guard me against all evils;
 and I tell her that I have greater desire
  to be able to do her will,
 all in all, than to be king of Tyre.

5 The lovely Lord God, with the glorious
  greeting *Ave*
 caused deity to become man,
 and by that *Ave* were saved all those
  who *Eva*
 and Adam had caused to perish.
 Through that *Ave* the son of God made
  of his body a martyr,
 he who redeemed the world by his
  sweet birth and his bitter death.

54 Toute riens ont commencement

1 Toute riens ont commencement
fors Diex qui onc ne commença,
mes cil fu espiritalment
adés, ne ja ne finera.
C'est li sires qui decevra
la rudesce ou li element
erent, et ordena comment
chascun d'eus doit estre et sera.

2 Jour fist par son commandement,
le ciel et la terre crea,
au secont fist le firmament,
au tierz erbe et eue habonda,
au quart jour le ciel estela,
li quinz poissons et oisiaus rent,
au sisiesme fist Adan,
au septiesme reposa.

3 En Adan mist soumeillement:
d'un costé qu'il li osta
fist Evain, cele fist Adan
mengier dou fruit qui le dampna.
Cest fruit devéé li dona
cil qui se dolose en torment
et fera parmenablement,
por ce que trop s'enorgueilla.

4 D'Adan et de son dampnement
devant Dieu grant estris monta:
s'il i avra alegement
ou s'ensi dampnéz demorra.
Joutice premerains parla
et dist, s'escripture ne ment,
[qu' Adans demorra ensiment]¹
et Veritéz si accorda.

5 Quant Misericorde l'entent,
Pitié sa sereur apela:
devant Dieu vindrent en present
et chascune li escria,
'Biaus douz sire, ce que sera
se vos alez si aigrement

en vostre deseritement,
vostre bouche se desdira!'

6 Quant Diex ot oï le contenz,
les deus parties accorda
si bien et si tres doucement
que l'une et l'autre s'en loä.
Dedenz la verge s'aömbra
et en nasqui tres dignement,
puis morut por sauver sa gent
et revint et les delivra.

7 Mere, si marveillousement
qu'onc virginité n'en quassa,
deffendez mon cors de torment
tandis com vie sera,
et quant l'ame s'en partira
si la recevez doucement
et conduisiez a sauvement,
quant Diex le monde jugera.

Sources: BN, Manuscript V, f. 153; Bern,
Stadtbibliothek, Manuscript C, f. 36;
R. 648
Text category: Ca
No music extant.
Rhyme scheme: 8a 8b 8a 8b 8b 8a 8a 8b
Edition: Järnström and Långfors, 1: 62
Contrafactum: R. 948
Remarks: Despite the missing line in manu-
script V in stanza 4, the text there is more
complete and coherent than in C. The
version in C conflates this song with no.
53, which also contains an allegorical
debate. This conflation explains the
appearance of no. 54 outside of the alpha-
betical sequence to which C adheres.

1 This line, taken from manuscript C, is
missing in V.

54 All things have a beginning

1 All things have a beginning, except
    God, who never began:
he has in spirit always been, and will
    never end.
He is the Lord who separated the
    elements from their crudeness,
and ordained how each of them should
    and would be.

2 By command he made the day,
he created the heavens and the earth;
on the second day he made the starry
    heavens,
on the third, plants and waters
    abounded;
the fourth day he attached the sky,
the fifth he rendered fish and birds;
the sixth he made Adam,
the seventh he rested.

3 He placed sleep upon Adam:
from one rib which he took, he made
    Eve,
she who caused Adam to eat the fruit
    which condemned him.
That forbidden fruit was given to her
by him who complains in torment, and
    will always do so,
because he was too proud of himself.

4 From Adam's damnation a great
    dispute arose before God:
whether he should have relief or
    whether he should remain in
    damnation.
Justice spoke first, and said, if the
    Scriptures do not lie,
[that Adam should remain forever],
and Truth agreed.

5 When Mercy heard, she called her
    sister Pity:

they came into the presence of God,
    and each cried out:
'Lovely sweet Lord, what will happen
if you go on so harshly with your
    disinheritance
will be something you will regret!'

6 When God had heard the case,
he accorded the two parties so well and
    so gently
that they praised each other:
he would cover himself within the
    Virgin
and be born of her with dignity,
then he would die to save the people
    and return to deliver them.

7 Mother, made so marvellously that
    your virginity was never broken,
protect my body from torment as long
    as life lasts,
and when the soul departs, receive it
    gently
and lead it to safety when God judges
    the world.

55 Ja ne verrai le desir acompli

1 Ja ne verrai le desir [acompli][1]
  qu'ai de loer la dame souveraine:
  com plus la lo et plus [m'i] abeli[2]
  a recorder les biens dont ele [est]
    plainne.[3]
  Bien av[e]rai emploié ma poine,
  et bien seront mi servise meri,
  se de celi sont mi chant conjoï
  qui des anges est dame et cheve-
    taine.

2 Ceste dame la joie nos rendi
  que nos toli la fame premerainne.
  Quant que cele nafra, ceste gari:
  cele ala bas, et ceste est [si] hau-
    tainne[4]
  que paradis est de son fil prochaine.
  cent mile tanz mieudre que je ne di,
  plus est bele que solaus a midi
  et clere plus que ruissiaus seur
    harainne.

3 Li fruiz planta l'arbre dont il issi,
  et dou ruissel descendi la fontainne,
  l'uevre l'ouvrier aleva et norri,
  li solaus vint de la tresmontainne,
  quant li filz Dieu vestuz en char
    humainne
  en Bethleëm de la virge nasqui
  por rachater ceus qui erent en peri
  la ou Judas son martire demainne.

4 Au concevoir nature s'esbahi,
  et au naistre fu ele moins certainne
  comment enfant puet naistre de celi
  qui vierge estoit entiere et pure et
    sainne.
  Si doucement ne descent pluie en
    lainne
  com saintement se mist et descendi
  en son saint [cors] de humilité flori,[5]
  cil qui Jonas sauva en la balainne.

5 Tres douce dame, a jointes mains vos
    pri
  qu'a nul besoing ne nos soiez loing-
    tainne,
  mes tensez nos encontre l'anemi
  quant vostre filz fera sonner s'arainne.
  Blanche com lis et vermoille com
    grainne,
  dame dou mont et dou ciel autresi,
  priez de cuer que de nos ait merci
  cil qui pardon fist a la Magdeleine.

Sources: BN, Manuscript V, ff. 153v–4r;
  Bern, Stadtbibliothek, Manuscript C,
  f. 108; R. 1389
Text category: Co
No music extant
Rhyme scheme: 10a 11b 10a 11b 11b 10a 10a
  11b
Edition: Järnström and Långfors, 1: 65
Contrafactum: R. 372

1 In both manuscripts V and C the word is
  'acomplir.'
2 Manuscript V reads: 'plus m'abeli'; in C:
  'plus m'i abeli.'
3 Manuscript V reads only: 'ele plainne'; in
  C: 'ele est plainne.'
4 Manuscript V reads: 'est hautainne'; in C:
  'est si hauteinne.'
5 In manuscript V the line reads: 'en son
  saint de humilité flori'; in C: 'en son saint
  cors d'umiliteit flori.'

55 I will never see fulfilment of the desire

1 I will never see fulfilment of the desire
      which I have
   to praise the sovereign lady:
   The more I praise her, the more it
      pleases me
   to recount the goodness which fills her.
   I will have spent my efforts well,
   and my service will be well rewarded
   if my song joins her who is lady and
      sovereign of the angels.

2 This lady returned to us the joy
   which the first woman took from us.
   As much as Eve wounded, Mary cured:
   the first went below, the second high as
      paradise,
   next to her son.
   A hundred thousand times better than
      I can express,
   she is more beautiful than the sun at
      midday,
   and more clear than a brook running
      over sand.

3 The fruit planted the tree from which it
      came forth,
   the spring came forth from its stream,
   the work raised and nourished the
      labourer,
   the sun came forth from the pole star,
   when the son of God, clothed in human
      flesh,
   was born of the virgin in Bethlehem
   to redeem those who were in peril,
   there where Judas found his martyr-
      dom.

4 Nature was astonished at this
      conception,
   and at the birth was less than certain
   how a child could be born of her

who was a virgin, pure, entire, and
   whole.
Rain falling upon wool did not descend
   so softly
as he who saved Jonah in the whale
placed himself and descended, in holi-
   ness,
into her blessed [body] that bloomed
   with humility.

5 Most sweet lady, with joined hands I
      pray you
   that you be not far from us in any need,
   but guard us against the enemy
   when your son makes the siren call to
      sound.
   White as the lily and red as scarlet tint,
   lady of the world and of the heavens
      also,
   pray from your heart that he who gave
      pardon to the Magdalene
   will have mercy upon us.

56 Droiz est que la creature

1 Droiz est que la creature
honneüre son creatour,
et cil droiz vient de nature,
ce nos dient li autour:
et por itant je m'atour
a servir la virge pure
en cui [cil] fist[1] norreture
qui fist la nuit et le jour.

2 Qui la sert sanz fauseüre
bien porte a son fil honnour:
si sont çaint d'une çainture,
d'un cuer et d'une douçour,
que li filz tient a amour
touz ceus dont la mere a cure.
Qui l'un en sert a mesure
conquis a dame et seigneur.

3 Toute clartéz est obscure
envers la sainte luour
de la mere Dieu, qui dure
ne set estre au pechëour.
Plus a en li de valour
que n'en die l'escriture:
c'est la flours et la verdure
qui ne change sa valour.

4 A Roume a une painture,
ce tesmoignent li plusor,
representant la figure
de la mere au sauvëour:
icelui fist Diex dou tour
de fame ençainte a droiture,
dont li Juis sa mesprisure
laissa, et guerpi s'esrour.

5 Or me soiez armeüre,
douce dame cui j'aiour,
vers l'enconchie pointure
dou soudoiant traïtour,
et priez au seïgnour
qui nos fist a sa figure,

la joie qui tout endure
qu'il nos doint par sa douçour.

Sources: BN, Manuscript V, f. 154; Bern, Stadtbibliothek, Manuscript C, f. 62; R. 2092
Text category: Co
No music extant
Rhyme scheme: 8a 7b 8a 7b 7b 8a 8a 7b
Edition: Järnström and Långfors, 1: 67
Contrafactum: R. 614 (Richart de Semilli)

1 In manuscript V, the phrase reads 'en cui fist'; in C it is 'en cui cil fist.'

56 It is right that the created

1 It is right that the created should
      honour its creator,
   and this right comes from nature;
   so the authors tell us:
   and for this reason I turn myself to
      serving the pure virgin
   in whom the one who created night
      and day took nourishment.

2 One who serves her without falseness
   also brings honour to her son:
   they are bound with one sash,
   of one heart and one sweetness,
   for the son holds in love all those in his
      mother's care.
   He who serves the one with modera-
      tion
   has won both lady and Lord.

3 All clear light is dark beside the holy
      radiance of the mother of God,
   who does not know how to be harsh to
      a sinner.
   She has more valour than the Scrip-
      tures can say:
   she is the flower and the greenery that
      never change colour.

4 At Rome there is a painting, as many
      have reported,
   which represents the figure of the
      mother of the Saviour:
   it shows God beside a woman honestly
      pregnant,
   because of which a Jew renounced his
      mistake and rejected his error.

5 Now be my armour, sweet lady I
      adore,
   against the fouled wound of the seduc-
      tive traitor,

and pray the Lord who made us in his
      image
that he give us through his sweetness
      the joy that lasts forever.

57 De l'estoile, mere au soloil

1 De l'estoile, mere au soloil,
 dont parmenable sont li rai,
 toute ma vie chanterai,
 et raisons le me conseille
 que de sa valour veraie
 aucune chose retraie
 que nus ne la sert bonnement
 que gent guerredon n'en traie.

2 Mere sanz acointier paroil,
 mieudre que je dire ne sai,
 qui portastes le roi verai
 a cui riens ne s'apareille,
 dame, por noient s'esmaie
 cil qui en vostre manaie
 se rent, car qui a vos s'atent,
 vostre secours ne li delaie.

3 Palais de l'ange de conseil
 de cui sont mi chant et mi lai,
 a vos servir tieng et me trai
 cuer et cors, oeil et oreille.
 Dame, or vuilliez que si m'aie
 qu'a son acort ne me traie
 cil qui dou mont traire en torment
 ades s'eforce et essaie.

Sources: BN, Manuscript V, f. 154; R. 1780
Text category: Co
No music extant
Rhyme scheme: 8a 8a 8a 8b 8b 8b 8c 8b
Edition: Järnström and Långfors, 1: 69
Contrafacta: none

57 Of the star, mother of the sun

1 Of the star,
  mother of the sun whose rays are per-
      petual,
  I will sing throughout my life,
  and reason advises me that I should
      not deny anything of her true valour:
  for no one who serves her well fails to
      receive noble reward.

2 Mother with no known equal,
  better than I know how to relate,
  who bore the true king to whom
      nothing is comparable;
  lady, he who puts himself in your
      protection will fear nothing,
  for you never delay in helping those
      who heed you.

3 Palace of the guardian angel,
  of whom I sing my songs and lays,
  I will hold to serving you with my
      heart and body, eye, and ear.
  Lady, please see to it that
  he who always strives to drag the
      world into torment
  does not succeed in drawing me
  to his side of things.

58 L'estoile qui tant est clere

1 L'estoile qui tant est clere
   qu'ades resplent nuit et jour,
   et a si fine colour
   que ne mue son estage
   par cler tens ne par ombraige,
   m'est achoison et matiere
   d'une chançon asevir.
   Or la me laist si fournir
   Damediex, par sa puissance,
   qu'ele me [mue] et avance
   et qu'anemis n'ait pooair d'enchanter
   ceus et celes qui la savront chanter.

2 Cele estoile est fille et mere
   a Jhesu le cr[e]atour:
   qui l'aimme et porte honour
   bien emploie cel usage,
   ne conquist en son aäge
   Alixandre l'emperieres
   qui dou mont fist son plaisir.
   Tant com fait en li servir,
   qui en la a s'esperance,
   ja n'avera mesestance
   ne morz ne vis, cui ele veut amer:
   tant est douce qu'en li n'a point d'amer.

3 Cele gent qui se font rere
   a loi de combatëour
   metent leur cors en labour
   de chanter devant l'imaige,
   et je fais tout lige homaige
   li et son fil et son pere
   de cuer, de cors, et d'espir
   a touz jourz sanz repentir,
   et por iceste lijance
   suis en certaine fiance
   qu'ele en pitié me voudra regarder,
   a mes besoignz et de touz maus garder.

Sources: BN, Manuscript V, ff. 154r–v;
   R. 902
Text category: Co
No music extant
Rhyme scheme: 8a 7b 7b 8c 8c 8a 7d 7d 8e 8e
   10f 10f
Edition: Järnström and Långfors, 1: 71
Contrafactum: The Provençal song,
   'Eissamen com la pantera'

58 The star which is so bright

1 The star which is so bright that it shines
      forever, night and day,
   and of such fine colour that it never
      changes its state
   through clear weather nor through
      dark;
   this is my cause and content for
      crafting a song.
   Now let the Lord God through his
      power
   so furnish me that I may be advanced
   and that the enemy may have no
      power to enchant
   those men and women who know how
      to sing to her.

2 This star is daughter and mother of
      Jesus the creator:
   one who loves and honours her puts
      these efforts to good use:
   in serving her, he will gain more
   than in his time did Alexander the
      emperor,
   who made the world his plaything.
   One who puts his hopes in her, and
      whom she wishes to love,
   will never meet misfortune in death or
      life;
   she is so sweet that there is in her no
      trace of bitterness.

3 Those who have themselves shorn in
      the manner of a warrior
   set their bodies to the task of singing
      before her image,
   and I pledge loyal homage to her and
      her son and her father,
   from the heart, the body, and the spirit,
      forever, without regret,
   and for this allegiance I have strong
      faith

that she will regard me with pity and
   guard me from all desires and evils.

59 De volenté desiriere

1 De volenté desi[riere][1]
que mes cuers maintenue a,
chanterai de la fine ierre
qui onc colour ne mua,
semblanz est a la verrierre
cui li solaus trespassa
ensi de tres bone maniere
que de riens ne la quassa.

2 Devant et apres entiere,
son fruit conçut et monstra
ceste douce dame [chiere][2]
cui Gabriel salua.
Tant est la pitié [pleniere][3]
dont Nature la para,
que ja nus qui la requierre
a s'aïde ne faudra.

3 Ceste dame est la lumiere
par cui Diex renlumina
la dolente gent chartriere
que li premiers hom dampna.
De li nos vint la baniere
que la deitéz porta
quant de la male ter[r]iere[4]
d'enfer ses amis geta.

4 Ceste dame est la [miniere][5]
qui le fin or nos livra,
de quoi li vrais ingierres
chierement nos rachata.
Virge desrainne et premiere
qui onques enfant porta,
esmeraudinne chiere
en cui Diex reposa.

5 Ja li soudoianz trichierres
en l'ame part n'avera
qui souvent est coustumiere
de dire 'Ave Maria,'
et qui en veraie proiere
vers li s'umeliera,

s'ame sera parçonniere
de la grant joie qu'ele a.

Sources: BN, Manuscript V, f. 154v; R. 1327
Text category: Co
No music extant
Rhyme scheme: 8a 7b 8a 7b 8a 7b 8a 7b
Edition: Järnström and Långfors, 1: 73
Contrafacta: R. 501; R. 1149; R. 1618;
  R. 1632; R. 2094; R. 2099
See also: *Analecta hymnica*, 20, no. 52; 21,
  no. 33

1 The word as given in manuscript V is:
  'desierree.'
2 The final word of this line is missing in
  the manuscript and the line has been
  emended to restore the rhyme as suggested by Järnström and Långfors, *Recueil
  de chansons pieuses*.
3 This line presents the same problem as
  the one two lines above it.
4 Manuscript V reads: 'terniere.'
5 Manuscript V gives: 'lumiere.' Järnström
  and Långfors substitute 'miniere' as more
  consistent with the sense of the passage. I
  find this argument plausible; since stanzas 3 and 4 begin the same way, an erro-
  neous duplication might easily have
  occurred.

59 From willing desire

his soul will have a portion of the great
joy which she has.

1 From willing desire which my heart
      has maintained,
   I will sing of the fine ivy which has
      never changed its colour:
   she is like the glass window
   which the sun enters in such gentle
      fashion
   that it does not break in any way.

2 Entire before and after, she conceived
      and brought forth her fruit,
   this [dear] sweet lady who Gabriel
      greeted;
   she is so full of pity, with which Nature
      adorned her,
   that she never fails to help those who
      call upon her.

3 This lady is the light by which God
      reillumined
   the miserable imprisoned people who
      the first man condemned:
   from her comes to us the banner which
      deity carried
   when he cast his friends out of the evil
      pit.

4 This lady is the [miner] who delivered
      fine gold to us,
   with which the true engineer ransomed
      us dearly.
   The last and first virgin ever to bear a
      child,
   precious emerald in which God rested.

5 The seductive trickster will never have
      a grip
   on the soul that makes a habit of saying
      'Hail, Mary':
   and one who humbles himself in true
      prayer to her,

60 En la vostre maintenance

1 En la vostre maintenance,
roïne dou firmament,
ont mis mon entendement,
desierrers et acoustumance,
si que seule remenbrance
de vos, quant plus suis plaignanz,
me sane si doucement
que mes cuers nuiés de pesance
de joie tresaut et dance.

2 Lumiere sanz defaillance
solauz sanz esconsement,
mere sanz dolousement,
terre portant sanz semence,
hauberz et escuz et lance,
espée clere et trenchanz
pour garantir toutes genz
qui fermes sont en creance
et en vos ont leur fiance.

3 Empereriz de vaillance,
virgene parmenablement,
m'ame et ma vie vos rens
et fais de mon cors lijance.
Or plaise a vostre puissance
que [vos] m'i soiez garanz[1]
contre le voiseus serpenz,
que mes cors n'ait mesestance
ne l'ame de moi grevance.

Sources: BN, Manuscript V, ff. 154v–5;
R. 229
Text category: Co
No music extant
Rhyme scheme: 8a 7b 7b 8a 8a 7b 7b 8a 8a
Edition: Järnström and Långfors, 1: 76
Contrafactum: Resembles a song by
Foulquet de Marseille.
Remarks: Järnström and Långfors
attempted to standardize the spellings of
the -ent/ -anz/ -enz/ -ens rhymes, which
seems both unnecessary and misleading.
It is precisely the levels of distinction
among them that are of interest to
linguistic historians.

1 Manuscript V gives 'qui m'i soiez.' The
additional word fills out the metre but is
not essential.

60 In your keeping

1 In your keeping, queen of the
        firmament,
   I have placed my purpose, desire, and
        habits,
   so that a single remembrance of you,
        when I am sorrowful,
   heals me so sweetly that my heart,
        wounded with heaviness,
   leaps and dances for joy.

2 Light unfailing, sun unhidden,
   mother without pain, earth bearing
        unsown,
   hauberk and buckler and lance,
   bright and trenchant sword for
        protecting all people
   who are firm in their belief, and put
        their trust in you.

3 Empress of valiance, perpetually
        virgin,
   I render my soul and life to you, and
        make of my body a tribute.
   Now may it please your power that I be
        placed in your protection
   against the malicious serpent,
   so that my body will not meet
        misfortune,
   nor my soul grief.

61 Tant [ne] me plaist toute phylosophie

1 Tant [ne] me plaist toute phylosophie
parfaitement savoir sanz meserrer,
[ne de terre] toute seignorie,
et d'air, de riviere, et de mer,[1]
con je desir en chantant recorder
la grant valour de la virge Marie,
non pas toute mes aucune partie,
se tout le mont en m'aïde en avoie.

2 Virge conçut au tesmoing d'Ysaÿe,
et enfanta sanz dolour endurer
celui par cui en deus fu departie
la Rouge Mer pour son peuple sauver:
puis la rejoint, et la fist reverser
seur Pharaön et sa grant conpaignie.
Bien doit estre loée et graciée
cele qui çaint neuf mois de sa courroie
celui qui fist si merveillouse voie.

3 En son cors fu humanitéz unie
a deité, [por] homme rachater:
si loiaument fu la chose establie
que quant la char couvint mort
    endurer,
la deitéz duranz sanz violer
ou sepucre li porta compaignie.
N'onques de lui ne fu l'ame guerpie
dedenz enfer, ne en toute la voie,
n'au resartir le laz d'or et de soie.

4 Ceste dame le buisson senefie
qui Moÿses vit sanz ardoir flammer:
lors qu'ele fu de grace raëmplie,
ençainte fu sanz li desvirginer.
De li nasqui sanz porte deffermer
li rois des rois et veritéz et vie,
qui trestouz seus fist tel chevalerie
qu'enfer brisa, et en retraist sa proie,
dont chascuns doit chanter et mener
    joie.

5 Chambre roiaus, d'umilité jonchie;
mout a le cuer despersement amer,
et desloial et plain de felonnie,
qui nuit et jour n'entent a vos amer:
quar qui vos set de fin cuer reclamer,
s'il vos avoit trente mil ans servie,
n'avroit il pas la joie deservie
que vostre filz doucement li otroie
en un moment, quant sa mere l'en
    proie.

Sources: BN, Manuscript V, f. 155; R. 1193
Text category: Ca
No music extant
Rhyme scheme: 11a 10b 11a 10b 10b 11a 11a
    11c 11c
Edition: Järnström and Långfors, 1: 78
Contrafactum: R. 1172 (Martin le Beguin de
    Cambrai)
Remarks: Järnström and Långfors construct
    an elaborate explanation for the final line
    of stanza 3, taking the lace and silk to
    represent grave clothes. The implied
    motion from hell back to the grave is not
    appropriate, however, to the theology of
    the Ascension. The image is far more
    likely to represent the garments worn
    in heaven, and thus to describe the
    Ascension as a physical event.

1 In manuscript V the three lines read as
    follows: 'parfaitement savoir sanz
    meserrer, / toute seignorie / de terre et
    d'air, de riviere et de mer.' The changes,
    which preserve both sense and metre, are
    my own.

61 It would please me to know all of philosophy

1 It would please me
   to know all of philosophy perfectly,
      without error,
   and [to have] all lordship over the earth
      and air, the rivers and seas,
   not as much as my desire to tell by
      singing
   the great valour of the Virgin Mary;
   not all of it, but a part,
   for I would not be able to tell even half
      of it
   if I had the whole world to help me.

2 Virgin she conceived,
   according to the testimony of Isaiah,
   and gave birth without enduring pain
   to the one by whom the Red Sea was
      parted in two
   in order to save his people.
   Then he rejoined it
   and made it turn upon Pharaoh and his
      great company.
   She should be well praised and
      thanked,
   she who for nine months fastened her
      belt
   around him who made such a
      marvellous pathway.

3 In his body was humanity united with
      deity,
   to redeem humankind:
   So loyally was it established
   that when the flesh had to endure
      death,
   the deity remained without harm
   and bore it company in the tomb.
   Never was the soul abandoned by the
      deity,
   not in hell, not on the journey, and not
      in putting on gold lace and silk.

4 This lady signifies the bush
   which Moses saw burning without
      heat:
   since she was filled with grace,
   she was pregnant without losing
      virginity.
   From her was born,
   without unfastening the door,
   the king of kings, the truth and the life,
   who all alone did such deeds of
      chivalry
   that he shattered hell and took away its
      prey,
   for which everyone should sing and be
      joyous.

5 Royal chamber, constructed of
      humility;
   he has a heart most full of bitter
      cruelty,
   disloyal and full of felony
   who does not seek, night and day, to
      love you:
   for he who knows how to call you with
      a refined heart,
   if he were to serve you for thirty
      thousand years,
   would not deserve the joy
   which your son sweetly brings him in
      one moment
   when his mother requests it.

Appendix B:
Additional Stanzas

11 Mere au roi puissant

quant nous morrons,
ta grase et t'amour.

3 Dame, tant fu pieus
Jhesu Cris vos fieus
glorious,
ki de maus Juieus[1]
fu tenus si vieus
pour nous tous,
que il l'escopirent
et si le batirent
mout fu angoissous.
Cil qui le serviront
et qui le crëiront
seront toudis
en paradis
la sus aveuc vous.

4 Dame, or vous proions
k'aveuc vous aillons
en clarté,
que nous ne soions
aveuc les felons
tourmenté.
Vierge glorieuse,
vierge presieuse,
aiiés en pité:
mout iert dolereuse
l'ame, et angoiseuse
que cil tenront
qui du ciel sont
en enfer bouté.

5 É las, que feront
cil qui la iront
sans retor?
Ja n'en isteront
ne ja bien n'aront
a nul jour.
D'icele conpaignie
nos desaconpaigne
par ta grant douçour,
et si nous ensaigne
que nos ne remaigne,
que nous n'i alons

1 See the remarks on the endemic anti-
Semitism of the period in the notes for
song number 36.

11 Mother of the powerful king

3 Lady, your glorious son Jesus Christ
 was to be pitied,
 he who for us all was taken so vilely
  by wicked Jews
 so that they beat him, and the more
  they beat him the greater was his
  anguish.
 Those who serve him and believe in
  him will be forever with you on high,
  in paradise.

4 Lady, now we pray that we might go
 with you into the light,
 and that we will not be tormented with
  the evildoers.
 Glorious and precious virgin, have
  pity:
 the soul would be most pained and
  anguished
 to be held by those who are cast from
  heaven to hell.

5 Alas! what will they do, those who go
 there without hope of return?
 They will never get out, nor have any
  good fortune ever.
 Sever us from such company, through
  your great gentleness;
 and show us that your grace and your
  love shall not be lacking,
 that we shall not go there (to hell)
  when we die.

12 'Qui bien aime a tart oublie'

Additional stanzas in manuscript i:

3 Mes trop sont nos cuers volage
et en mauvestié fichié
...
quant li mons sera jugiez
Jhesus vendra tous iriés,
ses plaiez et son costé
et dira: 'Mauvez fuiez,
tout droit en enfer alez,
ou serés mal hebergié.'

4 Cil mout mal ostel aront
qui en enfer seront mis:
ja redempcion n'avront
mes tous jours de mal en pis
et crieront a haus criz
...
'Mors, car tue ces chaitis
qui anc n'avront se mal non
mais tousjours de mal en pis.'

Additional stanzas in manuscript a:

4 Douce dame debonaire,
ki bien vous saroit amer
miex li venroit que prendre
    Aire
ne Bruges, ne Saint-Omer.
...
pöoir avés de douner
vostre amour, et de retraire
ceus qui vous voelent amer.

5 Or prion a celui sire
qui tout fist et deffera
que vers nous ne trestort
    s'ire
quant le jugement vendra:
chaitis et dolens sera
qui souffera le martire
que enfers li liverra,

quar ja n'i trouvera mire
ne d'ilec ja mes n'istra.

6 Or prions trestuit ensemble
la virge de grant valour,
mout i devon bien entendre
a lui servir nuit et jour,
qu'ele prit le haut seignour
qui en crois se lessa pendre
pour nous traire de doulour
qu'il de tout mal nous deffendre,
et nous doint la soue amour.

12 'He who loves well takes a long time to forget'

Additional stanzas in manuscript i:

3 But our hearts are flighty, and fixed on
    wrongdoing ...
When the world is judged, Jesus will
    come in anger, his wound in his side,
and will say 'Flee, you evil ones,
go straight to hell where you will be
    uncomfortably lodged!'

4 Those who are sent to hell will have
    poor lodging,
they will never have redemption,
    but will go from bad to worse,
and will cry out loudly ...
'Death, kill these wretches, who will
    never have it so bad
that it cannot get worse.'

Additional stanzas in manuscript a:

4 Sweet pleasant lady, he who would
    know how to love you
would get better result than from tak-
    ing Aire, Bruges, or St-Omer ...
You have power to give your love, and
    to carry away those who would love
    you.

5 Now we pray to that Lord who made
    and will unmake all things,
that he not turn his wrath on us when
    judgment comes:
he will be wretched and miserable
who suffers the martyrdom that hell
    will deliver to him,
for he will find no physician there, nor
    ever leave the place.

6 Now we pray all together to the virgin
    of great worth –

for we must set our minds on serving
    her night and day –
that she ask the high Lord who let him-
    self hang on the cross to deliver us
    from pain
that he may protect us from all evil,
    and give to us his love.

Appendix C:
Alternative Musical Notation

6a Chanter vos vueil de la virge Marie

Chan-ter vos vueil de la vir-ge Ma-ri - e qui main-te_ame a et sau - vé-e_et ga-ri - e.

Li doit on re - cla-mer et che-rir et a - mer: touz nos ge - ta d'a - mer et de grant vi - lai-ni - e.

Da-me, ne de - mo-rés, mes por Dieu se-cor - rés moi, qui sui de-vo - rés se je n'ai vos-tre_a - i - e.

9a Prions en chantant

Pri - ons   en   chan - tant   la   me - re   Jhe - su,
qu'ele nos soit   ai - dant   ne   soi - ons   per - du

en - vers son   en - fant   qui   de   li   nez   fu
qu'il   nos soit   ga - rant   par   sa   grant   ver - tu.

Bon fu on - ques   né - e   la virge ho - no - ré - e,   la flor de   bon - té,
da - me bien ai - mé - e,   ro - ï - ne cla - mé - e,   de grant roi - au - té.

23a Et cler et lai

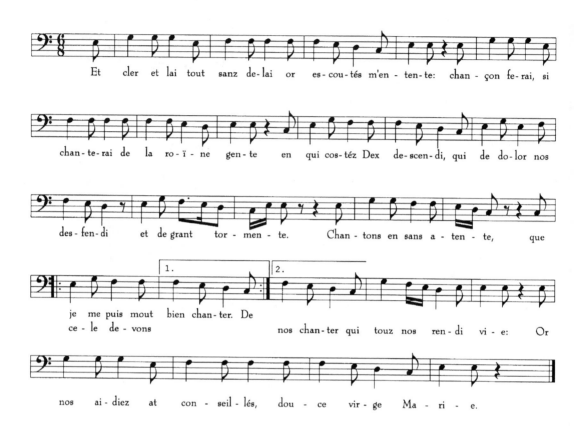

Et cler et lai tout sanz de-lai or es-cou-tés m'en-ten-te: chan-çon fe-rai, si

chan-te-rai de la ro-ï-ne gen-te en qui cos-téz Dex de-scen-di, qui de do-lor nos

des-fen-di et de grant tor-men-te. Chan-tons en sans a-ten-te, que

1. je me puis mout bien chan-ter. De

2. ce-le de-vons nos chan-ter qui touz nos ren-di vi-e: Or

nos ai-diez at con-seil-lés, dou-ce vir-ge Ma-ri-e.

31a Chanter m'estuet de cele sans targier

Chan ter me-stuet de ce - le sans tar- gier   qui de mer est luis-sans es - toi - le cler - re:
ser- vir la doit chas cuns de cuer en - tier,   car fors nos mist de la   tor-men-te_a-me - re

ou   mis nos ot   A - dans,   no pre- mier pe - re.   Le fruit man - ja par E -

vain   sa moil- lier   que Dex li ot   des - fen - du   a man - gier;

s'en che-ï-mes tres-tuit en grant mi- se - re,   quant de li fist li douz Jhe- sus sa me - re.

35a L'autrier m'iere rendormiz

L'au- trier   m'ie-re   ren- dor - miz   par un ma - tin en   e - sté:

a - don - ques me   fu a - viz   que   la dou - ce   me - re   Dé

m'a - voit dit   et   com - man - dé   que seur un   chant   qui   ja - dis

so - loit e- stre   mout   jo - ïs   chan- tas - se de   sa bon - té,

et je tan- tost   l'ai en - pris: Diex   doint qu'il   li   vieg - ne_en gré.

41a De fin cuer et d'aigre talent

De fin cuer et d'ai - gre ta - lent vuil un ser-ven-tois com-men - cier, pour

lo - er et pour re - gra - cier la ro - ï - ne dou fir - ma - ment: en

sa lo- en- ge_et de son non vi - vent tuit mi lai et mi son. En - si vuil u - ser

mon jou-vent en li ser-vir en bon e - spoir a quant que je por - rai mou - voir.

Title Index

General Index

TORONTO MEDIEVAL TEXTS AND TRANSLATIONS

General Editor: Brian Merrilees